TELEVISION STUDIES

The Key Concepts

Bernadette Casey, Neil Casey, Ben Calvert, Liam French and Justin Lewis

London and New York

First published 2002
by Routledge
11 New Fetter Lane, London EC4P 4EE

Simultaneously published in the USA and Canada
by Routledge
29 West 35th Street, New York, NY 10001

Routledge is an imprint of the Taylor & Francis Group

Typeset in Bembo by Taylor & Francis Books Ltd
Printed and bound in Great Britain by Biddles Ltd,
Guildford and King's Lynn

British Library Cataloguing in Publication Data
A catalogue record for this book is available from the British Library

Library of Congress Cataloging-in-Publication Data
Television studies : the key concepts / Neil Casey ... [et al.]
p. cm. – (Routledge key guides)
Includes bibliographical references and index.
1. Television. 2 Television broadcasting.
I. Casey, Neil (Neil James), 1955– II. Series.
PN1992.5 .T385 2001
791.45–dc21   2001031757

ISBN 0–415–17236–5 (hbk)
ISBN 0–415–17237–3 (pbk)

CONTENTS

INTRODUCTION

Even though a generation has grown up with it, television is still a comparatively new technology. Even in the context of the authors' own lives we have a lucid sense of its novelty. Some of us dimly remember a single channel of British television. Most of us recollect just two channels. Virtually all of us can recall black and white television. And every one of us can remember the advent of the video-cassette recorder, even if we have not yet mastered the knack of setting it for when we will be out. In the last few years the terrain has been altering dramatically, with a mushrooming of channels, interactive viewing, compact discs, internet links and other innovations that tax our imaginations.

Television is also enormously significant. In more developed societies virtually every household possesses at least one television, with ownership of a set per member becoming increasingly commonplace. Television viewing has become the dominant leisure activity for the majority of the population, with statistics suggesting that each individual in the UK watches television, on average, for nearly three hours a day, while in the US research has suggested that sets may be on for an average of seven hours (Macionis and Plummer, 1998). Although ownership in Asia and Latin America lags behind comparatively, these continents and that of Africa have already been targeted as the major areas of growth for the global television industry during the twenty-first century. Beyond these bare statistics, though, television plays a central role in most people's everyday lives. In the public sphere it has become the venue for political debate, religious evangelism and the exchange of 'news', as well as the major medium for entertainment (Macionis and Plummer, 1998). In the private realm, television has been seen both as a quasi-altar around which the family gathers and the harbinger of domestic fragmentation as everybody slopes off to different rooms to watch their own favoured programme. In addition, television is perceived as having an impact beyond the experience of viewing. It is blamed for encouraging violence and sexual promiscuity and for lowering educational standards. At the same time it has been lauded for raising political consciousness on issues as diverse as sexual health and global poverty. Academics of various hues have argued that it has helped people to become aware of their membership of nationalities, genders and even the human race − or, conversely, that it can dull the sensibilities of nearly every human who comes within its orbit. What is clear is that television as a bombardment of images and programmes, as a technology and as a world-wide industry, touches social life in profound ways. It has done nothing less than change the cultural landscape.

It seems appropriate and unarguable, then, that television as the major, global, contemporary mass medium should be subject to academic investigation. In some ways the emergence of television studies as an area of intellectual inquiry, to mirror the likes of literary, theatre and film studies, has been hesitant and, in certain quarters, resisted as a sign of the encroachment of popular culture on academe and the arts. Nevertheless, the last twenty years have seen the genesis of a recognisable, legitimate body of research on television as a cultural phenomenon. Academics and cultural critics had been interested in television since its inception and particularly so once sets were more widely available from the 1950s on. But the analysis of television tended to be subsumed under the study of mass communications and then, after that, media studies. For some the study of 'the box in the corner' should have been straightforward but, as Brunsdon (1998) notes, there is very little which is obvious about the television of television studies. Much early work, drawn from a broadly social scientific perspective, was stimulated by diverse anxieties about the effects and influences of television, be they cultural, behavioural, political or ideological. From the 1970s, analytical terms and models first developed in literary, film and cultural studies began to make an impact, while in the 1980s concepts have been drawn from psychoanalysis, philosophy and social psychology as well as, perhaps more predictably, sociology, history and economics. These other disciplines have also opened up new avenues of inquiry, so that Hartley (1999) points to the emergence of four separable but related areas. These he labels: television as mass society, television as text, television as audience and television as pedagogy. This book is intended to reflect the multidisciplinary origins of, and the breadth of diverse enquiry already managed by, television studies as a relatively new field of academic investigation. As such it says something about our own professional biographies, which have seen us coming from diverse subject and research backgrounds to end up teaching and writing about television. We hope, then, that this book can contribute to the development and maturation of television studies.

Using the book

In keeping with the genre we need to emphasise that this book is not a dictionary, nor a definitive guide to the precise content and boundaries of television studies. Rather, it is intended as a map of the territory, an indication of what has been covered, how and by whom. Each concept or topic is written to reflect what we consider to be essential information, to note central debates and to offer, where appropriate, examples relevant to television. As such the book seeks to debunk some of the more technical language which accompanies any field of study, helping visitors to television studies to gain a sense of the rationale and accomplishments of the field. But importantly, the book assumes that the reader will only begin here and will go on to use other relevant sources.

We should also offer some swift caveats. First, we have chosen seventy-odd concepts. We might have chosen more or less. Some are longer than others. Our choice in one sense, then, is idiosyncratic and points to our views on what is more and less significant in television studies, to our disciplinary heritages in sociology, cultural studies, history and media studies, to our employment in the United Kingdom and the United States, and to the historical moment. It is possible that a canny reader may be able to tell something about our various ages and our *tastes* from the examples we have used. Nevertheless, while we have been selective we hope that by writing more developed essays on a smaller number of topics we have covered the broad sweep of contemporary television studies. Second, with five authors we have sought not to impose a party line, and it should be possible to identify points of healthy divergence between entries in terms of theoretical and conceptual stance. Third, as those of you who have espied genres and theories among the entries will realise, we are defining 'concept' in a broad way to include any generally conceived notion. Fourth, as several entries starkly reveal, television dates quickly with programmes and technologies coming and going. Concepts are not immortal, but they are rather more durable than *Cop Rock* and *Eldorado* and you should be able to find your own examples to fill in the gaps.

The book should be simple to use. Each alphabetically organised entry has cross-references to other key concepts in the book (although the word may not be exactly the same, as in *postmodernity* referring to *postmodernism*) and an index to enable you to make more links. Every concept finishes with some suggestions for further reading and links to other relevant topics in the book.

Finally, despite our protestations of both idiosyncrasy and comprehensiveness, we would welcome any feedback (via the publishers) on suggestions for extra concepts, gaping omissions and alternative interpretations. Any weaknesses will be blamed on each other.

ACKNOWLEDGEMENTS

The book's genesis lies in our discussions in the last century about what students really want from academic texts. We would not for one moment pretend that we have an answer to this, but we would like to thank all our students who have contributed to our thinking. We would also like to thank Adrian Emerson, for his encouragement during the project's development, and Anne Murphy and Martha Casey, for their help in producing the finished manuscript. Finally we would like to thank editorial staff at Routledge and various children and partners for their impressive patience.

LIST OF CONCEPTS

Sign
Soap opera
Sport
Stereotypes
Structuralism and post-
structuralism
Synergy

Taste
Technology
Text
Uses and gratifications
Video
Violence
Women in television

ACCESS

Access television refers to those forms of programming that allocate televisual space to members of the public (non-media professionals) in order to ensure that all sections of society have an opportunity to be represented and to express their points of view. The basic philosophy underpinning access production is that there should be equality of access to television wherein anybody (and indeed, everybody) should have the chance to express their views. Advocates of access programming see it as a way of correcting imbalances (Corner, 1996) in mainstream television's output, especially where minority groups (ethnic or gay and lesbian, for example) are concerned. Quite often, it is the case that marginalised groups are either under-represented (e.g. the elderly and the disabled) or misrepresented (see *Stereotyping*) in mainstream programming.

Access television is more than just a generic term for certain types of programming – it implies a campaigning polemic (Corner, 1996). Within this context, access is not simply a 'right of reply' or reactive response. Ideally, access television should be proactive and involve a high degree of participation on behalf of the 'accessee(s)'. This involves not only access to the means of production such as cameras, sound and editing equipment but also to editorial and authorial control. On this basis, *game shows*, vox pop *documentaries*, docusoaps, talk shows, home shopping channels and other *audience*-oriented forms of programming do not strictly meet the criteria.

In the UK there is no guaranteed right of access (although there is right of reply) which means that access television in Britain is very much on broadcasters' terms, and there is no legal obligation for the provision of public access programming. Access programmes can be either institutionally produced (such as the BBC's *Video Diaries* produced by the Community Programmes Unit, and Meridian's *Freescreen*) or independently produced by small-scale producers. The US model for access production has possibly come the closest to realising the potential of public access television. During the 1970s, the Federal Communications Commission declared that with the introduction of cable television services there should be some provision for public access programming. Cable franchise owners had to provide admission to facilities and channel space for non-commercial public access and community programming. With the expansion of cable and satellite services the provision of resources also grew – by the mid 1990s there were over a thousand public access centres participating in regular access programming. One of the most

1

successful public access projects was the *Paper Tiger/Deep Dish Gulf Crisis TV Project*, which transmitted counter views and alternative messages concerning the Gulf War.

During the 1990s, access production flourished in both the UK and the USA, partly aided by the availability of relatively inexpensive video camcorders and editing equipment on domestic markets. However, while this development was seen as a significant step towards more democratic and participatory forms of media production, the use of camcorders has had some unforeseen consequences. To begin with, the availability of camcorder technology on domestic markets has reduced the emphasis on broadcasters making their facilities available to the public. Many programmes now consist of video footage shot and sent in by viewers using their own equipment. Furthermore, there has been an increasing trend towards individualism within access production. The use of camcorder technology has given rise to the production of what are known as 'first-person narration' texts (e.g. *Video Nation Shorts*) wherein individuals talk openly (and intimately) about themselves, their lifestyle or some emotive or personal issue. In conjunction with this, there has been an increasing trend towards professionalism within access production. This partly arises from broadcasters needing to maintain some degree of professional and institutional control over the quality and content of the programme, but also through participants having access to better equipment. Thus, it is not uncommon for broadcasters to receive relatively good-quality, edited tapes from viewers who strive to emulate professionals' techniques. Where this is not the case, broadcasters will generally re-edit videotapes sent in by viewers.

The need for television producers to maintain control over the final product goes beyond post-production practices. Through processes of gatekeeping and selection (who is allowed access and who is not) along with *agenda-setting* (what the context of access will be), broadcasters define the parameters of, and are able to manage, access production. Furthermore, as O'Sullivan *et al.* (1994) point out, broadcasters will not let simply anyone go on television and have their say – what is said and shown will always be, to some extent, mediated. *Representation* (including self-representation) is always in relation to, and mediated through, professional *codes* and *conventions* for producing entertaining, dramatic and interesting television. The recent trend towards reality programming, for example, has seen an increase in more dramatised, voyeuristic and visually appealing camcorder footage being produced by viewers (see *Reality television*). Critics have argued with some justification that these developments have contributed to the depoliticisation of access television wherein the personal, the sensational and the bizarre take precedence over the political and the progressive.

Access production is undertaken within the context of fundamentally conflicting sets of interests and is perhaps best understood as the site of a struggle – over representation, over meaning and, in the final analysis, over who has the power to define social reality (McQuail, 1994). Despite the well-meaning intentions of access producers and programme participants, it is often the case that, in practice, access television fails to accomplish much of what it sets out to achieve. While it seemed to hold possibilities for new forms of democratic intervention (Kellner, 1990), recent developments have somewhat undermined this potential. Access production (particularly in the UK) has struggled to realise the vision of a 'teledemocracy', the notion of television as a kind of electronic soapbox for the airing of diverse, critical and alternative viewpoints. Ultimately, as Garnham (1992) suggests, access to the means of production does not yield the same degree of *power* and control that *ownership* does.

See also: **Community television, Documentary, Reality television, Video**

Further reading: Corner (1996); Dovmunt (1994); Hood (1987); Kellner (1990)

ADVERTISING

Advertising is, in many ways, the most ubiquitous cultural industry. Many forms of media, such as *commercial television*, commercial radio, internet web-sites, magazines and newspapers, generate all or part of their revenue from advertising, and there are now few spaces free from advertising messages. In the United States – one of the world's most advertising-saturated societies – over 40 per cent of mail deliveries and over 25 per cent of television time consists of advertisements. From the advertiser's point of view, the sheer volume of advertisements creates what is often called 'clutter', with so many messages competing for attention that their impact is inevitably reduced. Current trends suggest, however, that the strategy for dealing with clutter is to search for new, additional advertising venues rather than reducing marketing budgets.

The purpose of advertising is fairly straightforward: to persuade people to buy goods and services in a market economy. From an economic perspective, advertising is seen as creating demand for consumer goods, allowing for the widespread proliferation of product names and brands – without advertising it would be difficult for consumers to negotiate supermarket shelves containing dozens or even hundreds of varieties of the same product. While many scholars see advertising as playing a key role in the development of a capitalist consumer economy, the evidence suggests that the degree to which advertising raises aggregate market consumption – particularly in an environment already saturated with advertising, and where consumer spending levels are already high – is inconclusive at best. Advertising is as likely to be about maintaining or protecting market share (or 'brand loyalty') as increasing it. As a consequence, the costs of advertising a product are generally not recuperated through economies of scale in increased production. Accordingly, the costs of advertising are generally passed on to the consumer. Thus it is that 'brand names' are generally more expensive. The consumer is, in effect, paying for the advertising campaign used to influence their purchase.

For this reason, the idea that commercial television is 'free' is a misconception. Consumers pay for commercial television indirectly, since the advertising costs will be passed on to the consumer in the store. Commercial television *appears* to be cheaper (than, say, if it comes from the government, licence fee or through direct viewer subscription) because the system of payment is indirect. In fact, commercial television may end up being more expensive than more direct forms of television payment, since the costs of commercial television involve paying not only for the programmes but also for the commercials that punctuate them. The popularity of commercial television, as an economic system, relies partly on the fact that its costs are hidden.

For some products – particularly in sectors where high levels of advertising expenditure have become the norm – the cost of producing the product may be less than the cost of advertising it. This means that what we are buying is not so much a physical object as the 'image' advertisers attempt to associate with that product. This is particularly apparent when people are faced with a choice between two equivalent products – whether sports apparel or shampoo – and they choose the more *expensive* brand name. It could be argued, in this sense, that unless people are aware they are paying for an image rather than the physical quality of the product, advertising leads to irrational consumer behaviour.

Proponents of advertising argue that advertising plays a vital and necessary role in a market economy because it provides consumers with information. However, critics of advertising point out that the quality of this information is suspect for various reasons: first because advertisers will necessarily skew information to suit their interests (and hence it is more like a propaganda system); second, because those larger companies with greater access to advertising budgets will dominate the message system regardless of product quality; and third, because the informational content of advertisements is increasingly low. The last point alerts us to the way in which advertising works as a *discourse*.

The proliferation of similar products in the marketplace in a cluttered advertising environment has led many advertisers to abandon informational advertising (which many consumers now find boring) in favour of what Roland Barthes referred to as a 'mythic' system, in which the product is juxtaposed with other images in the hope that the consumer will associate the product with the image. So, for example, often regardless of its attributes, the product will appear amid images designed to evoke such attributes as attractiveness, sexiness, popularity, healthiness, sophistication, style or success. The beauty of this strategy, from the advertiser's perspective, is that it avoids making any *overt* informational claims, so the advertiser is not constrained by the limitations of the goods or services being sold. Thus, for example, campaigns for fast food or soft drinks can use images of health and vigour to construct positive associations without making any direct (and false) claims about the healthiness of their product.

Advertising's mythic structure has influenced the political arena, as politicians and parties have become more adept at marketing themselves. Many commentators argue that political campaigns are therefore less attempts to explain and promote *policy* positions than attempts to associate a party or politician with positive images. So, for example, a politician promoting tax cuts whose main beneficiary will be the more affluent may attempt to construct a more populist image by surrounding herself with ordinary working people (or signifiers thereof). Modern political campaigns are, in this respect, run like any other marketing campaign, with the same underlying discursive logic.

Much of the academic research on advertising has focused less on its ability to sell products than on its broader cultural role. At its most basic level, advertising stresses consumption while ignoring various aspects of production (which may be dependent upon a poorly paid or poorly treated workforce). Raymond Williams (1980) described advertising as a 'magic system' that promoted capitalism and deflected attention away from social class differences, a critique that has been made more poignant as *globalisation* has highlighted differences

between first-world consumers and third-world sweatshop production. Environmental degradation has also highlighted the way in
which advertising ignores the *consequences* of consumption. The
pressure put on environmental and ecological systems by the
production and disposal of goods is, for obvious reasons, entirely
absent from the discourse of advertising. In advertising, consumption
is always good, while solutions to problems will always be through
consumption rather than social action. Within the discourse of
advertising, the only response to environmental problems is to buy
more goods (such as high-factor sun protection cream).

Advertising can therefore be understood as an ideological system
that not only speaks about the world of commodities but also paints
pictures of the world. This means promoting other forms of meaning
and identity as well as an *ideology* of consumerism. Viewed from a
semiotic or anthropological perspective, advertising can be seen as a
cultural industry that not only reflects certain social values but also
promotes specific values over others. Scholars like Erving Goffman, for
example, argue that the stereotypical representations of women in
advertising (as sex-objects or housewives) may reflect patriarchal values
within the society as a whole, but they solidify and reinforce those
values (Goffman, 1979).

While TV advertising is often regarded as creative and entertaining,
the widespread use of advertising in television has led to various
criticisms about its effect on other programming. In essence, the
function of TV programmes on commercial television is to attract
audiences to the advertisements that interrupt them (during
commercial breaks) or permeate them (through product placement
or sponsorship backdrops or logos). This means that programmes will
often be written, edited or produced *around* the commercial messages,
thereby delivering audiences to advertisers in a receptive mood. This is
not only a formal constraint, but one that can affect content. So, for
example, negative information about the car industry or about the
corporate world in general – whether in *drama* or *news* and current
affairs – may be regarded by advertisers as creating an unsympathetic
environment for the promotion of their wares.

See also: **Commercial television, Discourse, Political economy,
Semiology/semiotics**

Further reading: Ewen (1976); Goffman (1979); Leiss *et al.* (1990); R. Williams
(1980)

AGENDA-SETTING

The argument that television *news* and other genres such as *documentaries* and current affairs straightforwardly transmit an obviously biased view of the world has been rejected in most quarters of media studies. Nevertheless, while the majority acknowledge that television has no overt, direct and unambiguous *effects*, research has focused on the idea that television can 'set the agenda'. In other words, just as the agenda of meetings is set with more important items placed prominently on the agenda, television programmes can help define the boundaries of what *audiences* talk about and think. By the same token, other texts and meanings, for instance radical political views or more explicit sexual imagery, may be kept off the agenda. It is argued that television is especially vulnerable to those wishing to set the agenda because audiences, given the predetermined quality of the text and *narrative*, have less opportunity to structure their consumption in the way that newspaper readers can. This implies that agenda–setting is always covert or taken for granted. Certainly research on television news has backed this up (see, for instance, Glasgow University Media Group, 1976, for a seminal example) but broadcasters, as with the early BBC, may be open in their intent to structure the agenda in 'our' interests.

The concept of agenda–setting can be applied to any *genre*, including, for example, the ability of MTV and other *music video* networks to set a pop music agenda. However, it is in the field of television news that it has gained particular currency. News programmes, it is asserted, are able to set the agenda in choice and ordering of items, by the privileging of one voice before another, in more or less combative interviewing techniques, in allocation of 'the last word', and in any number of other techniques embedded in the everyday practices of the profession. Some journalists reject this position claiming that they simply select what is most significant on any given day or even that they have 'an eye for a story'. But this undervalues the ability of news and other professionals to shape texts. In particular it ignores the 'gatekeeping' role of editors, producers and others who make day-to-day decisions about media content. It also neglects the degree to which news programmes globally have become dependent on an agenda set by the agencies, such as Reuters and Associated Press, which supply pre-packaged news and film for television companies around the world. Agenda-setting is never, though, a question of news professionals determining what will be said and thought. They do have an influence but their agendas are set in a wider context of 'what is happening' in the world, deadlines, availability of film, and the existence of 'news values', those occupational *codes* used in the social construction of news stories.

Marxists have been concerned about the operation of a hidden agenda. The organisation of, say, a news programme seems normal and natural but they have argued that the selection, construction and presentation of news veils efforts to promulgate a dominant *ideology.* Democracy is therefore illusory because news, current affairs and documentaries act on behalf of the capitalist state to limit debate and discussion. So, news coverage might set an agenda concentrating on the events of a war rather than its political origins and propriety, or one which confines election coverage solely to mainstream political parties. The result is seen as the perpetuation of an agenda sympathetic to the ruling group. Watson (1998) describes a more complex model which identifies agendas belonging to various agencies. These include a *policy* agenda developed by governments and politicians, the media agenda of television (and other media) professionals, a corporate agenda and a public or audience agenda. This more *pluralist* model moves away from the idea of a single agenda set by very specific professional or political groups, acknowledging the possibility of alliances between social forces in the development of an agenda.

Discussion of agenda-setting has tended to become embroiled in much wider debates about the media's ability, not simply to generate a restricted spectrum of meanings but to ensure that those meanings are addressed and even believed by audiences. There is now a considerable body of research, particularly in the United States, that suggests the media's ability to set the agenda can often be a powerful influence on audiences. From the 1960s onwards, studies have repeatedly shown that public opinion often follows the dominant agenda reflected in news coverage, and not the other way round. This is particularly striking in those instances where the volume of news coverage has little to do with the scale of the problem being reported. So, for example, public concern about the environment tends to reflect media attention to environmental problems, and yet the degree of media attention to the environment has little to do with overall trends in levels of pollution or threats to the environment. Similarly, public concern about drugs in the United States went from 3 per cent to over 50 per cent and back down to 3 per cent in the space of a decade, shifts that directly followed increases and decreases in media coverage but that had little to do with the incidence of drug abuse or drug-related crime.

The more dramatic examples of agenda-setting involve incidence of what are called 'moral panics'. This involves an upward spiral of concern, in which increases in news coverage prompt responses from politicians and other elites (who are keen to be seen to be responsive), and the media's coverage of this elite response creates even more media interest. When public concern begins to *reflect* media coverage, this ups the stakes still further, and political elites and the news media then *appear* to be responding to public opinion, until action is taken to 'deal' with the problem. The first major study of a 'moral panic' involved the 'mugging crisis' of the 1970s, documenting a period in which little changed in terms of crime levels (Hall *et al.*, 1978), and yet media interest in the 'new' crime of mugging led to just such an upward spiral, with very real consequences in terms of judicial sentencing policy and police operations.

Initially, agenda-setting research was based on the premise that the media might not tell you what to think, but they do tell you what to think about. In recent years, this distinction has proved untenable, as it has become clearer that what we think about influences what we think. So, for example, the approval ratings of political leaders will often be influenced by which issues dominate the news agenda. The information we receive, in other words, will provide the building blocks on which our opinions are constructed.

See also: **Audiences, Ideology, News**

Further reading: Hall *et al.* (1978); Iyengar and Kinder (1987); McCombs (1981); McQuail and Windahl (1993); Rogers and Dearing (1987); Watson (1998)

AMERICANISATION

The concept of Americanisation is often used in discussions about role of the media in shaping contemporary popular culture. Broadly, the term refers to two aspects. First, it describes the dominance of American media organisations in world markets, and second, the transmission of a powerful American *ideology* to other nations through commercial media and culture, including television programmes, films and popular music. When the term is used, either by academics or by the public, it is often in a critical way. For example, people in Italy might regret the substitution of traditional cuisine with American food (e.g. pasta with hamburgers), or authentic musical culture with American pop or rock (e.g. opera with Celine Dion). The implication is that American culture is increasingly dominant economically and, related to that economic dominance, that it also damages local cultural traditions. The net result is that these cultures become rather like

America in their lifestyles, habits and behaviour. In short, they become 'Americanised'.

However, despite these concerns the process is not simply a one-way transaction. In part, the prominent global visibility of American culture is also determined by the strong demand that exists for commodities produced there. Whether they wear Levis jeans, drink Coca-Cola, listen to Nirvana records, use American phrases in speech or watch *South Park* on the television, many people, particularly the young, positively embrace America as the zenith of 'cool', modern culture. Television has become increasingly central to this expanding cultural influence, with American shows such as *Friends*, *The Cosby Show*, *Oprah*, *Jerry Springer* and *The Simpsons* dominating foreign *schedules* and ratings. Dahlgren (1995) suggests that America is the origin of four common television *genres* typical of contemporary cheap *commercial* programming: the tabloid-style news broadcast focusing on human interest stories and sensationalism; the vox-pop talk show (e.g. *Oprah*, *Ricki Lake* and *Jerry Springer*) which explore emotional and personal issues; the info-tainment magazine programme that tries to be informative, serious and entertaining (*Good Morning* being the British equivalent); and the transnational satellite news service offering 24-hour 'live' footage and immediate, spectacular, news stories (e.g. CNN). All of these formats are cheap to produce and to import, are mainly based around light entertainment values, and have a universal and international appeal that attracts a mass rather than minority audience.

The concept of Americanisation also has a cultural and political dimension and is often used alongside theories of *cultural imperialism* and *globalisation*. Rather like these concepts, Americanisation refers to two related processes. First, it describes how American companies dominate the market for the production and distribution of media products. For example, a quick look at the structure of the television industry shows us that most of the large international media companies involved in television production and broadcasting (e.g. Time Warner, Capital Cities/ABC, Gulf and Western) are American-owned. The other dimension concerns the textual and *ideological* messages of programmes produced by these organisations. Critics, particularly those taking a *Marxist* or *political economy* perspective, have argued that by controlling the economic means of producing *texts*, America can freely transmit its own liberal-capitalist values and ideology in the content of its television programming. American ideological *hegemony* is thus maintained at the expense of radical and minority voices, and at the expense of local cultures and values.

For example, Abercrombie (1996) discusses the largest company in the world with television interests, Time Warner. An American firm working in a transnational marketplace, its role is to produce and broadcast television programmes for an international audience using a world-wide workforce. Abercrombie argues that its economic power has been achieved by merging with other companies both in the television sector and in other media. As a result, it also has interests in media such as pop music and publishing, while owning television broadcasters including HBO and Warner Cable. Through the economic processes of multimedia and vertical integration, large companies like Time Warner have increased their efficiency and broadened their business interests.

Vertical integration allows a company to centralise all aspects of television production and distribution. For example, they may own their own television studios, technical equipment, editing facilities, promotion and advertising companies, and can broadcast their own programmes. Multimedia integration occurs when the company merges with other companies working in related fields, whose assets they use to make their television production more lucrative. This could mean, for example, merging with a publishing company. As a result, the publishing arm of the company will produce books about a television show that the company also makes. This allows the firm both to sell lots of books and to maintain an interest in their television output. When different parts of a firm come together in a mutual working relationship like this, the firm is exploiting a *synergy*, which only very large companies like Time Warner have the economic power to achieve. These processes have given powerful American media companies significant trade advantages in the global television market, further contributing to the relative international success of shows made by American media organisations.

This economic dominance can also have an effect upon global culture. America itself is a vast market, and successful television programmes broadcast there can make very good profits before they are exported elsewhere. Consequently, American companies can sell their programmes cheaply to foreign broadcasters in order to make excess or surplus profits. As a result, shows that have been very successful in America, such as *Cagney and Lacey*, *Dallas* or *Dynasty*, have frequently shown up on foreign schedules as well. These programmes are sold to other countries at differentiated rates depending on the size and economic strength of the buyer. For smaller or poorer nations programming is virtually given away, often as a strategy to stop competitors getting a foothold in markets that may in the future become more lucrative. As television shows are relatively expensive to produce it is thus difficult for a broadcaster from a small or poor country to compete with the American product on either quality or price. Branston and Stafford (1996) suggest that developing nations, particularly in Africa, have to buy in cheap American programming if their service is to be economically viable. This means that much of the content of television schedules world-wide is American in origin, even if that means reruns of old soap operas such as *Dallas*.

A consequence of this competitive imbalance is that poorer nations cannot make television programmes that articulate their own culture and values. Instead, their indigenous culture is 'crowded out' by that coming from America. Given these economic and cultural imbalances, it is of no surprise that America imports very little TV from abroad and exports a vast amount. For theorists like Lewis (P. Lewis, 1986), this one-way process is intensified by new technology, such as satellite broadcasting, which allows America to extend its economic and ideological reach still further.

To understand fears about Americanisation a little better we must also place the concept in a sharper theoretical and historical context. In particular, we must relate the issue to wider discussions of *culture* and consider, specifically, the distaste of many critics for *mass culture*. This antipathy derives from two main sources. First, mass culture is challenged for undermining traditional or organic 'folk' cultures. Second, it is perceived to be a threat to the enlightened values associated with 'high art'. The concept of 'folk culture' usually involves looking back into the past, to an older rural or pre-industrial era when people lived and worked on the land and constructed their own cultural traditions and entertainment for themselves. These traditional folk cultures, embodied in activities such as music, crafts or local fairs, have been celebrated because they emerged 'organically' from communities in an 'authentic' expression of values and ideals. In this view, the modern 'mass culture' that we buy in the form of commodities produced by commercial companies is set unfavourably against the 'genuine' culture of a romanticised past.

Similarly, the 'high culture' perspective also looks back to the past, but this time to an age of European cultural dominance where the plays of Shakespeare, or the music of Mozart, set standards of 'quality' and 'value'. High art has been celebrated because it teaches people to appreciate 'good things' by challenging the intellect. This view has become culturally dominant, and as a consequence it is widely accepted that it is 'good for us' to learn about classical music, poems or literature in schools, rather than about *soap operas* or MTV. The works of great artists are also celebrated and revered for being unique and individual expressions of elusive, creative genius. In contrast, popular culture, spread through the mass media of the press, the novel, radio, pop music and television, is associated with the industrial age of the nineteenth and twentieth centuries, and with urban life and leisure. It is not produced by the people but sold to them for a price, and is attacked by critics for failing to meet stringent cultural standards. It is often condemned for appealing to 'common' or 'base' instincts and for pandering to sensationalism and escapism.

Moreover, it is attacked for treating culture rather like goods on a production line, churning out an overabundance of identical cultural fare. Where we will go to a gallery to appreciate an original Monet painting rather than be satisfied with a reproduction on a poster, in mass culture we are fully accepting of what we are given. Some critics suggest that there is very little room for individual creativity to shine through in popular television. Week in and week out, the same episodes of *Friends* or *Ally McBeal* are played to millions of people and are screened world-wide, with each episode being predictable in terms of storyline, characterisation, dialogue and so on. Both the repetition of mass culture and the replay of *genre* conventions mean that many critics have dismissed these shows as bland and monotonous. Because they are produced industrially for a mass audience, the scope for individuality and creativity within them is also diminished. As time has gone on this 'trivial' mass culture has become synonymous with America, which is often perceived as the geographical epicentre of global mass culture. In this respect, Americanisation is defined as the creeping global influence of 'trash' culture.

Interestingly, this mass cultural perspective is common to commentators from both the left and the right of the political spectrum. Where their approaches differ, however, is in the political orientation of their critique. For radicals, such as members of the *Marxist* Frankfurt School writing in the 1950s, 1960s and 1970s, mass culture and Americanisation were viewed as a threat to a critical working-class consciousness because it distracted people from their 'real' oppression through bland entertainment. Radicals wished for a complete social, cultural and political revolution in order to turn society away from capitalism. They feared that this would not happen because *ownership* of the mass media by the capitalist classes would allow them unchallenged ideological dominance. Authors such as Theodor Adorno, who had a particular interest in popular music, suggested that the artefacts produced by American 'culture industries' stopped people from thinking critically about their lives, through providing passive entertainment and distraction.

In contrast, perhaps the most celebrated exponents of the conservative tradition are the British critics Matthew Arnold (1869) and later the literary critic F.R. Leavis (1930). Their books *Culture and Anarchy* and *Mass Civilisation and Minority Culture* were both classic indictments of mass culture and Americanisation. Herein, mass culture was seen as an attack on traditional forms of 'high culture' (such as poetry and art) and as a threat to the civilising influence that classical arts had on the people. Conservatives like Arnold wished for the maintenance of traditional hierarchical social structures (as many of them were educated aristocrats or bourgeois intellectuals), and saw popular culture as a threat to established order and authority. In both of these key texts America was frowned upon for creating little of intellectual or creative distinction in comparison to Europe. Perhaps the key difference between them was that Arnold was warning about what could happen through increasing Americanisation, from his position in the nineteenth century, whereas Leavis was writing about what had actually come to pass in the twentieth.

This conservative reaction was in part borne out of a fear of the democratic process and the political enfranchisement of the working classes. America often likes to present itself as a democratic, classless and modern culture, free from the political elitism of European societies. Yet for European critics like Arnold it is maligned for corrupting high culture with popular *taste* and for pandering to the masses in both the political and cultural spheres. In Arnold's view, democracy is equated with a lack of cultural standards and a threat to established political authority. If anything, this attack intensified in the twentieth century as America became the undisputed cradle of industrialised popular culture. This has led most critics, who have taken a mass cultural perspective, to identify America as a catalyst of cultural decline.

Another attack on Americanisation was made by critics keen to maintain and protect working-class communities rather than to preserve high art and traditional social order. The most significant example of this approach, again coming from Britain, is the work of Richard Hoggart (1957), exemplified in the book *The Uses of Literacy*. This text outlined two things. First, it mapped out Hoggart's positive feelings about traditional working-class communities and the fullness and richness of their culture. Second, it detailed how mass entertainment, media and art had attacked this culture. Again, the prime source of this cultural assault was located within America. For example, Hoggart compared British and American popular novels and condemned the latter for their use of superficial and futile sex and violence. Most vividly, however, Hoggart detailed the effect of American culture on British youth in his discussion of the 'milk bars' of the 1950s. The image conjured up here was of disaffected teenage malcontents voraciously consuming any American icon (from Humphrey Bogart to cheap milkshakes) in a bid to be modern and 'cool'. The tenor of Hoggart's writing leaves little doubt that this new culture of consumption was, as he himself suggests, 'anti-life'. Hoggart's critique reads almost as a moral warning about the effect of mass culture, including television, on traditional communities. In part, then, Hoggart's ideas preceded some of the concerns raised by the cultural imperialism thesis about the relationship between dominant and subordinate cultures.

It is also not surprising that *commercial television*, which after all is fuelled by advertising revenues promoting the wonders of the modern consumer society, would come in for its share of criticism. In Britain, which was home to many of the critics of Americanisation, the content and conduct of commercial broadcasters has been regulated so that they meet a *public service* responsibility to inform and educate, as well as produce 'quality' entertainment. In other words, it has been expected to avoid the vagaries of the American commercial model.

However, not all writers have been so critical about the influence of American culture. In particular, we need to consider the reasons why people enjoy consuming it and ask what sense they make of it. Most of the critical perspectives outlined are taken by people who are not engaged with this cultural transaction and who are 'looking down' on those who are. Indeed, emerging out of a *cultural studies* perspective, authors such as Hebdige (1979) and later Fiske (1987), have argued that people do not consume American culture passively, but engage with it in a range of diverse ways. Hebdige was interested in how young working-class British men drew upon American culture, such as fashion and music, in order to articulate a resistance to their own subordinate and relatively impotent class position. One can certainly see how American popular culture would be alluring to a young person being told to read good books, listen to some classical music or engage in 'traditional' cultural activities because they were 'good for them'. For youth, therefore, America offers both a romantic vision of a modern and exciting culture and an opportunity to reject dominant European cultural ideas. This may help explain the widespread popularity of American youth programming, such as *Party of Five*, and of contentious shows like *South Park* which carry with them the cultural condemnation of 'mature' adults.

Fiske also noted 'subcultural' readings of shows such as *Dallas* and *Dynasty*, which he suggests have become cult shows among gay communities. Likewise, Liebes and Katz (1993) examined cross-cultural responses to *Dallas* and found that it was subject to a wide variety of readings depending on the social and cultural circumstances of the viewer, or 'decoder'. For example, they found that some Arab viewers read the programme as an example of western decadence and declining moral standards, whereas Russian Jews read it as a self-criticism of capitalism. It is possible, then, for people to read popular texts in a myriad of unintended ways that reject, rather than absorb, the dominant mores of American society. This reveals to us a key limitation of the cultural imperialism approach, in that it assumes a passive and compliant audience when, instead, much evidence suggests the opposite.

Other critics, such as Tomlinson (1991), have argued that it is one thing to suggest that America is the economic leader in the global market for popular culture, yet quite another to say that this process has determined global cultural identity. Indeed, Tomlinson has questioned the conclusion of cultural imperialists that American companies flooding the international market with cheap products destroy local expression. Instead of a process of imperialism, which implies domination of one culture over another, he argues for the more neutral term 'globalisation', and suggests that different global areas are so 'interconnected' and dependent on one another that no one culture is able to dominate over all others. This has led some academics to suggest that America is itself influenced by other cultures, evidenced by the popularity of Latin American 'telenovelas', or America's historical fondness for *Monty Python* or *Benny Hill*. Rather than a one-way flow, we are witness to a positive exchange or cross-fertilisation of cultures that, in the long run, can create cultural hybrids (such as the telenovela, which contains many of the genre conventions of the soap opera) flowing into and out of American culture. In contrast, the cultural imperialism thesis reduces all American culture to a simplistic or essentialist category that fails to account for the diverse nature of American society.

This diversity is also reflected in American programming that is far from conventional in style or political stance. For example, cult shows such as *Twin Peaks* have challenged traditional notions of how to make 'good' television by using unorthodox narratives and visual *rhetoric*, while remaining very popular. In the political sphere the cop show

Cagney and Lacey has been celebrated by feminist scholars for its positive representation of female characters in a traditionally masculine workplace. Moreover, Chapman (1998) has argued that new media technologies, such as the camcorder and the cheap availability of satellite licences, have fuelled more politicised approaches to television-making. For example, he cites the *Gulf Crisis TV Project* (which broadcast anti-war programmes nationally in order to counter blanket mainstream media acceptance of the war) as evidence of a progressive development in television. Although operating on the margins of mainstream culture, the existence of this programming nevertheless offers a more rich and diverse view of American culture than is present in many of the positions set out earlier in this discussion.

See also: **Cultural imperialism, Cultural studies, Culture, Globalisation, Ideology, Marxism**

Further reading: Abercrombie (1996); Dahlgren (1995); Dowmunt (1994); P. Lewis (1986); Tomlinson (1991); Tunstall (1977)

AUDIENCES

An audience is best understood as a category rather than as a way of being. Just as we are members of different audiences at different times, so we are also members of a range of social groups. Being part of an audience is something we slip in and out of – it is part of who we are but does not capture or define us or how we think.

In media studies, the category of audience refers simply to the act of viewing, reading or listening to media texts (see *Text*). The development of mass media means that audiences are no longer linked by space or even time. Transnational media markets create audiences for globally exported TV programmes – from *Baywatch* to *Mr Bean* – that cross social class, nationality, occupation, education, race and countless other boundaries. While we can thus speak of 'global audiences', this term refers to the distribution of programmes rather than to a homogeneity of experience, since the meaning of a media text will depend upon the way viewers understand the world. Even programmes shown within a common cultural environment may be experienced very differently: viewers may watch alone, with family, with friends; they may watch a programme like *Baywatch* as a *soap opera* or as a form of sexual titillation; or they may watch avidly or inadvertently.

The dispersed, elusive nature of the experience of being an audience makes the study of media reception a complex endeavour. There are, accordingly, a number of ways of exploring what audiences are and how they relate to the specific media.

At the industry level, the way media audiences are conceived is fairly straightforward. Although some *public service broadcasters* like the British Broadcasting Corporation may carry out more sophisticated forms of research, commercial broadcasters are generally interested in only two things, the size of the audience and its composition (or more specifically, the amount of disposable income its members possess). This is because audiences are not seen as a category to be understood, but as a commodity to be sold to advertisers (see *Advertising*). Audience research – or 'ratings' – thus becomes a basis for negotiation between a television station and the people who pay for it (the advertisers). In this context, an audience made up of the elderly or people on low incomes is seen as less valuable than an audience of middle-class young adults. Television programmes on *commercial television* therefore tend to reflect the interests of the more 'valuable' audiences.

Academic audience research has a long history and a number of trajectories. During the twentieth century the development of urban, industrial societies led to speculation about the drift away from folk or community-based culture towards 'mass media' and 'mass culture'. By the 1930s, some theorists began to associate this sociological shift with the rise of Fascism in Europe. They described a mass society in which the breakdown of community structures created an atomised population with few defences against forms of mass propaganda. Members of the Frankfurt School of Social Research – such as Theodor Adorno and Max Horkheimer – argued that *mass culture* was crude, formulaic and ideologically repressive: mass audiences were therefore manipulated or merely distracted.

When members of the Frankfurt School emigrated to the United States to escape Fascism in Germany, their critique focused more explicitly on the capitalist commercialisation of culture. While their work was regarded by many American researchers as too pessimistic and sociologically unsophisticated, their thesis nevertheless provided a framework for the emerging *'effects'* tradition of audience research, which tested media influence against a backdrop of concern about its potentially harmful or persuasive effects.

Two areas of particular concern during the early years of television audience research were the questions of media *violence* and the coverage of politics. Specifically, did violence on the screen encourage violent behaviour and did the media coverage of politics sway the outcome of elections? The results of their work tended to alleviate concerns about excessive media *power* and defenceless audiences – audiences were not, studies suggested, merely 'cultural dupes', passive victims of a manipulative culture industry.

By the late 1950s researchers were beginning to develop different frameworks for the study of audiences. One of the most influential of these frameworks was the '*uses and gratifications*' approach or the 'functional analysis' of media. Uses and gratifications attempted, in a theoretical sense, to liberate audiences by substituting a concern with what media did to people with the more optimistic question of what people did with media. Although this switch in emphasis can be over-emphasised – uses and gratifications was still interested in media influence, albeit in a more negotiated form – it undoubtedly precipitated a conceptual shift away from the power of the media towards the power of the audience.

The uses and gratifications perspective was – and is – regarded by many as a step forward in audience theory, since it allows us to see audiences as active participants in the creation of meaning and as a heterogeneous population with different needs and motivations. The popularity of uses and gratifications in the 1960s and 1970s could also be seen as more in tune with the interests of a commercial media industry, who were keen to promote the idea that media were generally benign, existing to serve the various needs of groups of consumers.

During the 1970s, the influence of *semiology* and theories of ideology informed a *cultural studies* approach to the media audience. This approach, based upon the *encoding/decoding* model developed by Stuart Hall and colleagues at the Centre for Contemporary Cultural Studies in England, combined a more complex notion of media *power* with the idea that audiences were both active and constrained in making meanings. This approach was the point of departure for a number of studies in the 1980s and 1990s which have tried to explore the complexity of media influence to a range of forms, from romance novels and soap operas to *science fiction* and television *news*. A crucial question for much of this research involves the role media play in the construction of *hegemony* and the degree to which audiences resist, avoid or oppose dominant meanings.

Audience research today is a varied field encompassing a number of different approaches. The effects tradition, with its focus on direct causal relationships between media and audiences, remains popular with funding agencies (who tend to focus, as early effects research did, on potentially negative effects on audiences). At the academic level, the quantitative, survey-based study of media effects has become more sophisticated, incorporating approaches such as *agenda-setting* and *cultivation analysis* – both of which suggest that the broad content of mass media has a specific and sometimes powerful influence on the way audiences think. Indeed, the findings of cultivation analysis suggest that some of the early concerns of the Frankfurt School, while perhaps simplistic and overstated, were not entirely misplaced.

If the focus on media effects tends to take a macroscopic approach, retaining a notion of the 'mass audience', cultural studies and 'uses and gratifications' have enabled researchers to explore – on a more qualitative level – the different moments of being an audience. Although many studies attempt to capture more than one of these moments, these more qualitative approaches can be broadly identified under three descriptive headings:

1   A focus on the semiotic moment of meaning making, exploring how audiences read or make sense of specific texts, such as news programmes or situation *comedies*.
2   An ethnographic focus on how people behave when they are being an audience, on the ways in which media technology is used and perceived and what David Morley has called 'the politics of the living room' (Morley, 1992). Much of this work has explored issues of *gender*, use and power.
3   A focus on audiences who define themselves partly in relation to specific genres or media texts, whether as readers of romance fiction or as fans of shows like *Star Trek* (see *Fans*).

In some senses the qualitative focus on the diverse identity and behaviour of audiences signals a wider shift away from 'certainty' and 'unity' in media studies, as analysis recognises the fragmented experience of viewing.

See also: **Cultivation analysis, Effects, Encoding and decoding, Mass culture, Uses and gratifications**

Further reading: Dickinson *et al.* (1998); J. Lewis (1991); Morley (1992)

CHILDREN AND TELEVISION

Issues surrounding television and children are contentious ones framed by a range of interrelated concerns. A good deal of the research in this area has taken place outside of television and media studies – it seems that where children are concerned everyone (priests, politicians, journalists, parents, teachers, psychologists, sociologists) has something to say. With recent developments in communications *technology* giving rise to a whole new range of entertainment media within the home (satellite, cable and digital channels, computer games, the internet and *video*) anxieties concerning the *effects* of these new media on children have increased, lending a new urgency to contemporary research and debate. Before looking at the various approaches informing research into the influences and effects of television on children, it is useful to consider the ways in which children (and childhood) are perceived in western society. The concept of childhood is understood as being a stage in the lifecourse characterised by dependency and immaturity – both physical and mental. Children are conceived of as being unable to make rational and informed social, sexual, political, economic and intellectual decisions and are therefore dependent on adults to make these choices for them. Childhood is seen to be an important part of the socialisation process primarily associated with education and play wherein children are raised to be healthy functioning adults. Ariés (1973) suggests that such ideas concerning children and childhood are unique to western society – particularly in the ways in which children are almost quarantined from adult social life and are seen to be vulnerable and in need of protection. Ariés found that the way in which children are conceptualised varies both historically and culturally and that these variations have implications for the ways in which the lives of young people are understood and organised within societies.

Given the ways in which we have come to understand childhood in western society, it is not surprising to find that these dominant conceptions underpin a good deal of the research concerned with children and television. Most research undertaken in this field centres around children's access to unsuitable material (*violence*, *sexual* imagery or bad language), responsibility (of parents to regulate access and of broadcasters to provide suitable programming for children), morality and ethics (in terms of programme content), education (what, if anything at all, do children learn from television?), commercialisation (are children being exposed to market forces?) and the exposure of children to mass-produced entertainment which, it is argued, ultimately leads to declining standards in literacy and the erosion of spontaneous and creative play – the bedrock of childhood. All of these concerns, to a certain extent, assume that children are vulnerable and need protecting. They are, in effect, seen as being passive and receptive to corruption or manipulation. Television is often linked with the alleged demise of childhood, and children are often characterised as being 'couch potatoes' and TV zombies, waiting for their next viewing fix. The television set is seen as being an intruder into the protective environment of the home, bringing the harsh realities of the outside world into the living room and filling children's minds with sex and violence.

And yet, a good deal of research in both Britain and the United States has shown that, contrary to popular belief, children can be (and in most cases are) highly discriminating viewers. Television does not dominate children's lives – children often intersperse television viewing with other activities such as playing, talking and reading. Furthermore, *content analysis* of children's television such as *Batman*, *Superman* and *Teenage Mutant Ninja Turtles* indicates that children's programmes can have strong pro-social effects in that they often combine visually commanding and spectacular action sequences with a strong moral stance. For example, the cartoon series *Captain Planet and the Planeteers* successfully incorporated a strong environmental and ecological awareness message into an action adventure format. Similarly, programmes such as *Blue Peter* and *Sesame Street* have always included an educational and tolerant value system. Arguably, children are more likely to take notice of moral and social issues if they are presented to them in a context which is both appealing and entertaining for them.

Research findings in this field, then, have been contradictory and subject to fierce debate. For every study claiming evidence for the negative effects of television on children's behaviour and emotional development, there are just as many studies claiming quite the opposite – that television provides children with knowledge of world events, of different cultures and of ways to understand and experiencing things beyond their normal daily routines and lives. Research in the field of children's viewing patterns has, generally, tended to ignore children's perspectives and the ways in which they make sense of what they view on television, although this oversight is now being addressed by some researchers (Buckingham, 1993a; Gunter and McAleer, 1997).

Television, as a medium of communication, cannot be isolated from other influences in children's lives. Television (and media influence in general) is embedded in, and is part of, the matrix of social relationships which combine to make up the experience of childhood. Children do not completely identify with any single source or influence but are influenced by their families, peers, the school and so on. Television, then, is just one component, one source of identification and influence, among many. What is apparent is that television is more likely to reinforce pre-existing attitudes and experiences in children than radically to modify or alter behaviour. If this is the case, then the importance of teaching children media literacy and the responsibility of parents and teachers in influencing children's attitudes is paramount in shaping the perceptions and beliefs children bring to their experiences of watching television.

See also: **Audiences, Educational television, Effects, Violence**

Further reading: Buckingham (1993a); Gauntlett (1995); Gunter and McAleer (1997); Kinder (1991); Simatos and Spencer (1992)

CLASS

An understanding of class in relation to television studies can be gained in at least two ways: first, by examining the concept of class and the ways this has been conceived and developed by a variety of theorists, and second, by examining ways in which specific classes or the relations between classes have been represented (see *Representation*) on television. Readings of examples from television will be influenced by the different understandings of the concept of class itself.

The term 'class' has a complex range of meanings in social, economic and cultural theory, but refers primarily to economic and social position and the relative power, prestige and status that arises out of or is linked to it. Karl Marx (1818–83) wrote extensively on class and class relations, arguing that society was divided into two main classes, those who owned the means of production (capitalists or the ruling class) and those who owned only their labour power (the proletariat or working class). Under this system of class relations, the latter group were inevitably exploited and disadvantaged, not only economically but socially, and the interests of each group were bound to be in conflict. In Marx's analysis, then, economic class position was the key element in determining an individual's social position. Members of a given social class would share certain common experiences, besides economic advantage (or disadvantage), such as political attitudes, social values and beliefs. Marx argued (and hoped) that members of the proletariat would come to recognise their disadvantaged position and rise up to overthrow the capitalist system. However, Marx also realised that although large numbers of people might share a common economic and social position, they would not necessarily be aware of the fact. This state of affairs is called 'false consciousness' and is greatly aided by the successful circulation of ideologies reinforcing ruling-class beliefs and values. In Marx's analysis, the ruling class were in a uniquely powerful position to be able to influence ideas, values and beliefs (see *Ideology*).

From Marx's perspective, class relations imply a particular model of the way social, cultural and economic aspects of society fit together. The 'base/superstructure' model, as it has become known, rests on the idea that the economy or class structure, (the base) determines all other aspects of what we might broadly call *culture* (the superstructure). So the economically dominant class is able to dominate culturally as well. Economic dominance allows for a cultural dominance because members of the ruling class are in a privileged position to influence politics and ideas in society. The ideas of the ruling class become the acceptable, expected and dominant ideas. This is achieved through the articulation of ideology which then becomes the dominant ideology.

Thus, although Marx's writings preceded the advent of television, latter-day Marxists have pointed to patterns of *ownership* within television, and the mass media more generally, and have argued that the ideas of the economically dominant class come to predominate as an accepted 'world view'. What audiences are offered on television is thus inextricably linked to a set of ideas which support capitalism and ruling-class ideology. Other ideas are suppressed or marginalised. For example, much television *news* focuses on issues of international finance, world markets and domestic industrial conflict, with an inordinate amount of attention given to matters relating to, and in support of, capitalist economies (see *Agenda-setting*). Equally, it has been alleged from a Marxist perspective that television can function as a passifying narcotic, especially in the form of popular light entertainment such as *game shows*.

Marx's ideas have been modified and refined by Marxists and non-Marxists alike. Max Weber (1864–1920) modified Marxist theory by arguing that power, prestige and status, though frequently closely associated with economic class, are not by necessity determined by it. This analysis opens up the possibility of acknowledging how factors other than social class, such as *gender, race*, age or other aspects of status, might also play an important role in shaping life chances and experiences. Moreover, the debate about the relationship between the base and the superstructure has been extended and reformulated over time by neo-Marxists. Members of the Frankfurt School, writing mainly during the 1930s and 1940s, saw the development of a commercial mass media as central to the ways in which ruling-class ideologies are perpetrated and reinforced. In doing so, they elevated the importance of culture in helping to understand class relations.

Louis Althusser developed a more complex model of the ways in which dominant ideologies work. Key 'ideological apparatuses', such as the law and the family for instance, form a difficult, sometimes contradictory relationship with the economy rather than being simply determined by it. Thus, ideology is not regarded as 'false' but as a kind of framework through which people live and understand their conditions of life. Further, Antonio Gramsci's writings on *hegemony* provide a sophisticated analysis of the way ideologies and class relations operate within seemingly consensual democratic societies. An understanding of Gramsci's analysis can help to illuminate the interaction between different dimensions of power, such as gender and race, but also re-emphasises the shifting, dynamic nature of hegemonic relations, which are, he would argue, ultimately based on class. In this analysis, culture becomes the field on which class relations come to have real meaning. It is within culture that dominant and subordinate classes are able to negotiate, resist and contest hegemony. Thus, much of the academic work in this area, whether primarily theoretical or based on case studies (for instance, of television programmes), focuses on how underlying conflicts, based on material or symbolic inequalities between and within classes, are expressed and emphasised in media products and in the culture more generally.

The notion of economic class has been supplemented by the idea of social class, based not on ownership but on occupation. This conception of class has been used in a pragmatic way by the *advertising* and television industries as well as by market researchers, to identify and profile specific *audiences*. Social class groups, based on income, spending-power and lifestyle choices, are of particular interest to those television companies who are primarily reliant on advertising revenue and for whom, therefore, audience share is of vital importance.

Discussions about the ways in which class has been represented on television have taken a number of trajectories. In British *cultural studies*, the Marxian influence has largely predominated, so that class has been strongly emphasised as an explanatory category, as well as featuring in analyses of specific programmes or *genres*. The limiting effects of *stereotyping* and 'negative' representations, issues of under-representation and the undermining and/or distortion of working-class life in popular television, such as *soaps*, have been major concerns, along with studies of bourgeois dominance within the industry itself. See, for example, the series of studies from the late 1970s onwards by the Glasgow University Media Group (1976, 1985).

Appraisals of British television have continued to take the issue of class seriously, although given that the objects of study have ranged across television's output it is unsurprising that writers have observed a number of different treatments of class. For example, some work on soaps has looked at the way imaginary working-class communities are constructed (in contrast to the largely middle-class or monied communities in American soaps), while studies of sitcoms have noted the middle-class characteristics of most of the families featured. Authority figures on television (newscasters, voice-overs, hosts) have predominantly been middle-class in image. On the other hand, British television drama, particularly since the 1960s, has included some noteworthy examples of films and plays which have focused on working-class life or which have formed critiques of the class system. Some examples include the work of Ken Loach and Tony Garnett, such as *Cathy Come Home*, that of Jimmy McGovern, such as *Strike*, and work by Alan Bleasdale, such as *Boys from the Blackstuff*. But it is striking that in most popular television, the working class have been overwhelmingly represented as physical, simple, unsophisticated and parochial (*Bread* and *Auf Wiedersehen, Pet* being two examples). Moreover, even progressive dramas, with their emphasis on the economic and social circumstances of labour, have tended to produce working-class heroes rather than heroines, so that 'working-class-ness' becomes associated with masculinity.

In the USA, although some work has been produced on televisual representations of class, the focus has been very much more on representations of race and gender. This difference is partly accounted for by historic and social differences, in particular the anti-communist fever of the Cold War period, but also by differences in academic influence in which the US tradition has been far more linked to an empirical social science approach than a cultural studies approach. Nonetheless, it is agreed by many theorists that mass media portrayals of class tend to justify the existing class relations within contemporary capitalism. Butsch's (1995) survey of prime-time US television over four decades found that there was persistent under-representation of working-class/'blue collar' occupations and concomitant over-representation of professional and managerial occupations. Wealth and glamour were also over-represented. Butsch argues that while working-class males are frequently represented as buffoons, middle-class men never are, and while the wives of middle-class male characters could sometimes be portrayed as silly or irresponsible, in the main working-class wives were shown as sensible and mature in comparison with their menfolk. Butsch argues that this ideological hegemony is produced as a result of a number of structural and cultural factors. For example, the continuing dominance of middle-class masculine viewpoints within the television industry as well as the time constraints under which programme creators and executives are likely to work tend towards the quick-fix of class stereotyping rather than a more considered exploration of characterisation. In recent years, there have been some exceptions to the rule on prime-time American television, notably in such series as *Roseanne*. In general terms, however, American television is overwhelmingly dominated by a WASP minority, and the effect is that the estimated 60–70 per cent of the US population that can be regarded as working class becomes a televisual 'silenced majority' (Ehrenreich, 1995).

See also: **Comedy, Drama, Gender, Hegemony, Race, Representation, Soaps**

Further reading: Corner and Harvey (1996); Dines and Humez (1995)

CODE

At its most general, and particularly as it is used by *structuralists* and *semiologists*, a code is a system of *signs* which is able to communicate meanings. The signs might be words, lights within a traffic light system, musical sounds or images within a television *advertisement*. The system or code operates according to a set of rules which members of a culture learn and consent to explicitly or implicitly. Thus, etiquette is a system of symbolic actions used by people in rule-governed or coded ways in order to communicate. Codes may be simple, as in the case of traffic lights, or more complex, as with formal languages. They do not necessarily operate in isolation but interact in complex and intricate ways: for example, we can communicate using non-verbal, verbal and representational codes at any one moment.

Within media studies, the term 'code' is used to refer to a range of often unexplored audio-visual systems which have the capacity to construct and organise meaning in media texts. John Fiske (1987) attempts to describe the types of code which television uses, noting their conceptual separation but actual interrelationships. He begins by suggesting that 'reality' is already culturally *encoded* – that is, while there may be an empirical reality, we make sense of it in terms of cultural conventions (see *Realism*). Thus, things like appearance, dress and behaviour are culturally encoded. 'Reality' is then encoded electronically by technical codes, including camera, lighting, editing and sound. The close-up shot has come to signify intimacy, the fade-in often connotes beginning, a cut which moves from one shot to another can mean excitement or speed, and so forth. In his analysis of *Hart to Hart*, a 1980s American television series, Fiske mentions an editing code which gives heroes more time and shots than villains. Technical codes in turn transmit 'conventional representational codes' – that is, the conventional ways in which 'things' are represented. Here he includes, among others, narrative, characterisation and dialogue codes. Examples might be characterised representations of villainy and heroism, where traits such as accent, face-shape and colour of hair may encode meaning for audiences, and narratives within more traditional crime series (for instance, *Starsky and Hutch* or *Inspector Morse*), where the inevitable capture of the criminal signifies narrative resolution and a return to equilibrium. Codes of *representation* relate to, and help organise, ideological codes such as those referencing patriarchy, *class*, individualism, capitalism, nationality and *race*. In developing his example of villainy and heroism, Fiske cites Dorfman and Mattelart's (1975) observation that villainy in Disney cartoons is often expressed in characteristics of working-class appearance and manner. Similarly, the narratives of police series seek to ideologically situate the viewer with the police, and consequently the status quo (see *Crime series*). Writers in this essentially semiological stable are interested in the ways in which these various types of codes form a coherent and apparently natural unity. They see their role as deconstructing and exposing codes and their operation in organising a 'natural' reality.

It can be argued that some codes – those that audiences are more familiar with – are more accessible than others. *Genres* such as 'country house whodunnits' and *game shows* are based on the constant reworking of particular codes and conventions. Conversely, surrealistic advertisements or *postmodern* television drama such as *Twin Peaks* are based on disrupting codes, a process which may be 'difficult' for audiences, but which helps mark certain texts as avant garde (and simultaneously provides an opportunity for particular audiences to reveal their cultural capital in understanding complexity). In turn, disruption of 'normal' codes can become absorbed into 'mainstream' television, as with camera techniques in dramas such as *NYPD Blue* and *ER*.

In theory, codes can be *decoded* (that is, interpreted and understood) wherever audiences share the common code or language. Hence, some versions of *Marxist* media analysis have argued that television audiences almost unproblematically interpret codes of neutrality and formality conveyed by television *news* (Glasgow University Media Group, 1976). In so doing they decode in ways preferred by the programme-makers and implicitly by forces reproducing dominant ideology via the medium of news.

However, television audience research has become increasingly concerned with whether and how audiences actually decode preferred meanings. Eco (1972) talks about aberrant decoding where audience and preferred textual meaning do not coincide because message transmitters and audiences are operating with different codes. Similarly, Stuart Hall (1980) notes the possibility of audiences making negotiated and oppositional readings as well as dominant (preferred) ones.

See also: **Convention, Encoding and decoding, Mediation, Realism, Representation, Semiology/semiotics, Sign**

Further reading: Eco (1972); Fiske (1987); Hall (1980); Watson (1998)

COMEDY

Academic interest in television comedy has tended to focus on two sub-genres, the situation comedy (or sitcom) and political satire. Studies have addressed a range of issues, from mapping the *genre* conventions of sitcom to exploring the role of satire in provoking a general distrust of 'establishment' figures and institutions, particularly in the sphere of politics. Comedy is one of the most interesting aspects of television production in that it is, in a common-sense way at least, so clearly meant to provide 'escapist' entertainment. To explore its 'deeper meanings', therefore, might seem odd or even inappropriate. However, Bowes (1990) has argued that to acknowledge comedy only as 'light entertainment' diverts our attention from its content, which often works on the basis of *stereotypes* that may fail to challenge, or indeed may reinforce or legitimate, dominant *ideological* positions. These can function to relegate some social groups, who are often the butt of humour, to a subordinate position both within the *narrative* of a *text* and, consequently, outside in 'real' society. Because of its escapist function, however, the popularity of comedy, evidenced by its ubiquitous presence in television *schedules*, remains formidable.

Perhaps the most popular form of comedy is the sitcom. It has certainly provided the predominant focus for academics and has fallen under their gaze on many occasions (Bowes, 1990; Eaton, 1981; Goddard, 1991; Marc, 1989; Medhurst and Tuck, 1996; Woollacott, 1986). While emerging out of radio comedy in both Britain (e.g. *Hancock's Half Hour*) and America (e.g. *I Love Lucy*), by the 1950s the sitcom played a well-established role in the weekly schedule of television programmes that were on offer. Goddard (1991) has argued that by the early 1960s the sitcom was the pre-eminent form of television comedy in Britain, outstripping both sketch-based entertainment shows, which displayed the talents of comics such as Morecambe and Wise, and intellectual satirical shows such as *That Was The Week That Was (TW3)*.

Early in their development, however, differences in the form and content of British and American shows emerged. As McQueen (1998) has suggested, early American sitcoms tended to focus on the relationships between married, childless couples, exemplified by *Bewitched* and *The Dick Van Dyke Show*. These set the standard for what came to be known as the 'Hi Honey, I'm Home!' show. In contrast, British sitcoms centred on the lives of sullen, cynical men with frustrated ambitions and bleak dispositions. *Hancock's Half Hour* prefaced the 'naturalistic' or 'realistic' approach to character, dialogue and location that was a staple of later British sitcoms. Its sense of jaded social *realism* permeated through other popular shows such as *Steptoe and Son*, *Rising Damp* and *Porridge*. This sense of realism, Goddard argues, was crucial in assuring audience identification with characters and the situations that they found themselves in. It also played to the strengths of television as a medium, with its ability to represent a sense of reality in a way that other media could not. This was cultivated by the use of establishing shots to set the 'ordinariness' of scenes, close-ups for character expression, and quick editing to capture 'spontaneous' reactions to events. Given the availability of such devices, the naturalistic sitcom was always likely to flourish on television (Goddard, 1991).

As sitcoms became ever-present in the schedules, so authors turned their attention to identifying the distinctive conventions of the genre. Some basic rules were generally found to apply. Sitcoms usually adhere to the series format, with each continuing for a limited number of episodes. Individual shows last for thirty minutes at most, are repeated at the same time each week, and centre on the lives and activities of an established core of characters and locations. Eaton (1981) developed a 'typology' of sitcom, in which he identified three locations, or situations, in which the comedy tended to occur. First, the home, where humour derives from the interactions between family members (e.g. *The Cosby Show, Frazier, Roseanne, Only Fools and Horses*). Second, the workplace, where relationships between colleagues at work drive the humour (e.g. *Are You Being Served?, Dad's Army, Cheers*). Third, and less obviously, a location that is neither home nor work but contains some of the relationships and tensions that those situations generate. A recent example of this might be the popular American show *Friends*, where there is not a 'traditional' home or family environment, but where some characters take on 'family' roles which, at times, are the source of much mirth (e.g. Monica's motherly, almost obsessive, domestication). Bowes (1990) illustrates this third category through the example of the British sitcom *The Young Ones*, where the complications of communal living among dysfunctional students were parodied to excessive proportions. Here, the house hippy, Neil, was also the butt of many jokes due to his domestic and motherly function within the household.

The repetition of locations – and the simple interpersonal themes and issues that are addressed – also plays an economic or institutional function, in that it allows for sets to be recycled and for a limited number of actors to be employed. Over time, this repetition also provides the viewer with a sense of comfortable familiarity. In these ways, the sitcom serves as a distinct genre, organised according to recognisable rules and textual *conventions*. Audience recognition of these conventions, particularly the everyday situations and the antagonisms that they generate, contributes to the feeling of realism that the genre provokes and increases audience identification with both the characters and the humour. When we switch on, we know what we are going to get and, as McQueen (1998) has argued, the greater the friction or tension that is created the more we tend to laugh.

Eaton also suggests that the *narrative* of sitcom is driven by an 'inside/outside' division of plot and characterisation (Eaton, 1981). This means that characters and events from outside the immediate location can enter into it, and temporarily may even disrupt it. However, this outside influence will not change the fundamental nature of the established situation, which is reaffirmed at the end of each episode when the narrative closes. As Woollacott (1986) has proposed, this reaffirmation occurs because the narrative of sitcom tends to follow a 'classical' pattern. Here, the situation is in some ways disrupted, which leads to a sequence of events to resolve that disruption. The episode will then end in a narrative closure characterised by a return to the original, now stable, situation. The viewer, who is fully aware that the narrative is always 'circular' and expects it to return to normal, is not placed in a position of suspense but is located in a position of amusement as they anticipate how the circle will be closed. Our pleasure in sitcom therefore derives from the efficiency, particularly in respect to comic timing, with which this 'return to normal' is enacted. As McQueen (1998) has suggested, the primary situation of the sitcom, therefore, is that nothing ever changes. Our knowledge that this is so is also our foremost *pleasure.*

Other devices reinforce this circular narrative, which lends itself to an easy recognition of, and identification with, the genre. McQueen also notes that many characters have recurring motifs that provide a ritual element to proceedings. Joey's chat-up line, 'How you doin'?' (*Friends*), or Del Boy Trotter's range of colloquial catchphrases, 'Lovely jubbly'/'You plonker' (*Only Fools and Horses*), are liberally sprinkled throughout the dialogue to provide us with familiar pleasures. Another source of gratification and humour comes from the glut of *stereotypes* that are ever-present in the sitcom format. Medhurst and Tuck (1996) suggest that sitcom cannot function properly without recourse to stereotypes. Given a short thirty-minute slot in the schedules, the emphasis of the sitcom is on immediacy. As a result, characters are necessarily packaged according to easily distinguished 'types' which themselves tend to play upon wider cultural clichés such as the nagging mother-in-law or the middle-aged male 'queen'. Medhurst and Tuck imply that there are progressive and regressive aspects to the sitcom and to the issue of stereotyping. First, sitcoms provide a sense of collective experience for a working-class community that, in reality, has been fragmented and disrupted by the break-up of traditional communities. This sense of community is established not only by the focus being, in the main, on working-*class* people in everyday situations, but is manipulated through other devices. For example, canned laughter gives the viewer the impression that they are laughing along with others and that their response to the text is a shared one. This provides the mythical sensation of a public engaging in a collective experience. By way of example, Medhurst and Tuck (1996) suggest that this simulates earlier 'organic' experiences of social solidarity, such as the music hall.

The myth of a defined community that is created, however, also functions to distinguish between those who are inside and outside of that community. Those on the outside are often constructed as 'deviant', particularly through being the objects of ridicule and through stereotyping. In their study, Medhurst and Tuck were primarily concerned with representations of gay men in sitcoms, suggesting that groups that are subordinate or marginalised by the dominant *ideology* in the 'real' world are frequently depicted as comic within the televisual one. However, they warn against the temptation for us to simply dismiss stereotypes or reject them out of hand. Drawing on the work of Richard Dyer, Medhurst and Tuck rightly argue that, however principled or well intentioned, such punitive action will not make a stereotype disappear. It will also preclude us getting to grips with the power of the stereotype by examining how its ideological work is done. After all, it is precisely because the dominant heterosexual ideology has a fear and apprehension of the conspicuously extravagant, effeminate man (lesbians have been largely invisible in sitcoms), that it insists on him being ridiculed. If a stereotype so obviously threatens the intolerant status quo, we might argue, then why not celebrate its power to confront and resist by embracing rather than rejecting it? Stereotypes are thus more complex than they may seem on first reading. Bowes (1990) also warns against thinking about sitcom stereotypes too simplistically, and asks us consider whether or not the stereotype is the subject of the humour or the producer of it. For example, he argues that gay stereotypes in the sitcom *Agony* served to reveal and ridicule the intolerance of other, heterosexual, characters, presenting them (and, by implication, the 'straight' status quo) and their conservative views as aberrant.

Outside of sitcom, the study of political satire has also proved a fertile ground for some theorists. Peter Keighron (1998), in an exploration of television satire in Britain, has argued that the strong tradition of satire reflects a general disrespect for politicians and political life, particularly for the Conservative Party. From the 1960s, when *TW3* could secure an audience of thirteen million, until the present, when *Have I Got News for You*, *The Day Today*, *Rory Bremner* or *Michael Moore* continue to do healthy business, satire has had a place at the heart of comic programming. Wagg (1992) has argued that the tradition of satire reflects a general erosion of political life, parliamentary democracy and the public sphere in post-war Britain. This has been accompanied by an ascendancy of the private/individual sphere. As a result, the world of politics is easily ridiculed as we have little direct commitment to it, other than voting once every four or five years (if we bother to do so). For many of us it appears burdensome and more or less irrelevant to our day-to-day lives. This is even true of those in the middle and upper classes who, traditionally, have provided the intellectual raw material and personnel for the political sphere. As Wagg notes, many of the satirists who have appeared on our screens, such as Peter Cook, were Oxbridge-educated scholars. Satire, then, has tended to provide the subversion of choice for a literate and educated elite.

The objective of such satirists has often been to expose the falsity and fabrication of politics. The idea that politics is 'only a game' (and, consequently, is 'fair game' to the satirist) has come through strongly in much television satire. For instance, Wagg alludes to an incident where

Graham Chapman, of *Monty Python* fame, silently addressed members of the Cambridge University student union, then a seedbed for aspiring politicians, while dressed as a carrot (Wagg, 1992). Interestingly, much satire found a home at the BBC, which had often been perceived as the traditional voice of the elite establishment. This access to the nation's principal broadcaster gave the satirists' mockery of public life an extra and unexpected legitimacy. For Wagg, however, this has come at a price, as politics and individual politicians *do* have the power to supervise our everyday lives in quite concrete ways. By passing legislation determining the conditions of groups or individuals, such as ethnic or sexual minorities, it can impact on those lives in a direct manner. By customarily writing off the public sphere as absurd, we thus willingly evacuate a site of considerable power. In doing so we make no investment in the important decision-making processes that are central to democratic citizenship. Ultimately, then, we should make few complaints when the 'mad world' of politics, as satirists would have it, acts against us.

See also: **Genre, Ideology, Narrative, Realism, Stereotypes**

Further reading: Bowes (1990); Goddard (1991); Keighron (1998); Marc (1989); Medhurst and Tuck (1996); Wagg (1992)

COMMERCIAL TELEVISION

The history and development of commercial television has taken very different forms on each side of the Atlantic. In the USA, television has always been a fundamentally commercial enterprise, financed predominantly by advertising revenue. From early in US television history, commercial sponsors and advertisers have exerted a good deal of direct and indirect control over content, style and scheduling of programmes. This continues to be the case today, with US television based solidly and unapologetically on commercial principles and on the concept of television as primarily an entertainment medium.

By contrast, in Britain the history of television has been dominated by the ideals of *public service broadcasting* (PSB), even though commercial television has existed for some four decades. It is, though, too simplistic to perceive commercial and PSB television as opposites. In Britain at least, the principles, ethics and assumptions underlying each type of broadcasting have infected and permeated the other, but the balance between PSB and commercial principles has changed over time. It is also worth noting that both the BBC and commercial terrestrial channels have been subject to tight controls throughout their existence.

The governing conditions of pre-war television in the 1930s explicitly forbade *advertising* and sponsorship and were committed to an 'uplifting' cultural tone. But, as Branston (1998) has pointed out, the rejection of advertising as a means of raising funds for broadcasting was not wholly based on pure principles of public service. Rather, the powerful press of the time exerted a great deal of pressure to retain its advertising revenue, while the licensing of the BBC by the Post Office provided an opportunity for the latter to make a healthy profit. Thus, from an early point, commercial drives and the principles and practices of PSB were both in tension and in collaboration.

Nonetheless, it is possible to argue that the early days of British broadcasting were dominated by Reithian notions of 'serving the nation' through a combination of education, information and entertainment. The early period was also flavoured with a suspicion that all things American, and especially American popular culture, were vulgar, downmarket and morally dubious (see *Americanisation*). By the 1950s, partly as a result of the wartime experiences of US radio broadcasting which proved highly desirable to British listeners, these attitudes became increasingly questioned by broadcasters and audiences alike. The underlying tensions surfacing during the 1950s, when television established itself as the premier popular medium, have arguably continued in a struggle between competing views of the role and purpose of television in society which remains largely unresolved today. Either television is regarded as an informing and potentially liberating medium – in which case its essential role in a democracy suggests the need for some degree of regulation and a strong tendency towards PSB principles and practices – or, alternatively, television is regarded primarily as a medium of entertainment. In this view, commercial forces are seen as providing the best chance of giving viewers what they want, as well as being regarded as less elitist than PSB. Commercially based systems, however, ultimately depend on viewers' ability to pay, thus possibly shutting out poorer sections of the population (McQueen, 1998). With the increasing spread of commercial channels delivered by satellite, by cable and digitally, *audiences* fragmented and defined by subscription patterns are no longer a possibility but an increasing reality.

Nonetheless, the relationship between PSB and commercial television is not straightforward and it is too simple to regard commercialisation as synonymous with 'dumbing down' or loss of 'quality', although this fear has fuelled much recent and on-going debate. Historically, the gradual increase of commercial influence, especially from advertisers, fuelled by a certain degree of public discontent in the particular forms of television available in the post-war years and teamed with increasing affluence, led to the 1954 Television Act and the creation of ITV in 1955. Far from heralding a commercial 'free-for-all', however, the setting up of Britain's first commercial television channel, funded by advertising rather than the television licence, was framed by numerous regulations and controls, suggesting that a PSB ethos prevailed, albeit in somewhat masked form. Thus, ITV at this time can be seen as an extension to the idea of PSB rather than an alternative (Scannell, 1990). On the other hand, commercial broadcasting was distinctive in certain ways, not least in its programming, which tended to provide more in the way of light entertainment and US imports. This move proved to be popular with audiences and thus commercially successful. Undaunted by diminishing audiences, the BBC responded in a number of ways, eventually bidding for a second channel in the early 1960s. The Pilkington Committee reported in 1962, approving the introduction of BBC2 (which began broadcasting in 1964), criticising the quality of some commercial output and laying to rest the need for commercial advertising on BBC channels. The recommendations of the Pilkington Committee also included tighter controls on commercial television via the ITA (Independent Television Authority), who were empowered to punish such misdemeanours as 'triviality'. Again, we see here how PSB ideas of cultural improvement are threaded through the controlling mechanisms of commercial TV. While the introduction of BBC2 allowed for 'quality' television to be concentrated on the new channel, with BBC1 somewhat popularising its programming, the ITV networks from 1966 re-examined their output and began introducing a larger diet of 'serious' *dramas*, current affairs programmes and *documentaries*.

Since then, a number of changes in the regulations surrounding television have worked to break the BBC–ITV 'duopoly' and to destabilise the balance between commercial and PSB tendencies. In particular, the Annan Committee Report of 1977 heralded the introduction of Channel 4, the UK's fourth terrestrial channel, in 1982. Its remit was to provide programmes for those sections of the population not adequately served by the existing channels, such as minority groups. Annan also enabled a far greater proportion of programmes to be commissioned and made independently (and commercially) than had previously been the case. Channel 4, owned by the IBA (Independent Broadcasting Authority), would boost the independent sector by acting as a publishing house rather than a production company.

In the 1990s, commercial pressures and the Broadcasting Act of 1990 have had the net effect of moving television in Britain further towards a position of deregulation. The most significant elements of change brought about by the Act have included the replacement of the IBA by the ITC (Independent Television Commission) which oversees a system of franchise bidding for the television regional networks. The inevitable commercial pressures to win large audiences at low cost have, arguably, resulted in a lowering of production values and a loss of 'quality'. In addition, the 1990s have seen a number of mergers and take-overs, so that a few large companies now rule terrestrial commercial television. The introduction of Channel 5 in 1997, the massive proliferation of satellite and cable channels, and the introduction of digital *technology* have further solidified the influence of commercialism.

Debates about commercialism in Britain continue overwhelmingly to focus on fears of loss of quality and have recently been associated primarily with increasing deregulation. Within the BBC, the influence of the commercial channels and the growing competition arising from the development of satellite, cable and digital technology have acted to influence programming styles, schedules and content. The BBC's commitment to serve 'the nation' has had to be re-evaluated in the light of pressures to retain a significant audience share.

It may not be too extreme to argue, then, that what we see on television is currently shaped far more by commercial interests, via sponsorship and competition for advertising, than by ideas of PSB, despite government's proclamations to the contrary (O'Malley and Treharne, 1993; Williams, 1994). Certainly, the Reithian notion of a 'national audience' is largely dead and buried, with the concepts of niche audiences, segmented audiences and even channels as 'brands' becoming common currency.

See also: **Advertising, Americanisation, Public service broadcasting, Technology**

Further reading: Branston (1998); McQueen (1998); O'Malley and Treharne (1993); G. Williams (1994)

COMMUNITY TELEVISION

Since the 1970s community television production has existed in various forms in America, Britain and parts of Europe. It can be defined in a number of ways, but perhaps can best be regarded as having two main objectives which are, first, to inform people of events and second, to mobilise citizens for bringing about social change (Hollander, 1992). Community television, then, is often framed in terms of strengthening local communities and serving to maintain local identities and local culture. Programmes produced by community broadcasters are generally those made by people who live in the community rather than media professionals. Local concerns, grassroots social issues and community *news* are the backbone of community television output. For its advocates, community television is seen as a communicative tool which can be instrumental in strengthening local culture and identities in an increasingly commercial multi-channel media environment.

A number of developments (technological, economic, political and social) gave rise to the beginnings of small-scale community media production and the emergence of community television. To begin with, the growth of various social reform movements in the 1960s led to more demands (from some sections of personnel working within broadcast organisations as well as from interest groups and viewers) for fairer *representation* and equality of *access* to the electronic media. Coupled with these demands was a growing dissatisfaction with the output and performance of existing broadcasting *institutions*. Prior to the 1970s, the *technology* was not readily available in terms of equipment for production, frequency space for transmission and suitable apparatus for reception. Technological developments, such as the increasing availability of broadcast channels with the introduction of cable (and subsequently satellite and digital) technology, created a possible space for community and access programming. Technological advances also saw the development of portable *video* production equipment which meant that production outside of the main broadcasting organisations was now a possibility. Finally, the increasing trend towards commercialisation and deregulation also gave rise to a weakening of the broadcasting monopolies established in the initial post-war period.

Community television programming is characteristically low-budget and of 'amateur' quality, although the technology is now available to facilitate higher-quality production. Staffing usually involves a mixture of fully trained and experienced media professionals who offer their services on either a part-time or a full-time basis, regular part-time volunteers who have been trained, and volunteers who are in the process of being trained. There are various tensions and antagonisms underpinning community television production and programming which centre around a number of interrelated concerns to do with finance, *scheduling*, content, channel identity, professionalism and, inevitably, *audiences*. Each of these concerns, to a greater or lesser extent, can produce tension and a conflict of interests within community television production, and it is sometimes the case that its initial ideals and non-commercial philosophies which provided have to be compromised in order to survive in the contemporary broadcasting environment.

Finance is probably the biggest single issue affecting the success or failure of community television projects. Staffing, programme production and transmission, as well as the technology to achieve all of these, cost money. It is quite often the case that franchise owners have to put what would otherwise be profits back into community programming and production, which means that community television can be a financial burden rather than an asset. This is the case in the US, where cable operators are required by law to provide some form of community access programming. For some franchise owners this legal obligation is met unwillingly. In the UK the Annan Committee (1977) pledged support for community television and tied its future development into the cable industry as it was being developed in the 1970s and 1980s. However, the structures for financing and supporting community television production were never really specified, hence community television has struggled to survive in the UK.

Problems relating to funding have a cumulative effect, and ultimately influence factors concerning quality of programming, scheduling and programme content, which in turn have implications for establishing and maintaining a distinctive channel identity and service. Because of the costs of creating and sustaining a distinctive 'quality' service, it is difficult for community projects to compete with the established broadcasters (Wilson, 1994). Furthermore, with inadequate resources the output of community television is, inevitably, of a lower standard (technically) than that produced by professional broadcasters. Audiences have certain expectations and ideas associated with professionalism and broadcasting which community television often fails to achieve. In addition to this, the small-scale arrangements of community television production mean that regular and diverse programming is often not possible. Realistically, the most a community channel can hope to produce is ten to fourteen hours of new broadcast material a week.

An equally important consideration (and one which has implications for the various manifestations of community television) is the term 'community' itself which, while being rich in associations, is notoriously difficult to pin down (Rushton, 1993). Thus, 'community' can be defined in various ways: neighbourhood communities, cultural and ethnic communities and communities of interest. Any geographical location, then, may embody a variety of different communities each with a legitimate claim on fair and equal representation. Carving out and establishing a distinctive (and representative) channel identity is, in itself, a considerable task for community television channels. With lack of funding this task is made all the more difficult.

The future of community television production is uncertain. On the one hand, the technology is now available for high-quality programming and the multi-channel environment can enable transmission of broadcasts from a diverse range of sources. In sum, the conditions for a truly *pluralistic* and democratic media environment have never been better. On the other hand, the media industries are becoming more competitive and commercially oriented. Whether or not community television can survive in such an environment remains to be seen. Future developments in community television are now, more than ever, dependent on the established broadcasting corporations and their practices and wider developments in media *policy*, national and international broadcasting initiatives, commercialisation, deregulation and *globalisation*. Ironically, it may be the case that the homogenising tendencies of a global media culture may in fact produce a demand for more community-oriented programmes (Wilson, 1994), and if this is so then the technology is available to achieve this. But in light of competition from the transnational media organisations, community television production is likely to remain, as it has always been, marginalised.

See also: **Access, Globalisation, Representation, Technology, Video**

Further reading: Jankowski *et al.* (1992); Kellner (1990); Rushton (1993); Wilson (1994)

CONTENT ANALYSIS

Content analysis is a type of research technique used extensively in communication and media studies. It has a long history, preceding the development of television, in the analysis of propaganda and political bias. It has come to play an important part in the repertoire of tools available to media analysts, particularly in conjunction with other techniques such as interviewing and observation. Content analysis is an empirical, systematic approach that analyses texts by breaking them down into their constituent parts. At its most basic, it examines the frequency of words or of images occurring within a *text*. Supporters of content analysis applaud the technique for its comprehensiveness and scientific reliability compared to other, more subjective approaches.

Although content analysis was used in the early part of the twentieth century to document the content of newspapers, Harold Laswell and others developed it more fully in the 1940s to study the effects of political propaganda on popular beliefs and opinions. At this time, the main purpose of the research was to ascertain the intentions of those sending media messages and to attempt to gauge the *effects* that this might have over time on the population receiving them. Given the wartime context of much of this research, attention was paid to the possibly far-reaching influence of media forms such as radio in relation to perceptions of international conflict and change. Later, work by George Gerbner and his colleagues combined an extensive quantitative analysis of the content of American television programmes with a survey of audience opinions and values. The research (see *Cultivation analysis*), combining a range of techniques, examined the interrelationship between television content and changes in public opinion.

A simple application of the technique today might be to quantify the frequency of specific minority groups appearing on prime-time television. Initially, the researcher would need to define the group or groups to be identified as well as the types of television programme to be considered. Frequency of appearance, time on screen, incidence and coincidence of other items defined in the same 'set' would then be coded and analysed. The advantage of this approach is that it requires adherence to systematic rules and procedures to ensure a basis for textual analysis. While the method might not in itself provide deep insights, it can provide a beginning for more complex forms of research which not only quantify the elements of the text but relate the information gained to an understanding of underlying textual and social meanings.

So an initial mapping of how certain social groups are over- or under-represented on television, compared to their occurrence in the population, can provide insight into the way dominant ideologies and values are reflected and reinforced by mainstream television (see *Ideology*). In order to arrive at this type of understanding, however, it is usual for more qualitative approaches, such as *semiotics* or ethnography, to come into play alongside content analysis.

Although it has a number of strengths, content analysis has attracted criticism since its inception. It has sometimes been regarded as naïve in its assumptions and therefore limited in what it can reveal. For instance, claims to *objectivity* and value-freedom have been challenged by those who regard such ideals as either impossible to achieve or, more crucially, flawed in their over-reliance on positivist assumptions about meaning. Such critics point to the inherent problems in selecting and defining categories for analysis, since the categories themselves do not have a value-free reality. The categories a researcher chooses might well belie their theoretical orientation and interests. The influential series of studies on television news by the Glasgow University Media Group during the 1970s and 1980s, for instance, focused primarily on issues of balance and bias, using social *class* divisions as basic conceptual tools, in keeping with their *Marxist* perspective. Similarly, the validity of quantitative methodology has come under criticism for its reliance on surface, manifest content to reveal the meanings of texts. It has been pointed out that quantification of words, images or concepts in a text tells us little about the ways in which the text is understood by those consuming it. Nor can quantification adequately account for meanings derived from the contexts of production. Our understanding of a text is not fixed but can come from a variety of interacting factors. It is shaped by what is absent as well as what is present in the text, by the way elements are combined, by our expectations as members of an *audience* and by generic conventions and production values.

Because of these perceptions of its drawbacks, contemporary content analysis tends more often to be used as a starting point or in conjunction with other methodologies than as a method standing alone. As a popular approach to understanding television, it has been largely replaced by more qualitative forms of analysis. Nonetheless, the place of content analysis in television studies remains a significant one and a useful starting point for appropriate research projects.

See also: **Cultivation analysis, Effects**

Further reading: Hansen *et al.* (1998); Jensen and Jankowski (1993); Priest (1996); Stempel (1989)

CONVENTION

The term is often used interchangeably with *code* but in actuality the latter has a more specific meaning embedded in its *structuralist* roots. A convention can be defined as any kind of social, cultural and hence textual practice shared by members of a particular culture. In terms of television it refers to 'normal' or established practices understood by both programme-makers and *audiences*. An audience's familiarity with the conventions of television explains the ability to tune in midway through a previously unseen programme and understand what kind of programme it is and, indeed, what is going on.

In fact, conventions tend to be so taken for granted that they come to seem 'natural'. Narrative closure within children's cartoons (for instance *Thundercats* or *Teenage Mutant Ninja Hero Turtles*), the use of music to herald the start of a programme, or the newscaster looking directly at the camera are conventional and seem 'right'. Similarly, the convention of the male voice-over on documentaries seemed natural during the 1950s and 1960s, and as such helped reinforce an *ideology* of male authority.

For the television industry, 'successful' conventions – i.e. those that audiences enjoy often in generic forms (see *Genre*) – can provide a framework for programme development. The result, according to some critics, is the production of formulaic and cheaper television. Confessional chat shows which emphasise audience participation, such as *Jerry Springer* or *Kilroy*, provide an example of a genre which relies on easily understood and cheaply reproduced conventions. Ideologically, there is an argument that the genres which depend on regularised conventions can be both reassuring for audiences and deeply conservative.

Innovation breaks with convention. Television advertisements which veil the name of the product, apparently realist programmes which employ surrealist and postmodernist techniques (*Ally McBeal* or *The Young Ones*) and situation *comedies* which do not use 'canned' laughter all disrupt conventions. Disruption can cause misunderstandings and provoke displeasure among audiences, but it can also help define more experimental televisual forms, exemplified by cult programmes such as *The X-Files* and, in Britain, *This Life*.

It can be argued that in a culture increasingly saturated by the media, audiences are becoming more knowing about television conventions and ways in which they can be disrupted or 'played with'. Contemporary audiences have a more developed sense of *intertextuality* – that is, an awareness of ways in which texts and their conventions interact and are self-referential.

See also: **Code, Genre, Intertextuality, Semiology**

Further reading: Fiske (1987)

CRIME SERIES

Television, like many cultural forms, has seen an abundance of writers, producers and viewers attracted to crime and deviance. Reflecting the popularity of crime genres in literature and cinema, television drama in Europe and North America has recurrently used fictionalised accounts of 'cops' and 'robbers' as a resource, while programmes about 'real' crime have gradually occupied more of the schedules.

As with any *genre*, the crime or police series is not an unchanging structure but evolves in a complex relationship with *audiences*, media *institutions*, social contexts and other genres. However, some writers have identified core qualities of a classic crime or police genre from its emergence until the present day. Its *narrative* structure begins with some kind of challenge to social order being posed by criminal forces. The threat to normality is dealt with by police officers, or perhaps private investigators with the freedom to operate outside legal convention. In the past, criminals were obviously 'bad' and police invariably 'good'. However, in recent times the definition of the moral and the legal has become clouded by the representation of 'bent cops' and sympathetic 'villains'. The tension, and indeed *pleasure*, within the narrative emanates from the conflict between the police and the criminal and uncertainty as to whether the criminal will be caught or, in the case of a 'whodunnit' such as *Murder She Wrote*, revealed. Narrative resolution, and hence familiar pleasure, is achieved at the climactic and almost inevitable moment of capture or revelation.

Oppositional characterisation provides the genre's dynamic. The chief narrative agent is the police officer (or team) who is essentially 'positive'. He – or, less frequently, she – appears regularly, with the audience being positioned within their occupational and domestic worlds. But the central character is also made 'interesting' by virtue of perhaps a lollipop (*Kojak*), an ethnic identity (*Banacek*) or an unusual car (*Starsky and Hutch*). *Morse* epitomises the kind of sleuth based on Sherlock Holmes. He is distinguishable from the rest of us and his sidekick by an over-fondness for beer, a love of opera, moodiness and sheer special intelligence, as well as the requisite custom car. In contrast, 'villains' are virtually invisible, often making single appearances and adopting stereotypically 'evil' identities at odds with 'normal' identity.

During the 1970s and 1980s, British crime series were subjected to a powerful attack from media scholars influenced by Gramscian *Marxism*. Many critics had pointed to the inherent conservatism of formulaic genres within a capitalist media industry, but writers such as

Hurd (1981) and Clarke (1986) went further in their analyses of crime series. They argued that the genre, in its depiction of the world of 'law and order', functions ideologically. Crime series employ conventions of *realism* which represent and naturalise aspects of social life as *the* definitive reality. In so doing they veil not only the 'constructedness' of the text but also the ideological meaning which the text has been given. The end and continuing result is that texts – in this case crime series – are able to support existing relations of domination as long as audiences go along with the preferred reading.

How, then, do specific texts contribute to these ideological aims? First, they represent a 'real' world of recognisable identities, places, times and events in which stories unfold in familiar ways. So *Dixon of Dock Green* begins with a genial 'bobby' speaking to camera and telling 'us' about a crime which has occurred in Dock Green, a fictional but recognisable part of London. Programmes like *Miami Vice* and *The Streets of San Francisco* in their use of actual places make an equivalent claim to realism. Production techniques culled from documentary television and cinema verité – for instance the grainy film of *Z-Cars* or the roving hand-held camera of *Homicide: Life on the Street* – have been used to bolster the sense of realism.

The narrative unfolding in this realistic world is one in which the police are able to solve the problems experienced by a society or community. It might be by regular police work, violent action or intellectual puzzle-solving, but the outcome is invariably the same. Furthermore, they are sympathetic characters. Furillo in *Hill Street Blues* may be a recovering and sometimes lapsing alcoholic, and Regan in *The Sweeney* may beat 'villains' up in the course of a case, but at heart these are 'good' people committed to improving society in difficult circumstances. And, of course, they are in direct contrast to anonymous but wicked criminals, often assuming the role of stereotypical folk devils. Marxist critics, though, argue that crime series are acting ideologically to represent the police as social benefactors when in actual fact they are agents of the state committed to maintaining a status quo of inequality and repression. The classic *narrative* of crime, pursuit and capture omits corruption, ineffectiveness and the iniquity of laws as well as any number of other legal and punitive processes in favour of closure. The main source of conflict, beyond that of the police officer and the criminal, is between ordinary cops and their bureaucratic managers ('top brass' or City Hall), a schism which only acts to conceal other tensions between the police as an institution and disempowered groups within society.

Clarke (1986) looks at how the genre adapts its ideological role to different social circumstances in twentieth-century Britain. He notes how *Dixon of Dock Green* employed a procedural, televisual style to depict a consensual Britain threatened by a growing lawlessness, and particularly juvenile crime, and a police force able to reasonably and efficiently deal with the problems. In contrast, *The Sweeney* borrowed innovations such as a stress on action and the buddy format of two lead policemen (*sic*) from American cop shows such as *Kojak* and *Starsky and Hutch*, themselves products of the application of Hollywood conventions to television. The programme was set in 1970s London, where the morally strong but legally dubious character of Jack Regan sought to stem a rising tide of lawlessness using whatever means necessary. Here the text suggested a real need for increased and harsher policing to maintain a harmonious social order. Clarke (1986) relates this to a wider political agenda, suggesting that the text articulated with New Right views on the need to strengthen the powers of the state in response to various challenges – a process which Hall *et al.* (1978) referred to as *Policing the Crisis*. In short, the crime genre is seen as naturalising and legitimising repression and thereby contributing to the maintenance of a hegemonic order.

But, as Hurd explains, to make their representations convincing texts must work with familiar or known contradictions (Hurd, 1981). Whether this is corruption (*Between the Lines*), police sexism (*Prime Suspect*) or institutional racism (*NYPD Blue*) the question boils down to how far these problems are mythically resolved or ultimately concealed. Where there is narrative closure – and this can go from a 'bent copper' being thrown out of the force in *Dixon of Dock Green* to the textual suppression of Sipowitz's racism in *NYPD Blue* – then it could be argued that crime series continue to displace contradiction and repression. Only traditionally radical British examples like *Law and Order* and *Cops* could be said to challenge the hegemonic order of the genre, and they are less likely to be widely distributed, nor indeed have they tended to be hugely popular. A lack of co-operation from police authorities has not helped their cause within the BBC. A more optimistic reading is obtained by considering the ways in which the genre has changed over time to reflect wider historical developments. While the narrative of *The Bill* still tends to uncritically and ideologically situate the viewer within the police station, its representations of gender, criminality and race nevertheless set it a world apart from, say *Softly Softly* and other British police dramas of the 1960s and 1970s.

Crime series have also attracted criticism from feminist media researchers questioning the masculinity of the genre in its traditional form. Texts have tended to have male protagonists both as police and as criminals, female victims and criminal accomplices, and a focus on conventionally male crimes such as robbery and murder. Crimes are solved using traditionally masculine qualities such as strength, courage, violence and self-sufficiency, so that there is no need for exploration of feelings. But it is the narrative, with its orientation to a single action-based goal and a movement towards climactic resolution, which confirms the masculinity of the genre (Fiske, 1987). Early British responses to a feminist critique (for example, *Juliet Bravo* and *The Gentle Touch*) simply placed individual female characters in what were historically male policing roles. While these programmes began a redefinition of crime, introduced narratives around sexual politics and the workplace and included domestic plot-lines, some critics were dissatisfied (Baehr and Dyer, 1987). It was felt that texts such as *Prime Suspect* made policewomen individually 'super' rather than everyday members of a discriminated-against gender, isolated them from other women and tended to explain their professional success in terms of a domestic 'flaw' such as a failed marriage. At the same time they also suggested that police forces had become more 'caring', an ideological assertion countered by much sociological research. However, two other generic developments were more far-reaching.

Cagney and Lacey directly challenged ideological notions of masculine social authority and the marginalisation of women in the genre from within mainstream television (Gamman, 1988). The programme placed two women detectives with different private lives within a 'buddy' format, thus allowing collective female experience and difference to be articulated. The women work within an obviously masculine environment but are able to take on sexism using mockery to deflate the office machismo and displace power relations. In their work they are efficient professionals, but are not seen as unusual because of their gender. At the same time the characters hang on to familiar aspects of their feminine world, not least in the programme's interweaving of public workspace and private lives. Crimes – and there is a concentration on gendered crimes such as sexual abuse and rape – have an impact on their respective domestic situations, and vice versa (Gamman, 1988).

The second significant development was the employment of characteristics of *soap opera* within the crime genre. Soaps are characterised as a feminine genre. They have a serial form which resists narrative closure in favour of the pleasures of uncertainty, multiple narratives, an emphasis on 'emotions', and strong female characters alongside sensitive males (Fiske, 1987). A soap format was applied in British series like *The Bill* and American ones like *Hill Street Blues* and *NYPD Blue*. These American examples have succeeded in bringing new audiences – and notably higher-income women – to the genre, attracted by relatively complex textual strategies and a liberal political stance which have earned the soubriquet 'quality television'.

More recently, postmodern theorists have rejected the search for truth behind ideological texts. They point to *Moonlighting* and *Twin Peaks* as two of the television series which have subverted the conventions of the crime genre. While programmes such as *Homicide: Life on the Street* have employed the techniques of factual television, *Crimewatch* in the UK, *LAPD* and even television news have increasingly employed dramatic narrative and characterisation in their re-enactment of 'real' crimes. For some this is evidence of a dissolving of the distinction between realist and non-realist television texts. Similarly, it is suggested that the inherent meaning of a text is largely irrelevant. Audiences understand what texts can 'do' and are primarily interested in simply gaining a range of pleasures from a constantly evolving genre.

See also: **Gender, Genre, Ideology, Narrative, Realism, Soaps**

Further reading: A. Clarke (1986); J. Clarke (1996); Sparks (1992)

CULTIVATION ANALYSIS

Cultivation analysis grew out of the 'cultural indicators' project developed at the University of Pennsylvania in the late 1960s. The cultivation approach provides a model for analysing the broad influence of television messages. It begins with three basic assumptions. First, while it is possible that individual television programmes or *genres* may influence people, this is a very difficult thing to measure. Television's more pervasive influence is long-term. It is therefore important to focus on the totality of the television world and on those stories, messages and images that are repeatedly shown. Second, television's influence will, on the whole, be symbolic rather than behavioural. So, for example, *violence* on television may not influence the way someone behaves, but it may influence the way they see the world and their perception of the risks the world presents to them. Third, television's influence is likely to have more to do with maintaining social order and *ideological* systems (such as patriarchy or consumerism) than changing them. This is a notable departure from traditional media *effects* approaches, which tend to look for media influence in changing people's ideas rather than as a source of support for the status quo.

The cultivation approach is preceded by an examination of the *institutional* pressures and limits on programme production and distribution. The desire for appeal to a global market, for example, will favour simple, formulaic programming (sex, violence, slapstick comedy) over more subtle forms of drama. It is also dependent upon a 'message system analysis' that quantifies and describes patterns of stories and messages in order to map the broad symbolic structure of the television world. On US television, for example, men outnumber women by a ratio of three to one; women appear in a more limited range of roles and tend to disappear once they reach a certain age While this ratio may vary from one genre to another (the imbalance is greater on *news* programmes and less on *soap operas*) most television viewers will, across time, see far more men on their screens than women. This pattern is also true of British television.

The 'cultural indicators' project has, since 1967, been tracking week-long samples of US network television *drama*. This allows the researchers to make comparisons between the television world and the 'real world' beyond it. So, for example, in terms of the cast of characters that populate television in the US, old people are under-represented by a factor of five to one while middle-class professionals – such as lawyers and doctors – are significantly over-represented. These TV characters, on the whole, live in a far more violent world than most TV viewers, and one where problems are solved – whether by violence, comedy or wisdom – with extraordinary speed.

Cultivation analysis then poses the question: does consistent exposure to these repetitive *representational* patterns – particularly in television entertainment – influence television viewers' beliefs about the real world? Does television, in other words, cultivate a view of the world that looks – either symbolically or literally – like television? If it does, as cultivation analysis suggests, we would expect to see a correlation between the amount of television someone watches and the degree to which their view of the world corresponds to television's representations of that world.

Exploring this hypothesis is complex. It involves screening out other factors that may lead to differences in perception between heavy and light television viewers. Suppose, for example, we find that heavy viewers are more likely to hold traditional moral values. Since the average amount of television people watch tends to increase from young adulthood to old age, differences between the moral outlook of heavy and light viewers may be a function of age difference rather than television viewing. In this instance, isolating television as the significant causal variable means comparing light and heavy viewers within age bands and asking 'Do older heavy viewers hold more traditional views than older light viewers?'

Cultivation analysis thereby establishes correlations between television viewing and the way people see the world only after it has tested for a variety of other possible explanatory variables (*race*, *gender*, education, occupation and so on).

In the US, the findings of cultivation analysts have tended to confirm their hypothesis. In some cases, the relationship between content and perception is fairly straightforward. Heavy television watchers, for example, appear to interpret the absence of the elderly on television literally, and are therefore more likely than light watchers to regard the elderly, in numerical terms, as a declining group in the population as a whole. In the case of television's gender imbalance, the cultivation effect seems to be more subtle. Personal experience obviously makes the idea that there are three men for every woman implausible. Nevertheless, cultivation analysis has found that heavy viewers are more likely to hold sexist or *stereotypical* views about gender roles. This suggests that the gender imbalance on TV – particularly among authoritative figures (such as advertising voice-overs, serious news reporters) – encourages associations between maleness and authority.

In the midst of the long-running debate about the influence of violence on television, cultivation analysis has focused on the way in which the dramatic over-representation of violence on American TV influences people's perceptions of violence. Their findings point to a phenomenon they describe as the 'mean world syndrome'. Television is an abnormally violent world, with crime on prime-time television in the US occurring much more routinely than in the real world. On average, at least five acts of physical violence per hour occur involving half of all major TV characters. This repetition of murder and assault appears to cultivate a feeling of fear and distrust. In brief, the more television someone watches, the more likely they are to regard the world as a violent, dangerous place, a world where strangers are more likely to be untrustworthy or threatening than benign. These results have not been replicated so clearly in research outside the US – possibly because in other countries levels of television violence are generally lower.

Cultivation researchers have described television's influence on political attitudes as producing what they describe as a mainstreaming effect. Television, they argue, operates within the fairly narrow confines of a political mainstream – usually defined as such by political elites – while celebrating the value of 'moderation' over 'extremism'. While this is reflected in the propensity of heavy viewers to identify themselves as moderates, the attitudes they tend to embrace are not necessarily in the political centre (on some issues they tilt to the right, on some to the left). The essence of mainstreaming is that it narrows the range of opinions people are inclined to hold. Television is thus described as producing homogeneity and limiting diversity and divergence.

Overall, cultivation analysis suggests that television – as the dominant storyteller of our age – is a powerful symbolic and ideological force in contemporary culture. It is important to note, nonetheless, that the correlations it traces are statistically significant but not absolute. The finding that heavy viewers are more likely to think one thing rather than another must be understood as a tendency rather than a rule. Not all heavy viewers, in other words, correspond to the types that cultivation analysis describes. This suggests that television, though important, is one among many ideological influences on the way people think. It has the power to prefer, not to insist.

See also: **Audiences, Content analysis, Effects, Mass culture**

Further reading: Shanahan et al. (1999); Signorielli and Morgan (1990)

CULTURAL IMPERIALISM

The cultural imperialism thesis holds that dominant societies are able to impose their *culture* on that of subordinate societies as a means of establishing and perpetuating control. This is seen as part of the historical development of a wider economic and political imperialism illustrated particularly in the relationship between developed and underdeveloped nations. More specifically, cultural imperialism refers to the spread of cultural values, ideas and practices which reflect and reproduce the 'superiority' of the dominant culture (Christianity, Shakespeare and McDonald's are but three examples). At the same time it describes the devaluation and destruction of indigenous culture (for instance, polygamy or witchcraft).

Media imperialism refers to the way in which the mass media is able to organise and purvey cultural imperialism. The concept has been especially popular among *Marxists*, who lay stress on the determining role of political economy – and more precisely, ownership of the world's media by major capitalist interests – in understanding the world media order and culture. It has been particularly associated with the rising power during the twentieth century of the US and its ability to shape systems of information and entertainment for ultimately ideological purposes, a process sometimes labelled *Americanisation*. The US is the biggest domestic producer and the largest exporter of television programmes, while many of the major international media corporations are American (for example, Time Warner and Fox). Thus, many societies in Africa, Asia, Latin America and other parts of the world experience a diet of television drawn overwhelmingly from North America, and indeed Europe. O'Sullivan *et al.* use the example of television schedules in Fiji composed almost entirely of European and American programmes, including various sports, the British comedy *Porridge* and the American programmes *WKRP in Cincinnati* and *Hollywood Wives* (O'Sullivan *et al.*, 1998). One of the primary motives in such cases is financial as American corporations sell media products to third-world buyers way below the cost of producing domestic programmes. The problem is compounded by the fact that media products and processes are perceived as flowing in one direction only, with American audiences being unused to anything but American programmes.

In the context of a world information order, multinational corporations (MNCs) own the mass media and are therefore able to control *technology* such as satellites, the flow and distribution of images and information and textual content itself. For example, major *news* agencies such as Reuters form parts of large MNCs which control the technology of news production, the distribution of news programmes (tending to be exported from developed societies to developing societies), and the content of news texts (Gurevitch, 1991). The result is that television news sets an *ideological* agenda that favours the advanced capitalist societies. Cultural imperialism, then, is closely bound up with economic imperialism. This kind of approach would also point to the mass media's ability to develop new markets by *advertising* the imperative of consumption, the rapid world-wide spread of MTV being a prime illustration. Satellite technology has exacerbated the situation as media products – an example here would be the availability and popularity of American basketball in the Caribbean – are able to ignore borders and, in the process, threaten existing national identities. Attempts in a number of countries to regulate the import of American material have been thwarted by media corporations and the American government. The labelling of this homogenisation as 'McDonaldization' (Ritzer, 1993) or 'Coca-Cola culture' is not incidental.

Proponents of the cultural and media imperialism thesis see the result of these economic and cultural processes as dissemination of dominant capitalist ideology throughout the world. For example, in their seminal text *How to Read Donald Duck*, Dorfman and Mattelart (1975) point to the racial *stereotyping* of 'other' nationalities and the promotion of capitalism and consumerism in Disney comics. Television, then, has the capacity to veil the exploitative reality of economic relations (via, say, advertising) and compensate for the miseries of everyday life with the provision of so-called 'prozac television' such as *Dallas*. It can legitimate the superiority of 'western' culture (*Upstairs, Downstairs*) and the inferiority of 'the other' via *racist* representations (e.g. Warner Bros and Disney cartoons). In this model, audiences cannot fail to be affected. Both first- and third-world populations come to see the world through a 'western gaze', with the former becoming 'armchair conquistadores' (Shohat and Stam, 1994).

Theorists of a Gramscian bent have rejected what they see as this mechanistic and determinist account, arguing that cultures are able to resist forces of imperialism. In other words, culture should be seen as an arena of political struggle or 'cultural politics' rather than imposition. This allows for, among other things, consideration of different and competing *representations* – for instance, of 'Africans' on British television – and of the capability of governments and others to reject 'western' media products. However, the analysis is still couched in terms of a fundamental organising relationship between two societies or formations within those societies.

It is this dimension of the thesis which has attracted criticism from *globalisation* theorists who reject the idea of a unidimensional flow of culture. They argue that the development of a global system has seen the emergence of infinitely complex cultural flows in various directions (Barker, 1997). While American cultural products such as CNN news or *Friends* are consumed all over the world, there are equivalent cultural flows from Japan (*Pokemon*), Latin America (telenovelas) or India (videos of Bollywood films) to other parts of the world. Even where a potentially 'imperialist' text is viewed in most societies, there is much evidence to negate the idea that ideological inculcation is the inevitable outcome because local audiences actively consume television in line with local culture and circumstance. The considerable amounts of research on *Dallas* have noted the diversity in reception among different nationalities and identities (Ang, 1985; Tomlinson, 1991). Growth of new media technologies, democratisation of ownership and indeed continuing non-ownership in some parts of the world are all cited to criticise the cultural/media imperialism thesis (Tomlinson, 1991).

The cultural imperialism thesis, then, has proved to be a durable approach within the study of television. It has pointed to the role of first-world nations and corporations in owning and controlling television production and distribution, and shaping content and hence ideology for international audiences. However, in the context of an increasingly complex media environment it has been seen as rather a blunt, deterministic tool of analysis in its focus on the unit of the nation and imposition as a process.

See also: **Americanisation, Globalisation, Ideology, Marxism**

Further reading: Abercrombie (1996); Mattelart *et al*. (1984); Tomlinson (1991); Tunstall and Palmer (1991)

CULTURAL STUDIES

At its most obvious, 'cultural studies' is the study of *culture*. But the term 'culture' is itself so complex that untangling what studying it might entail or include is fraught with difficulties. Television is an aspect of culture, at least if an inclusive, democratic definition of culture is used that includes popular forms (pop music) as well as more established forms of 'high' culture. This is the sense used by Turner when he writes of culture as aspects of our lives that are so unquestioned and powerful in their influence that they are almost invisible and unnoticed (Turner, 1990). Television is part of *lived* culture, the culture of the everyday and ordinary. Its output (*texts*, programmes) and its organisation (industry) can similarly be regarded as significant aspects of cultural life. So it might be suggested that television studies is an area within cultural studies. While this is correct on one level, on another it must be acknowledged that the relationship between television studies and cultural studies is complex and changing. As Brunsdon (1998) has pointed out, television studies has evolved only since the 1970s and is based on the premise that television be regarded as both worthy of study and as conceptually specific and separate as a medium. The broader study of culture has a longer history. It has been through a number of phases, some existing before the invention of television. However, there are some noteworthy parallels between the study of culture (particularly what was known as '*mass culture*') and the study of television, in that both have been regarded with fear, hostility and suspicion by various commentators and critics. It is only in more recent times that the study of television has taken on a somewhat less elitist hue, and this shift has also been evident within the discipline of cultural studies.

More recently, the term 'cultural studies' has come to imply a set of theoretical, methodological and critical positions which have become extremely important in the body of work concerned with understanding television. However, these positions have not combined to create a distinct approach and television studies can be undertaken from other perspectives (for example, by examining the development of television *technology* in its own right). As a result, there is no simple equation between television studies and cultural studies. One does not equal the other because television has its own specific history, characteristics and elements. Rather, it can be suggested that cultural studies has been an important influence within television studies. A fuller flavour of this relationship can be gained by retracing the history of some key developments within cultural studies.

Although there had been some studies of leisure and recreation before the mid-nineteenth century, only at this time can the beginning of what is now usually known as the 'culture and civilisation' tradition be seen to emerge. An important early figure in this tradition was Matthew Arnold, who in his book *Culture and Anarchy* (1869) argued that the cultural pursuits of the population should be perceived as 'mass culture' directly associated with the development of industrial capitalism. Mass culture was compared unfavourably with two earlier pre-industrial forms. These were 'folk culture', which included rural-based sports, traditional songs, dancing around the maypole and other long-standing leisure activities, and 'high culture', which referred to such pursuits as classical painting, orchestral music and serious literature.

The new mass culture – music halls, popular sports, the public house – was largely commercial and was regarded with distaste by Arnold and some of his contemporaries. He saw it as debasing the standards of civilisation and society as crystallised in the high arts. To Arnold, 'culture' meant 'the best that could be achieved', a definition that excluded most popular forms. This culturally conservative view also carried with it political implications, as it was feared that the debased cultural diet of the (urban, industrialised) masses would lead to social upheaval, even anarchy (hence the title of his book). Arnold's position on mass culture was both disapproving and fearful, and was one that did not (would not) actually deign to study the new culture, only comment on it from afar.

This approach dominated until the 1930s when – again in response to a perceived 'cultural crisis', this time the Depression – it enjoyed a new lease of life through the work of critics coming from a literary studies tradition, such as F.R. Leavis, Q.D. Leavis and T.S. Eliot. While these writers were still scathing about mass culture and its supposed dangers, their contribution was important because they did consider the new forms of culture such as film and popular literature and used the techniques of analysis previously reserved for 'high' culture and 'serious' literature. Even so, Q.D. Leavis was not appreciative of the new cultural forms, calling them 'masturbatory' (Storey, 2001).

What is interesting is that while these British thinkers were decrying the new culture, *Marxists*, in the form of the Frankfurt School, were doing exactly the same thing for entirely different reasons, in the USA. These writers – Adorno, Horkheimer and others – were European émigrées, and they analysed a number of aspects of modern American culture, looking upon the whole scene with some horror. They argued that industrial capitalism had successfully hoodwinked the working classes into accepting (and seemingly enjoying) a numbing, pacifying type of commercial culture. This 'culture industry', it was argued, used dominant *ideology* to instil false consciousness into the proletariat, ensuring that the needs of capitalism could be met with the minimum of disruption. Later, Herbert Marcuse (1964), another Frankfurt School theorist, was to write that the only true culture was a culture of revolution, a genuine counter-culture.

This second phase lasted up until the late 1950s when, according to Tony Bennett (1981), there was a radical 'break' with the old, traditional ways of looking at culture. As can be gleaned, Leavisism, valuable though it was, basically extended and confirmed notions of the decay and degeneracy (and dangers) of mass culture. This was also true for the theorists of the Frankfurt School, whose writings are imbued with pessimism. But by the 1950s these attitudes were becoming out of step with the political atmosphere of democracy that prevailed after World War II. The boundaries between high and low culture were no longer meaningful or adequate. It is thus significant that what was previously called 'mass culture' shifted to become 'popular culture' in the next phase.

Since the 'break' at the end of the 1950s a number of theoretical directions have been taken, and out of these what is now called 'cultural studies' has properly emerged. The first wave of theorising became known, retrospectively, as 'culturalism' and is mainly British. The second is a European-influenced approach, using the umbrella title of 'structuralism'. *Post-structuralism, feminism* and latterly, theorists of *postmodernism* have added complexity to an already diverse field. Moreover, many of the key figures within cultural studies have resisted the labels attached to them or have combined different approaches in their writings. The academic leanings of some writers have shifted and developed over time.

The 'break' at the end of the 1950s came in the form of a small number of books by (then) young British academics, with socialist principles and from working-class backgrounds. Collectively, Richard Hoggart (1957), Raymond Williams (1958), Stuart Hall (1964, with Paddy Whannel), and the historian E.P. Thompson (1968) later became labelled 'culturalists'. Although there were differences of emphasis within their work, their outlook held enough in common to warrant the umbrella term. Each of them took seriously the new popular culture, although in the case of Hoggart some shades of the Leavisite approach remained in his evident distrust of the new 'candy floss culture'. Rather than comparing it with 'elite' culture, however, he compared it with the traditional working-class culture of his own youth, which he remembered fondly and nostalgically.

These writers formed a challenge to the liberal/idealist tradition (culture and civilisation) in which values and ideas are essentially autonomous and free-floating, separate from the economic and political life of society. But they also challenged the earlier, reductionist Marxist theories that saw culture as ultimately determined by the economic base of society. The new theorists tried to explain culture as having a complex interrelationship with other aspects of political and social and economic life. Thus, in a term borrowed from Louis Althusser, culture is seen as 'relatively autonomous', not a simple reflection of economic structures. It influences – and has consequences for – economic and political relationships, rather than being simply influenced by them. Culture is actively produced – it is not simply a passive receiver, influenced by economic structures. It can be, in its turn, influential.

For example, in Britain the BBC exists within the framework of the capitalist state but it is not directly controlled by the government (except at certain moments, such as wartime). The BBC is influenced by the state but it can also exert influence on what goes on in other parts of the social structure. It influences its viewers and listeners by how it presents *news* and by the values it supports, and it can also be influential in high places. While for the most part it will be supportive of the status quo, it can also afford to allow a limited number of dissenting or radical or critical voices. A somewhat controversial example of this tendency was the documentary *Death on the Rock*, which was critical of the British army's handling of the shooting of suspected IRA members in Gibraltar. However, the concept of relative autonomy can be applied to many examples in television.

The theoretical 'break' in cultural studies signified an important change of attitude towards cultural products and practices. Theorists no longer talked of an impoverished 'mass' culture; what they were studying was a rich, diverse and familiar 'popular' culture. Moreover, this relativist position takes the largely non-judgemental view that all forms of culture are worthy of investigation. Thus the study of television, as perhaps the clearest form of truly 'popular' culture, came eventually to be seen as a more respectable, if not entirely respected, academic practice. This initial body of work culminated in the setting up of the Birmingham Centre for Contemporary Cultural Studies (CCCS), founded by Richard Hoggart in 1964. Its first director was Stuart Hall. The centre became extremely influential in developing a new tradition of cultural studies in Britain, both in relation to its initial interest in everyday life and later by a focus on media, and particularly their ideological functions.

The culturalist approach emphasises the active response by social groups, with assumed shared values, to the conditions of social existence. This has been exemplified in numerous studies of 'lived culture' (see, for instance, Hall and Jefferson, 1976 and Hall et al., 1980) as well as, more specifically, in ethnographic studies of television audiences that are concerned with the social experience and meaning of viewing for various groups. Marie Gillespie's study of young South London Punjabis' relationship to television is an astute, more recent example of this type of work (1995).

During the 1960s, a rival way of approaching popular culture was imported from Europe in the shape of structuralism (and later, post-structuralism). This completely different way of thinking emanated from writers such as Lévi-Strauss, Saussure and Barthes. In its purest form, structuralism is a highly rational, highly abstract, non-interpretative form of analysis which challenges the idea of an essential meaning in any text. It seeks to uncover and elaborate upon the rules, or 'signifying systems', underlying the texts of popular culture and to demonstrate how these rules exist independently of the individual user or consumer. Structuralism developed in a number of ways, into semiology/semiotics, discourse analysis and post-structuralism (including psychoanalytical approaches) during and since the 1970s. All of these variants have been applied to the study of television.

Unlike culturalism, structuralism in its many facets begins not with the notion of shared experience but with systems and structures that produce meaning. All cultural phenomena are *signs* in that they produce meaning but the meanings are produced by reference to an underlying system of *conventions* (a kind of grammar), which help organise and categorise objects in relation to each other. The system of signs is not natural, however, but more or less arbitrary.

A method used in the structuralist analysis of media is the exploration of 'binary oppositions' in the text. Originally used by Lévi-Strauss in his analysis of myth, it can be adapted for an effective analysis of media texts by examining oppositional elements that reflect latent meanings. Extensive use has been made of this method for analysing the Western film and popular literary forms such as the James Bond novel, while in the analysis of television texts Berger (1995) provides an analysis of the British TV drama series *Upstairs, Downstairs*. In his table of paired opposites, the Upstairs is signified by (and comes to mean) wealth, mastery, leisure, champagne and so on, while the Downstairs is signified by their opposites – poverty, obedience, hard work and beer.

While culturalism and structuralism, with their obvious differences in concern and approach, provided an initial jumping-off point for cultural studies, a number of developments have subsequently shaped the field (some of which are discussed elsewhere in this book). For example, the translated writings of Antonio Gramsci (see *Hegemony*) formed a bridge between the two perspectives and provided a more nuanced account of popular culture for Marxists. Similarly, Louis Althusser's influence has been keenly felt (see *Ideology*), as has the work of Pierre Bourdieu (see *Taste*) and that of Michel de Certeau (1984) in relation to 'everyday life', so that the field is now more complex and more diverse than ever. Additionally, in recent years there has been a further switch of emphasis towards investigating *pleasure* and inter-rogating the postmodern condition. Much contemporary work within cultural studies rejects the notion of the 'grand discourse' – that is, internally coherent systems of explanation such as Marxism or feminism – and looks instead to the fragmentation of meaning and experience within culture.

All of these developments have had an impact on, and have contributed to, television studies as it is now practised. Whether through textual analysis, audience studies or an understanding of television as an institution in different historical and social contexts, cultural studies continues to inform and partially frame the more specific study of television.

See also: **Convention, Culture, Hegemony, Ideology, Postmodernism, Semiology, Structuralism**

Further reading: Bennett, Martin *et al.* (1981); During (1993); Hall *et al.* (1980); Storey (2001); Turner (1990)

CULTURE

The late Raymond Williams once wrote in *Keywords* (1976) that the term 'culture' is one of the most complex in the English language. Certainly, it is a term central to almost every debate about television, and our understanding and particular usage of the term is likely to connect with assumptions made about the place of television in society.

Williams noted a number of ways in which we can use the term 'culture'. In its broadest sense, culture refers to that part of the total range of human action which is socially rather than biologically transmitted (nurture rather than nature). However, in its long history the term has been narrowed and made more specific in a number of different ways. For instance, it can refer to a particular way of life, of a people or period or group. This is the sense often used by anthropologists and sociologists and the sense in which the term 'cultures' (plural) is most often used. The emphasis here is on 'lived cultures', that is to say customs, practices, rituals and so on. Gift exchange, eating habits, religious ceremony, leisure activities and television viewing are examples of ritual practices that can be easily recognised within contemporary societies. A second way in which the term has been narrowed is to mean the works and practices of artistic or intellectual activity. In other words, this definition includes the recognised products, artefacts and *texts* of a group or society. Songs, films, books, stories, dances, language forms, paintings, architecture and television programmes might be counted here. So, in this version, we are talking about practices that result in the production of symbolic forms. In reality, although it is possible to distinguish between lived culture and the texts arising out of a culture, they are part and parcel of the same thing. We engage in watching television programmes – this is an important aspect of our lived culture – but the programmes themselves are the texts emerging from dominant cultural values, ideas and beliefs.

In the past, this second definition of culture was frequently used to acknowledge a hierarchy of texts. That is, while Shakespeare's plays might be regarded as 'true' culture, romantic fiction would be excluded as not 'intellectual and artistic' enough. The same distinction might be applied to music, elevating classical European music to the realms of 'culture' while devaluing popular forms such as rock'n'roll or blues. Today, the notion of culture has been broadened, democratised and made more complex to include popular and commercial forms, so that now, for explanatory purposes, any simple definition is inadequate in that it is unable to provide a full, nuanced understanding of the diversity of products and practices in which people engage. In fact, some theorists of postmodernity have argued that there is a total collapse of the division between high and low culture (see *Postmodernism*). Nonetheless, although our understanding of culture has become more inclusive, fierce battles continue to rage about what counts as culture and what can be regarded as a valuable cultural product or practice. This battle is not new, however, but goes back to the early cultural theorists (see *Cultural studies*). An indication of the complexities can be gained by examining some of the descriptive terms put alongside the word 'culture', such as 'elite', 'mass', 'folk' 'popular', 'sub' and 'counter'. We can see that the use of such terms is often evaluative rather than just descriptive, and the use of specific terminology generally implies that the user is taking a particular attitude or stance towards the object of study.

In the case of 'high' or 'elite' culture, we know that the boundaries of what we call 'elite' culture are notoriously difficult to establish. To begin with, there are cross-cultural differences. In Italy, opera has long been regarded as part of popular culture; in Britain and the US it is still largely seen as part of 'high' or 'elite' culture. Moreover, things are never static. Recently, opera has been used a great deal in television advertisements and as theme music for televised sports events, so while it may not yet be regarded as popular culture it is used within popular cultural forms, thus indicating a collapse of boundaries. The main point, though, is not simply the cultural and historical relativity of this example but that just using the term 'elite' implies a value judgement. Whether one approves of elite culture or not, using the term suggests that there is something else, some other kind of culture ('low', 'popular', 'mass'?) which can be identified and compared. The early cultural theorists (such as Matthew Arnold in the nineteenth century) made exactly these kinds of value judgements. They assumed that there was an identifiable culture (high/elite) which was somehow better or purer than some other kind of culture (low/mass).

Early theorists were concerned with what they called '*mass culture*'. In particular, they were worried about its long-term effects on civilisation. Both conservative and *Marxist* theorists worried that the new mass culture thrown up by the Industrial Revolution was an impoverished form of culture. These theorists used the term 'mass culture' pejoratively and to compare it (unfavourably) with both high/

elite culture and 'folk culture'. Folk culture was seen to be a simple, mainly rural form of culture, somehow 'authentic' and arising out of the 'creative impulses' of the people. This term has its roots in the work of some German philosophers' concepts of *Volk* (especially the ideas of Herder). So the new mass culture was compared unfavourably with both of the older forms.

What we have seen more recently, since the late 1950s, has been the use of the term 'popular culture', and this assumes a very different stance and attitude, much less critical and more fond. Its origins are in Richard Hoggart's *The Uses of Literacy* (1957) and in the work of Raymond Williams, and the approach is very much a result of the democratisation of education and culture in the wake of World War II. It is also a stance that places importance on the idea that popular culture is a site of struggle between competing groups in society. This new understanding of culture was developed in the 1970s and 1980s by Stuart Hall and other British cultural theorists.

From this standpoint, it is possible to note, describe and evaluate 'sub-cultures' and 'counter-cultures'. A sub-culture is generally taken to mean a marginal or subordinated section within a dominant culture. This might be a youth culture or perhaps an immigrant culture. Sub-cultures are usually characterised by having oppositional elements to them (so the Boy Scout organisation is a youth movement but not really a youth sub-culture). This opposition, however, is rarely overtly political. The opposition is displaced into symbolic forms of resistance via consumption patterns. Sub-cultures that have been identified and studied (mainly in the 1960s and 1970s) have generally been working class in origin.

On the other hand, the term 'counter-culture' usually means, according to Dick Hebdige (1979), a mix of 'alternative' middle-class youth cultures in which more explicit political and ideological resistance to the dominant culture is expressed. Examples of counter-cultures might include the Hippies of the 1960s or contemporary New Age travellers. Both sub-cultures and counter-cultures, as part of popular culture, are regarded as being 'relatively autonomous'. In this perception, culture is neither free-floating, as suggested by a liberal *pluralist* perspective, nor determined by the economic base of society, as argued by some Marxists (e.g. the Frankfurt School). An important issue in relation to television is whether or not it is always part of the dominant culture. While much of television's content appears to be shaped and limited by what might be seen as dominant cultural norms, some television, notably satire, some youth television, the occasional critical *drama* or *documentary* and possibly some open access/public access television may have at least the potential to be counter-cultural.

Contemporary theorists using the term 'popular culture' have defined it as an 'area of exchange' between dominant and subordinate classes, played out in contestation on the field of culture and ideology (Bennett, 1981). John Fiske (1989) has re-emphasised this idea, although his work further stresses the importance of the struggle for social meaning as an aspect of popular culture. He suggests that popular culture becomes a contest to make meanings that are in the interests of the subordinate rather than those preferred by dominant groups.

How might culture be thought of as a site of struggle or conflict? Examples are numerous: the conflict between parents and *children* over viewing, eating and drinking habits and loud music; the legal restrictions on drug use and some sexual practices; the existence of censorship; and the continuing public debates about pornography and violent material. All these examples illustrate an understanding of popular culture as a site of conflict. The terrain of these struggles is constantly shifting; debates about the boundaries of 'decency' on TV, for example, while seemingly endless, are nonetheless relative and subject to the changing standards of viewers. Even seemingly 'innocent' forms of children's culture, like cartoons and comics, can be and often are the focus of cultural struggle, in public debate (the 'what does this do to our kids?' approach as evidenced by recent debates over *Teletubbies*) as well as in the private domain. More recently, debates over the meanings of 'culture' have entered a new phase with the development of theories of *postmodernism*. The old boundaries between 'high' and 'low' culture are seen not only to have broken down, but to have become irrelevant in societies where the 'real' and 'authentic' may be impossible to define and where we are increasingly bombarded with images having no definite meaning, but rather a range of possible meanings. Strinati and Wagg (1992) have explained this as a theory of culture 'sans frontières': a flow of culture which pays no heed to national boundaries or centres, and which is simultaneously becoming fragmented and *globalised*. In some respects, they argue, the postmodern debate returns theorists to some very old concerns about the 'value' and possible 'decline' of culture.

Thus it is possible to say that the term 'culture' is complex and elastic. It can be very broad or narrowed to a number of variants, such as elite culture, sub-culture, mass culture and popular culture. These differences in terminology are not frills but are crucial in telling us something about the implied theoretical positions of their users and the traditions from which they stem.

See also: **Cultural studies, Postmodernism**

Further reading: During (1993); Strinati and Wagg (1992); Turner (1990); R. Williams (1958)

DISCOURSE/DISCOURSE ANALYSIS

The widespread usage of the term 'discourse' throughout a variety of disciplines (linguistics, sociology, literary theory and so on) highlights the extent to which the term has infiltrated, and been applied within, social and cultural theory. In fact, Fiske (1987) suggests that the term 'discourse' is itself 'multidiscursive' as its meanings can vary depending on the context of its employment. Most simply, discourse (as developed in linguistic analysis) refers to any unit of language (spoken or written) that is greater than a single sentence and which is amenable to analysis. Within the field of media and communication studies, however, the term is expanded to refer to all types of signifying practices which produce meaning, such as film, *video*, photography and television (Fairclough, 1995).

The concept originates from the French word *discours* (meaning 'conversation', 'speech', 'dialogue') which in turn is derived from the Latin *discursus* meaning 'to run around'. The term, then, is dualistic in that it is both a noun and a verb. This dualistic property has been developed within *post-structuralist* thought wherein 'discourse' refers not only to the formal organisation of language and the processes of language use and meaning production, but also to the outcomes of those processes (Thwaites *et al.*, 1994). Thus, discourse as a concept, following the work of the French theorist Michel Foucault, relates to ways of thinking, talking, representing, doing and acting as well as to specific forms of language use and social interaction (van Dijk, 1993). But it is also seen as linking language to social practices (embodied in the phrase 'discursive practice') so that discourses are able to shape the attitudes, beliefs, behaviours and power relations of the people involved in a given 'communication event'. This recognises that language is a mode of action that is both socially and historically shaped and shaping. Discourses, then, do not simply offer 'neutral' descriptions of social reality – they actively work to constitute it.

Discourses are central to our lives in that they help us to make sense of (construct and negotiate) social reality, and in this way they are both constitutive of and the products of society and *culture*. Hence there are different discourses – medical, legal, scientific, televisual – each with their own sets of culturally accepted conventions. Certain discourses have become institutionalised (legitimised) and may carry cultural authority over other discourses. For example, in advanced western capitalist societies an institutionalised and then 'naturalised' patriarchal discourse of *gender* still carries cultural authority over and above feminist discourses of gender in spite of the challenges presented by *feminism* as a social and political movement. An understanding of discourse raises issues concerning *ideology* and *power*. Discursive practices can have ideological effects in the sense that they work to produce and reproduce unequal power relations in the ways in which they represent things and position people (Wodak, 1996). In this context, ideology can be understood as a consequence of specific discursive effects – it is through an understanding of discourse that ideology becomes 'visible' (Thwaites *et al.*, 1994). Discourses, then, can be defined as particular sets of beliefs and attitudes which are embedded in specific socio-historical contexts and which embody cultural practices that function to shape the identities and actions of social participants.

To understand how this is applied to the study of television it is useful to consider discourse as a set of textual arrangements (Thwaites *et al.*, 1994) which function to organise and co-ordinate the actions, positions and identities of the individuals involved – both the producers and the consumers of the *text*. Fiske (1987) provides an account of the ways in which ideology is structured into television texts through the discourses and conventions that inform the practices and processes of television *production*. Television, as a medium for communication, occupies a cultural space which straddles both the public and private spheres in social life. It brings public discourses into the private domain and private discourses into the public domain; that is, it *mediates* between the two spheres. In doing so, television has effectively reconfigured (*postmodernists* would say 'blurred') the boundaries between the public and private spheres, thus significantly redefining the boundaries between social reality and its *representation* (Fairclough, 1995). But, as Fiske (1987) suggests, television hides its discursive nature (its 'constructedness'), presenting itself as an unmediated product of social reality. This self-effacement occurs through a range of techniques and modes of signification which erase traces of the discursive practices and ideological labour that have gone into the processes of meaning production. Thus, television mediates between the public and private domains, bringing the discourses of one into the other but rarely drawing attention to its own 'discursivity'. For instance, television *news* presents itself as being 'a window on the world' – impartial, neutral and *objective*. Its (re)presentation of events in the world is held to be immediate, authentic and unmediated. Our attention is never drawn to the social, cultural and institutional processes involved in the construction of news as a text.

The study of discourse (discourse analysis) is primarily concerned with identifying the unwritten rules, structures, patterns, functions and conventions of language use and how these work to organise various discourses in different contexts. Within the context of media studies (and particularly with reference to television) discourse analysis is employed to make sense of the ways in which media convey meaning. It is able to open up questions concerning *representation* because discourses are always articulated from an ideological standpoint in that they present a particular (partial) view of social reality. What is included and excluded in representation is, ultimately, determined through discourse, which in turn is structured by ideology (Thwaites *et al.*, 1994).

Discourses exist in hierarchical relations, so that one of the key objectives of discourse analysis is to make explicit which discourse(s) is the prevailing one and in whose interests it can be seen to be operating. A news broadcast may articulate a range of discourses – competing and alternative – to impose order and sense on events happening 'out there' in the world in an attempt to control, contain and define the parameters of potential meanings. However, it may well be the case that certain ways of understanding events may be given prominence over others so that alternative interpretations may be represented as illegitimate, deviant and nonsensical – they may even be excluded altogether. An example of this would be anti-capitalism demonstrations in Britain, where police and protesters clashed on the streets of London. National monuments were defaced, roads were blocked and property was damaged in the ensuing chaos. Television (and press) news coverage of the event primarily drew upon official and institutionalised discourses concerning law and order and law enforcement, and combined these with liberal discourses expressing the rights of 'law-abiding' citizens to go about their daily routines without being impeded by political activists. The views of the protesters were more or less excluded and their actions were represented as deviant, extremist and criminal.

Discourse analysis has certain limitations. It is useful for identifying the forms of discourse structuring a text but it cannot identify the discourses that the viewer brings to bear on the text (Fiske, 1987). We all draw upon different discourses based around factors such as social class, *race*, *gender* and nationality, so that the same text may be interpreted in different ways via different discourses (see *Audiences*). Furthermore, as Wodak (1996) points out, ultimately it is difficult to determine the extent to which a discourse is self-contained. They are not closed systems but are episodic and fragmented, and can change over time as well as in terms of how they relate to other discourses. Locating the exact ideological origins and 'endings' of a particular discourse, then, is fraught with theoretical and methodological problems.

See also: **Ideology, Intertextuality, Structuralism and Post-structuralism**

Further reading: Fairclough (1992, 1995); Fiske (1987); Thwaites *et al.* (1994); van Dijk (1993); Wodak (1996)

DOCUMENTARY

The television documentary is a *genre* of programming which, as far as is possible, is 'factual' or based on 'real' events. The closest equivalent to the documentary is *news*, in that it is also based around presenting facts and pertains to real people, places and experiences. The aim of a documentary is to inform viewers of occurrences within society by offering them a convincing and balanced account of events. In a literal sense, documentaries attempt to 'document' and record events using evidence and 'facts' as 'proof'. As long as the documentary-maker reports fairly and evenly, weighing up all of the evidence available to them, the claim is that they can produce unbiased and objective readings of the subjects under their scrutiny. Sometimes, the balance of evidence will lead to a point of view that the documentary-maker will present to the viewer as an argument. Documentaries that set out to advocate a particular position are often referred to as 'authored documentaries'. The notion of *objectivity*, however, echoes the language of journalism, and it is of little surprise that, in Britain at least, much early television documentary-making had its origins in radio journalism (Corner, 1991).

The idea of documenting an event also relates to the methodology of historians, who rely on written documents and manuscripts (e.g. diaries, official government sources, letters, etc.) as primary sources of evidence. When writing an historical account the researcher will reference these documents and reflect on their content as they proceed. Similarly, the television documentary will also reference documents and will use sources as evidence. However, historians have recently begun to recognise the merits of other kinds of non-written sources, including oral testimonies, photographs or television and film footage, and have incorporated these into their work. For the documentary-maker, access to these visual sources is essential if the subject is to 'come alive' on the screen. For instance, when historical documentaries are made with little visual material about the event available, re-enactments of incidents may be staged to give the viewer a sense of what the '*reality*' might have been like. This is important as, despite highbrow claims about making 'serious', 'factual' and 'impartial' programming, television is essentially an entertainment medium that must be visually provoking if viewers are to stay tuned in. Indeed, Winston (1998) has argued that there is a trend in documentary towards subjects that satisfy the traditional *pleasures* of television or film viewing, such as programmes about *sex*, which invite a voyeuristic gaze from the *audience*.

Moreover, documentaries are also like fiction in that they are organised into *narratives*, which 'tell' events in a particular way. In the process of building a narrative, which essentially involves making a story out of the materials available, claims of objectivity are difficult to sustain. Concerns that the documentary form is therefore flawed have been evident from the beginnings of documentary production, when it was confined to film-making (the term 'documentary' was actually coined in the 1930s by documentary film-maker John Grierson, who was a part of the British Documentary Movement). In choosing which shots to show, by using the camera for emphasis (e.g. using close-ups to identify with particular individuals or taking shots from below to make people appear authoritative), or by editing tape into a particular sequence, the documentary-maker privileges a particular story over a number of possible alternatives. The time and cost restraints of making a short documentary may also prohibit a full exploration of all of the evidence available.

Despite concerns about impartiality, many documentaries are made with an *educational* intention in mind and are perceived as having a crucial role in stimulating discussion and debate around important topics. Chapman (1998) has argued that this has led to a perception of the documentary as a 'progressive' political instrument, particularly by those on the political left who celebrate them as a way of providing a critical voice on society. For example, in the 1980s a documentary called *Death on the Rock*, produced by the British channel ITV, challenged the government's version of how and why two members of the IRA (Irish Republican Army) were shot by British forces in Gibraltar. Despite the progressive potential of this programme in terms of opening up a delicate issue, it provoked a retrograde and authoritarian response. For some observers, *Death on the Rock* was instrumental in speeding up the deregulation of the television industry and its movement towards a commercial system. McQueen (1998) has proposed that the then prime minister, Margaret Thatcher, was furious that the programme had been produced, and that it fuelled her determination to break up the 'cosy duopoly' that the BBC and ITV had long enjoyed.

Generally, however, the instructive function of the documentary has made it essential to broadcasting systems based on a *public service* model, where programme-makers have a remit to inform and educate as well as to entertain. In countries where there is no public service tradition, or where *commercial television* is the dominant system, the supply of documentaries is often limited. Winston (1998) suggests that in the mid 1990s the BBC dedicated up to 23 per cent of its output to documentaries in response to its public service commitments. This compares to as little as 0.1 per cent of output found on the Italian commercial station Mediaset. Winston also suggests that American networks have produced documentaries as 'cultural loss leaders' rather than because they have had a genuine commitment to the form. As a result, the documentary units established by major players including NBC (who produced the *NBC White Papers* documentary series) and CBS (who produced the *CBS Reports*) were designed mainly to secure public faith in a broadcasting infrastructure widely condemned for producing cultural trivia. With the onset of commercial satellite and cable television, this limited commitment to documentary production has been further undermined. In 1984 it was dealt a fatal blow when programming guidelines designed for the networks, which included the provision of some documentary programming, were terminated in a general climate of deregulation.

Some commentators, such as Chapman (1998), have argued that the documentary is also under threat in Britain as the public service broadcasting system is eroded by the increasing provision of cheap programming from cable and satellite broadcasters. Given increasing consumer choice it is harder for the traditional home of the documentary, the BBC, to justify its collection of a licence fee from all television viewers. This has been recognised by its current Director

General, Greg Dyke, who has considered (but, as yet, has rejected) the possibility of the BBC becoming a subscription service. The commercialisation of television has, Chapman suggests, made broadcasters much more sensitive to audience ratings in order to attract advertisers. This militates against documentaries as, historically, they have proved to entice fewer viewers than other popular genres, despite having a high status within the industry. While some documentaries have succeeded in crossing over to a mass, even international, audience (McQueen (1998) estimates that the British-produced programmes *The Dying Rooms* and *Return to the Dying Rooms*, which explored conditions in Chinese orphanages, reached an international audience exceeding 100 million), they have tended to be exceptional rather than typical. Despite this generally pessimistic outlook, however, it is true that some non-terrestrial broadcasters have provided documentary services, such as Sky's Documentary Channel.

Some commentators have argued that with the decline of the public service ethos, the future of the documentary lies in its hybridisation with other genres. In particular, distinctions between information and entertainment, and fiction and non-fiction, are gradually collapsing (see *Drama*), as evidenced by the emergence of the 'drama documentary' (dramadoc) and the 'documentary drama' (docudrama) (Paget, 1998). Caughie (1980) makes a useful distinction between these superficially similar genres. The dramadoc is like a documentary in that its content aims to replicate a real-life situation; for example, the British dramadoc *Hillsborough* re-enacted a tragedy at the Hillsborough football stadium where over ninety Liverpool fans were crushed to death during an FA Cup semi-final. The programme was a mixture of 'fact', in that it was based on documentary evidence, including personal accounts of the tragedy and television footage shot on the day, and drama, in that actors were used to play the roles of people involved. In this instance, the desire to record an event truthfully was combined with an effort to make an emotionally charged programme. The twin aim was to create a reliable account while engendering a powerful affective response in viewers. In contrast, the documentary drama is like a documentary in that its style and form draws on a *rhetoric* of *realism*. The use of conversational language, real locations and real time, hand-held camera shots or naturalistic lighting combine to give a fictional programme the appearance of being like a documentary. In film, the most recent (and successful) example of this is the *Blair Witch Project*, which emulates the style of an amateur documentary filmed on home video. On television, popular shows such as *Hill Street Blues* in America, or *This Life* in Britain, also draw upon a documentary style to give them a feeling of 'authenticity'.

See also: **Genre, Objectivity, Public service broadcasting, Realism, Rhetoric**

Further reading: Chapman (1998); Corner (1986, 1991); McQueen (1998); Paget (1998); Winston (1998)

DRAMA

Although drama is one of the most varied, complex and popular of contemporary television forms, to understand its current significance it is necessary to start well before the invention of television, with the origins of drama in the Greek classics.

The term itself means 'action' or 'enactment' and the notion of 'performance' is a key element. The enactment of the 'real' through symbolism also highlights the ritual aspect of drama, and most known societies have shown evidence of dramatic, often religious, rituals. Certainly, from the fourth century BC, when Aristotle outlined the main forms (tragedy and comedy), drama has been linked to mimesis – the idea of imitation or *representation* of reality. Aristotle studied written rather than oral forms of drama and this, along with his hierarchical assessment of tragedy and comedy, has led to modern divisions between 'high' and 'low' *culture*, echoes of which remain today (for instance, in 'serious' drama being ranked more highly than television situation *comedy*). As well as this hierarchical ranking, drama developed in a number of ways from the Renaissance onwards, with naturalism (including illusionism and the idea of the 'willing suspension of disbelief') taking hold from the nineteenth century, along with the anti-illusionist 'epic theatre' of Bertolt Brecht in the early twentieth century. Brecht believed that drama was intrinsically political, and he placed great emphasis on the modes of production as well as the content of the dramatic script. Alongside these ideas, the influence of a commercially produced popular culture and the development of film and experimental fiction helped mould newer vernacular forms as well as a modern tendency towards *realism* in drama. Today, the expectation is that drama should be eclectic, constantly changing, challenging and innovative (McLeish, 1993). Moreover, certain tendencies associated with *postmodernism* – parody, playfulness, loss of realism, added emphasis on visual spectacle – have become evident, not least in popular television drama.

The strong association, and uneasy partnership, between theatre-based drama and television is evident from the earliest days of television when, in the 1930s, large-screen televisions were set up in a number of theatres in the UK. The intention was to show, among other items, dramatic productions (to be known as 'tele-oramas') for public rather than domestic consumption (Stokes, 1999). This 'theatre television' (also exhibited at cinemas) was doomed to failure for a number of reasons, mainly linked to objections from the BBC. So a division between the consumption of drama in public places (theatres and cinemas) and the private, domestic viewing experience of television took hold. Whereas theatre-based drama has continued to be somewhat shaped by long-standing traditions, television's more obvious associations with entertainment and commercialism have influenced the evolution of specific modes of television drama, while further blurring the distinctions between 'high' and 'low' culture.

Initially, television drama took the form of theatrical production transposed, live, to the small screen, and was based overwhelmingly in the traditions of theatre. In Britain, especially on the BBC, drama series and one-off plays were regarded as a high-quality product, relatively expensive to produce and conforming very much to Reithian notions of the democratisation of culture (see *Public service broadcasting*). Their high reputation and prestige meant that they sold well abroad and attracted large audiences. The USA, with its emphasis on commercial broadcasting and a less well-established tradition of 'quality drama', formed a regular buyer for this product, especially in the form of historical dramas. In terms of visual and *narrative* innovation, however, the early examples of television plays were generally unremarkable. By the 1960s, this was beginning to change with the single play format, as in *The Wednesday Play* and *Play for Today*, becoming known as a vehicle for greater risk-taking and innovation. The best work by dramatists of the period was, arguably, written directly for television rather than being transferred from the theatrical stage (Mullan, 1997). Subject matter was sometimes controversial or socially critical, and the form and techniques used in television drama began to incorporate elements of *documentary* on the one hand (the docudrama) and to play with a range of non-realist devices on the other. But alongside some ground-breaking dramas, a seemingly contradictory set of tendencies seemed to be taking hold, especially from the late 1970s onwards. That is, the bulk of television drama appeared to be increasingly formula-driven and bound by the rule of the lowest common denominator. Moreover, disapproval of *American-isation* became fuelled by the increasing importation of drama series, in particular soaps, from the USA. Media theorists began to argue that much television drama was ideologically conservative (see below).

In the USA, the first televised drama was broadcast in Schenectady, New York, in 1928 by the General Electric Company, and from the beginning of the 1940s American television stations regularly featured drama programmes of one sort or another. Sitcoms, such as the massively popular *I Love Lucy*, and Westerns (e.g. *Gunsmoke*) were major prime-time viewing during the 1950s, although 'prestige' drama in the form of original, one-off plays also made an impact at this time, for instance through the *Kraft Television Theater* (Hiebert *et al.*, 1991). Much drama began to be made on film, aiding reproducibility and national distribution. After the development of videotape in 1956, live broadcasting began to decline and this clearly affected the way drama was televised. Pre-recording meant that mistakes could be eliminated and a 'smoother' overall appearance was possible.

But from the late 1950s, issues of increasing cost intervened and the single play took a serious nose-dive. Some drama series in the 1960s (*Peyton Place*, *Alfred Hitchcock Presents*) began to include more 'adult' themes and greater realism, thus partially plugging the gap that had appeared as a result of the decline of the one-off play. Today, prime-time prestige drama is rare, with the exception of some British imports and network specials, but drama series such as *ER* and *NYPD Blue* remain immensely popular.

The commercial financial base of US television had an impact on the way in which drama was experienced. Unlike British television, where a play or film can be seen uninterrupted, US audiences were used to regular commercial breaks, and had been since the days of radio. This is one of the reasons why one-off plays, requiring greater concentration, were largely overtaken by serials and series with shorter episodes.

So today, drama on television in the US and the UK comes in many formats: the one-off play is still in existence, but more often than not contemporary television drama is seen in the form of serials, such as *soaps*, or in series. The mini-series, along with two-parters and three-parters, is a variant, and in recent years made-for-television films as well as cinema-distributed films transferring to television have become the norm. Far from the studio-bound, conventional cause-and-effect narrative, television drama now offers a variety of viewing experiences including overlapping, multi-narratives, postmodern self-conscious-ness and what Robin Nelson has called 'flexiad drama' (Nelson, 1997).

This is said to be a mode that draws on the flexibility and aesthetics of advertising and music video, rejecting realism and meaning in favour of spectacle. *Ally McBeal* and *Spaced* are two possible contemporary examples. Varying the format of drama has also meant radical shifts in scheduling, such as showing episodes on consecutive nights or several episodes on the same night, and it is now commonplace to show omnibus editions, repeats and preambles as reminders of previous episodes or series.

Much television drama, though, continues to rely on certain familiar formulas. Those most favoured and popular include *crime series* (*NYPD Blue, The Sopranos*), hospital dramas (*ER, Casualty*) and domestic or community-based narratives. The latter most often take the form of soaps or sitcoms and include youth-orientated series such as *Friends, Hollyoaks* and *Dawson's Creek*. Family sagas, often generated from popular fiction, generally appear as mini-series, while traditional historical dramas or adaptations of the classics (Shakespeare and Dickens in particular), more common in Britain than America, may utilise comparatively conventional approaches to format and *scheduling*.

Since the 1960s, then, television drama has incorporated numerous changes in format, content, style and production conditions. Alongside these changes, television analysts, audiences and professionals have heatedly debated the meanings and implications of the genre's evolution. The tension between 'quality' and 'popularity' has been at the heart of debates about television drama and the alleged 'dumbing down' of television more generally.

In Britain, a seminal moment in critical debates in this area came in 1978 with Colin McArthur's treatise on historical drama. Beginning with the notion that television claims a commitment to showing the 'truth' (see *Objectivity*), he acknowledged that historical events filtered through drama or drama-documentary are inevitably prone to fictionalisation. But he also argued that the past has been overwhelmingly shown from a bourgeois and nostalgic (and therefore, conservative) perspective, for example through individualised, personalised 'great men' narratives (McArthur, 1978). He believed that this tendency could be countered via politically radical, naturalist/realist drama (such as the contemporary series *Days of Hope*). This was the extension of a debate, largely between McArthur and Colin McCabe, which centred around the limitations of the 'classic realist text' (see *Realism*). McCabe maintained that it was necessary to shift away from the formal conventions of realism, with its emphasis on closing down contradictions, visually and in the narrative, in order to produce a text that would make viewers think for themselves and that would offer non-bourgeois versions of history (Bennett, Boyd-Bowman *et al.*, 1981). Although the debate was never fully resolved, it is interesting that during this period writers including Dennis Potter were embracing the technical and aesthetic possibilities of television to produce highly innovative, non-realist yet popular drama, such as *Pennies From Heaven* and *The Singing Detective*.

Despite the existence of figures like Potter, George Brandt (1993) claims that the 1980s probably heralded the end of high-quality television drama in Britain. His pessimism centred around increasing commercialisation (see *Commercial television*) and lack of investment in innovative or critical plays. Numerous cultural critics and television professionals have echoed Brandt's feelings in the last decade. On the other hand, Nelson (1997) argues that change is not always for the worse and suggests that television drama is in an exciting period of transition. He outlines some important shifts in television drama and in the way theorists have analysed these shifts. For instance, the predominance of 1970s spectatorship theories, which saw the passive positioning of the spectator by the text, later gave way to reception theories where what readers actively do with texts to produce meaning became paramount (see *Audiences*). Placing himself somewhere between these two positions, Nelson refuses the 'high'/'low' dichotomy (arguing that a 'highbrow' novel can also be a popular, commercially produced television series) and concentrates on elucidating the varied and complex forms of contemporary television drama. He is concerned to take account of the socio-historical and technical conditions of production as well as the agency of both writers and readers. Most of all, Nelson acknowledges the importance of a move away from familiar realist drama with its roots in naturalist theatre (such as *Boys from the Blackstuff*) towards television highly influenced by postmodern style and sensibilities (his example is *Twin Peaks*). The former is characterised by recognisable characters, cause-and-effect narratives and a sense of real historical events. The latter is likely to disobey narrative convention, be influenced more by the conventions of other media texts than by 'reality' and utilise the 'visuality' of film rather than the verbal nature of theatre. Postmodern drama is also more likely to invoke pastiche, parody and playfulness than a sense of locking in on a slice of life. While these developed forms of narrative provide a good deal of pleasure for viewers, focusing as they do on lifestyle and values, they do not, according to Nelson, encourage citizenship through a critique of public issues.

While drama may no longer offer the certainty and reassurance of its traditional forms, and while some critics perceive its quality to be under threat, there is no doubt that it remains a highly popular form of television, and that the very variety of its televisual manifestations offers progressive potential.

See also: **Commercial television, Culture, Documentary, Objectivity, Postmodernism, Public service broadcasting, Realism, Soaps**

Further reading: Brandt (1993); Nelson (1997); Potter (1984); Tulloch (1990)

EDUCATIONAL TELEVISION

Educational television covers a wide range of programming, from pre-school-age children's programmes (*Sesame Street*, *The Tweenies*) to broadcast material designed for schools, colleges and universities (*The Learning Zone*, *Channel 4 Schools*) to documentaries and lifestyle programming. With the emergence of cable, satellite and digital television, whole channels devoted to educational programming (such as *Discovery Channel*, *History Channel*, *BBC Knowledge*) are now a regular feature of the multi-channel environment. The increasingly diverse amounts of educational programming currently available across a variety of channel schedules confirm the position of television as not only being the central medium for popular entertainment, but also the central medium for the dissemination of popular information (Groombridge, 1972).

Research in this field is generally characterised by a concern with understanding the ways in which television *encodes*, (re)produces, transmits and circulates symbolic *representations* of knowledge (Livingstone, 1999) across a variety of genres and in different contexts. Within this framework, there has been a considerable focus on the *effects* of the medium on the message and the production of '*mediated* knowledge'.

The idea that television can 'educate' has been contested and subject to considerable debate and scrutiny. First, television, it is argued, cannot 'teach' because it is widely perceived as being a recreational medium, used primarily for entertainment and relaxation. Second – and this criticism is closely related to the above point – television viewing has often been thought of as a passive activity whereas the acquisition of skills and knowledge is believed to be an active pursuit. Third, television presents a one-way flow of information whereby the viewer (learner) has little or no control over the pace and delivery of information. In other words, the learner is not given the opportunity to actively engage with the material presented in the same way that s/he would be able to in a classroom situation. For example, if a student has a problem comprehending information in the classroom the teacher can be asked to further explain, reiterate or expand upon the material being taught. Fourth, television relies heavily upon what are traditionally thought of as being non-literate modes of teaching which are characteristically oral and visual. Televisual tuition is often seen as a degraded form of learning in comparison to print literacy which, as a means of acquiring knowledge, is still privileged over and above other forms of learning. For example, the assertion that *'children* shouldn't spend so much time watching television and should instead do something more con-structive like reading a book' illustrates the extent to which this privileging of print literacy over visual literacy informs our commonly held ideas. Finally, as Crisell (1997) points out, the actual processes involved in extracting information from a highly detailed and ambiguous *text* can also be problematic for the transmission of knowledge. Over the years there have been various research programmes designed to establish the extent to which the formal features of television (editing, graphics, camerawork, music and narration) act as a distraction from, and interfere with, the processing of information for viewers.

Some theorists have been less concerned with the formal features of television, focusing their attention on the *ideological* content of educational programming. Ferguson (1984) analysed an edition of the BBC programme *Blue Peter* (which strives to fulfil the BBC's remit of educating, informing and entertaining the younger audience) and found the programme to be an obstacle to the extension of knowledge. Far from 'opening up' the minds of its young viewers *Blue Peter* was ideologically reactionary – articulating imperialist, racist and sexist *discourses*.

Huston *et al.* (1992) suggest that, for the most part, the bulk of television programming is not explicitly designed to educate or influence viewers (although *Marxist* theorists might argue otherwise – drawing attention to what is 'implicit' rather than 'explicit') but, rather, some programmes may be produced as educational texts aimed at the effective transmission of knowledge. They go on to cite *Sesame Street* as an exemplary text in terms of teaching young children a range of cognitive, numeracy and literacy skills. Because of its unprecedented success, *Sesame Street* has been the subject of numerous research programmes designed to elucidate the extent to which the programme teaches pro-social behaviour in young children. Comparative studies between groups of children who watched the programme on a regular basis and those who rarely (or never) watched it indicated that the children who were regular viewers had a greater capacity for processing information, along with significantly more developed literacy and numeracy competencies (Huston *et al.*, 1992).

Groombridge (1972) advances a similar argument, envisaging television as potentially the great liberal educator of 'our times'. He suggests that television's provision of sounds, images and *narratives*, from a variety of social, cultural and geographical sources beyond the viewer's immediate, everyday life experiences, provides frameworks within which audiences can compare, evaluate and assess their own position in the world. Thus, television 'liberates' through access to new ideas and new information. There are, however, according to Groombridge, limitations to the extent to which television can actually 'educate' audiences, and these relate to the characteristics of the medium. Television's capacity for immediacy, for dramatisation and 'impact' reduce information to spectacle. The spatial and temporal dimensions of television mean that there is little time for in-depth, critical analysis of the information presented so that it is limited in its capacity to inform and educate the audience.

More recently, issues concerning the ways in which information is mediated by and through television have been considered in relation to *audiences*, their viewing practices and social contexts of viewing. The emphasis of research has shifted from a singular concern with the formal characteristics of the medium, and the extent to which these affect the message of texts, to a consideration of the prior knowledge audiences bring to their consumption of television texts and the processes of meaning production where viewers and texts come together.

See also: **Audience, Children and television, Encoding and decoding**

Further reading: Eco (1979); Groombridge (1972); Huston *et al.* (1992); Simatos and Spencer (1992)

EFFECTS

'Media effects' is the term given to a school of media audience research that looks at direct relationships between media and the attitude and behaviour of *audiences*. The effects research tradition dominated mass communications research during the early years of television and mass media. The widespread use of propaganda during World War II inevitably created concern about the rapid growth of television in the years thereafter – whether from McCarthyites fearing the power of a potentially 'leftist' media or Marxists concerned about the control of the masses by corporate or government elites (see *Marxism*). Others were simply pessimistic about the effect of mass media on *mass culture*, and media effects research sought to investigate how television and other mass media might influence public opinion and behaviour.

The rise of effects research coincided with the availability of two forms of social scientific inquiry: the public opinion style survey – which, by the 1940s, had attained a certain respectability – and psychological models of experimentation (in which subjects would be tested in controlled conditions). While there were attempts at more ethnographic forms of research, media effects is very much associated with these two methodologies.

In the 1940s and 1950s, the results of this research often seemed contradictory: some studies – particularly those using 'experimental' methods in which 'before' and 'after' exposure could be controlled (such as in advertising campaigns) – suggested clear patterns of media influence, while others – usually of the survey-based kind on more complex phenomena (such as political attitudes) – did not. The work of Bernard Berelson and Paul Lazarsfeld on media and voting behaviour in the 1940s and 1950s was particularly influential in assuaging fears of mass propaganda and in emphasising, instead, the importance of more interpersonal forms of influence.

When compared to the unambiguous power of wartime propaganda, the failure of much of this research to consistently report effects that were either alarming or direct seemed more notable than evidence to the contrary. The term 'minimal effects' thus became associated with the first few decades of research on media influence.

The lack of clear, positive and coherent results also alerted media researchers to the difficulty of investigating the relationship between media and audiences. The effects tradition has been subsequently criticised for its failure to overcome a number of conceptual or methodological problems. In particular, the following criticisms apply:

1   Media effects research has a tendency to see mass communication as a simple, linear relationship between message and receiver. This has been referred to as a 'hypodermic needle' approach to media influence, a metaphor that invokes an analogy with medical research in which the message/medicine is simply 'injected' into the receiver/patient and the researcher measures its effect. In this model the audience member is seen as a passive recipient, rather

than as an active agent who participates in the process of making meaning.

2   Media effects has found it difficult to resolve the difficulty of tracing long-term, more diffuse effects – such as television's influence on *gender* roles – meanings that may be built up over time and therefore be beyond the scope of a simple 'before and after' survey or experiment.

3   The effects tradition has tended to ignore the ideological complexity of media messages. So, for example, the media coverage of politics is regarded as having an effect if it has tilted voters one way or another. This ignores some of the more subtle ways in which media frame issues, discourses and agendas, and discounts the role media might play in defining what elections are about and what the result of an election means, without clearly invoking support for one well-established party over another.

The finding of 'minimal effects', in other words, might simply be a function of theoretical and methodological limitations. The researchers, in short, were not looking in the right place or in the right way. Thus, while a fairly crude 'hypodermic needle' model of media effects still dominates mainstream discussions of media influence, as well as the interests of government of non-profit funding agencies (informed by questions like 'Does *violence* on television make people more violent?'), the inconclusive nature of much of the early media effects research led a number of researchers to look for different ways of investigating the relationship between media and audiences. By the early 1960s, for example, *'uses and gratifications'* research chose to ask very different questions that emphasised the active role of audiences. More recently in the 1980s and 1990s, more qualitative forms of research from within a cultural studies tradition – informed by *semiology* – have seen meaning as a complex, ideological process whereby media and audiences engage one another.

Media effects is, for many, still associated with simplistic conceptions of influence, informed by a pessimistic view of mass culture in a media age. A number of researchers – most particularly in the United States – have nonetheless been reluctant to abandon the basic model and have created more sophisticated approaches to the exploration of effects. In the late 1960s, agenda-setting research, for example, began to isolate clear and specific evidence of media effects (see *Agenda-setting*), and in the 1970s cultivation analysis also began to

report powerful links between media use and views
Cultivation analysis).

This and other more recent research has also cas
notion of 'minimal effects', suggesting that the way
media frame issues, the topics they cover and the stor\
influence assumptions and attitudes about the world.

See also: **Agenda-setting, Cultivation analysis, Mass culture, Uses and
gratifications**

Further reading: Lazarsfeld et al. (1944); Lazarsfeld and Katz (1955); McQuail
(1994)

ENCODING AND DECODING

Stuart Hall's 'encoding/decoding' model of media production and
reception was developed – notably by David Morley – at the Centre
for Contemporary Cultural Studies in England. The model was an
attempt to move beyond linear, transmission theories of mass
communication and to incorporate *semiotics* and theories of *ideology*
and *representation* into media research. Although the model has been
used flexibly (and sometimes as a point of departure) by various
researchers, it has been extremely influential in providing a general
framework for the analysis of media *power*, particularly in the study of
audiences and reception.

The model takes its key terms – based on the notion of 'coding' –
from semiotics (see *Code*). The premise behind this conception is that
the production and consumption of media texts (see *Texts*) are social
processes in which meaning is constructed (although that meaning is
never inevitable, permanent or fixed). The media message or text is, in
this sense, a complex series of *signs*.

Encoding refers to the ideological, professional and technical
processes that inform how the world is represented or signified in
media texts. These processes may or may not be conscious or
intentional. So, for example, the decision to lead the news with a
publicity stunt by a leading politician is ideological, in the sense that
politics is seen as defined and informed by political elites. It is
professional in that the form and style of coverage of politicians is part
of the routines of news journalism, and lastly it is technical, because
the decision to lead with the item may have been informed by the
availability of a clip of the politician, together with clips of reactions to
it.

What is important here is that there is little about the action itself that makes it the most important event of the day. When President Ronald Reagan started the 'Indy 500' car race in the United States it was the lead item on all three US networks, even though the event would not affect the lives of any viewers. It is the process of encoding that makes it so. Indeed, one should include Ronald Reagan's campaign staff among the encoders, since they crafted the event as conveying a positive message about the President in a form the news media would regard as 'newsworthy'. Nothing on television – whether it is the way women are represented or the way crimes are reported – is natural. It is the product of a series of encoding processes.

The encoding processes not only produce a message, they give that message certain meanings. In keeping with the semiotic status of the model, however, those meanings cannot be guaranteed by the encoders. Even if a message is produced with an overt, propagandist meaning, we cannot be sure how a viewer will interpret it. The message is, nonetheless, heavily structured to encourage certain meanings over others ('structured in dominance'). It has, in other words, a *preferred meaning*.

Since the process of encoding involves both conscious and unconscious decisions, the preferred meaning should not be confused with the intended meaning. The intentions of the producer, writer, editor or actor will certainly be important, but the preferred meaning may also involve assumptions of which they were unaware. So, for example, an advertiser making a TV commercial for a floor cleaner may decide to show a woman in the kitchen using the product and choose a man to provide the voice-over. These decisions may be regarded as purely aesthetic – the woman looked like an attractive housewife and the man's voice had the 'right' tone to it – without any awareness that they are being informed by an ideological assumption that housework is something that women do and that, even when selling a domestic product, men's voices are perceived by advertisers as having more authority than women's. The advertiser's intention was simply to sell the floor cleaner: nonetheless, the commercial contains preferred meanings not only about the product but also about *gender* roles.

Once the message has been produced and inscribed with a preferred meaning, it will then be decoded by viewers, readers and listeners. Again, the model does not assume that the preferred meaning will automatically be reproduced: the model therefore posits three 'decoding positions' that the audience may occupy.

The first is the preferred reading, or an interpretation of the text that will closely reflect the assumptions and intentions of the encoders.

So, for example, the viewer may find the floor cleaner commercial persuasive and not question its assumptions about gender roles. The second is the negotiated reading, or an interpretation that may accept one of the text's preferred meanings but not another. This can take a number of forms: the viewer may be indifferent to the floor cleaner but find the commercial's use of gender roles perfectly natural; or they may find the portrayal of the housewife stereotypical while failing to notice that a man has been chosen to do the voice-over. Alternatively, the oppositional reading is an interpretation in which the preferred meaning of the text is understood but rejected. In this instance the viewer would reject the commercial, seeing the use of gender roles as part of a persistent pattern of sexist imagery and distrusting the ad's claims about the floor cleaner.

While these three decoding positions have little in common in an ideological sense, they share a common understanding of what the text is about. A viewer who interprets the commercial within a completely different frame of reference might disregard the preferred meanings entirely, noting only that the actress cleaning floors looks like their sister. Since this reading takes place outside the range of the preferred meanings, it might be described – using a term from Umberto Eco – as an aberrant reading or decoding.

For critics of other audience research approaches such as *effects* and *uses and gratifications*, the model has a number of strengths. In particular it allows us to see meaning as dependent upon both the text and the audience: to paraphrase Marx, people make their own meanings but not in conditions of their own choosing. It also defines the relationship between producer, text and audience as an ideological relationship: it therefore allows us to examine the role television and other media play in reinforcing or asserting certain attitudes and assumptions. So, for example, the floor cleaner commercial may play a part in the power struggle between an ideology of male dominance – or patriarchy – and an ideology of gender equity – or *feminism*. If its preferred meaning is accepted, it can be seen as instrumental in the reinforcement or development of patriarchy.

Although the model has not always been precisely replicated, the overall thrust of the encoding/decoding approach has informed much of the qualitative audience research carried out since the 1980s. Subsequent research also suggests that some of the model's technical terms might be modified, clarified or developed. Most notably, there has been much discussion about the status of the preferred meaning: in short, is it the property of the producer, the researcher or the audience? One answer is that there may be some interplay between them to establish the range of preferred meanings. Suppose, for example, that a black audience member dismisses the floor cleaner commercial because the actresses in them are always white. Is this an oppositional reading or an aberrant decoding? In this instance the viewer would see the ad as part of a racist system of representation – something the researcher might not have foreseen. The researcher then needs to decide whether the commercial is indeed informed by racist assumptions and, if it is, to use this audience reading to broaden their analysis of the preferred meanings.

A number of studies have suggested that what might be described as instances of 'aberrant decodings' can play an important and systematic part of decoding. This may be the case, for example, in the viewing of films or programmes across cultures, or in the decoding of programmes – like the *news* – that are routinely watched inadvertently. One can conclude from this that the category of the preferred meaning needs to be more flexible or that aberrant decodings may play an important part in the media's ideological role.

In connection with this, researchers such as Janice Radway (1984) and John Fiske (1989) have developed a notion of the 'resistive reading'. Although this sounds like an oppositional reading, it is both different and distinct. The resistive reading is one that goes against the grain of (rather than rejecting) the preferred meaning. So, for example, a woman reading traditional romance novels might enjoy them not for their broad endorsement of patriarchal stereotypes, but for those moments when the hero displays a sensitivity that allows her to question those stereotypes. Or a viewer of the floor cleaner commercial might interpret the actress less for her role in domestic drudgery than for the strength and exuberance she displays in spite of it.

While these points may depart from some aspects of the encoding/decoding model, they build upon its basic premises: that media production and consumption is an ideological process and that meaning resides not in the text or in the audience, but in the interplay between them.

See also: **Audiences, Effects, Ideology, Polysemy, Semiotics**

Further reading: J. Lewis (1991); Morley (1980, 1992)

FAMILY/DOMESTIC VIEWING

When deciding on the *scheduling* of programmes, broadcasters often base their decisions on a rather outdated view that people watch the levision in family units. In Britain, for example, this approach is set in ˛islative stone with the creation of a 9 p.m. 'watershed'. Between 5.30 ˎ. and 9 p.m. programming on terrestrial television is aimed mainly at ˙ly audience who, it is assumed, watch together. In contrast, more ˎoriented material is screened after 9 p.m., when *children* are ˎsedly safe in bed. As a result, some scenes portraying *sex, violence* or ˎring cannot legally be shown until after the watershed.

The decision to mould schedules to suit family viewing is not ˎcidental or arbirary. It represents an effort by broadcasters to ˎnderstand and control viewing habits, which is helpful when they are trying to sell time slots to advertisers keen to address clearly demarcated audiences. If broadcasters have to work around a watershed, for example, then advertisements for products aimed at adults (such as cars, perfume or alcoholic drinks) will obviously appear later in the schedule. However, the notion that families watch in predictable ways is questionable given that many homes now have more than one television set, or receive satellite or cable as well as terrestrial television. As a result, viewing habits are now much more fragmented and personalised. A child particularly keen on music may stay in their bedroom and watch MTV, while the father and mother may tune in to different channels which suit their own personal tastes and interests.

Despite these changes, the old model of family viewing remains very influential in deciding the content and scheduling of television. This view remains because television is widely regarded, both by the industry and by academics, as a domestic medium. For example, we usually watch it in the home and place the set in the corner of our living rooms in clear view. We also tend to build our home routine around the times of our favourite programmes. The clearest way to understand this domestic context is to compare watching television to watching a film. John Ellis (1982) has argued that analysts have too often treated television as if it were like film. Certainly, there are similarities in the use of visual *rhetoric*. Like film, television is composed of a mixture of visual images, sounds and verbal language. Both media are also primarily used for entertainment, and are often concerned with telling stories of one kind or another. However, there are some essential disparities that make them very different in the way that they are made and watched.

First, Ellis argues, simple distinctions, such as the size of a television set compared to a cinema screen, make our relationship with the medium different. Unlike film, television is not physically imposing or grand. The viewer is usually much bigger than the television screen, which means that we tend to dwarf it and often look down at it when we watch. When in a cinema, by contrast, we are eclipsed by the physical presence of the screen. We gaze in awe at its detailed and spectacular images and listen intently to stirring, crisply produced soundtracks. The quality of the cinema's apparatus cannot be replicated in the home. Moreover, watching a film is very much a public occasion. We go out with friends to see a film and sit in a large theatre with many other people. We pay an entrance fee to get in and, when seated with the lights turned off, we are encouraged to stay silent so that all of our attention is focused on the spectacle unfolding in front of us.

Television, on the other hand, is a private medium that we watch in the comfort of our own homes. We usually do not darken the room or stay quiet when watching it, and may well be eating a meal, doing the ironing or holding conversations while it is on. It often functions simply as a background distraction while we do other things, so that we pay close attention to it only at interesting or tense moments in a programme. Sometimes we ignore it completely, but leave it on all the same because we find its presence comforting. Television, then, fits into the routine patterns of home and family life in which our attention is inevitably distracted.

This distracted, domestic context is vitally important, for it also helps to determine the form that television *texts* take. For example, the content of many popular shows often mirrors the family or domestic setting in which the viewer is situated. Sitcoms and *soaps*, such as *Friends* or *Coronation Street*, are set in home environments with stories that revolve around interpersonal relationships, problems and situations. The characters have conversations in real time, interact in everyday locations (the apartment, the coffee house, the bar, the workplace) and speak in ordinary language, much as we do in our daily lives. In fact, their lives are so similar to our own that we spend countless hours discussing their encounters with friends or family, as if they were real people rather than fictional characters. Also, many television programmes, particularly *news* shows, talk to the viewer as if they were sitting on the other side of the room. For example, when reporting live, a news journalist will look straight into the camera (and by implication at *us*, the individual audience member) and will use plain, conversational language when speaking. In news bulletins the presenter may well say 'hello', or 'good evening', or a chat show host will 'welcome' us to a show. This gives the illusion that we are being directly addressed, as if in a real conversation.

The domestic context also affects the way that stories are told through *narrative*. Unlike films, many television texts are not single-

...ory narratives, in which there is a clear 'closure' as a problem or enigma is resolved at the end. Instead, the most common television *genres*, such as soaps or sitcoms, are classified in the serial or series format where the stories do not end. While there may be a temporary resolution of an issue at the end of an episode, the story will be picked up and moved on later in the series. The narrative of television, therefore, is usually on-going and is potentially infinite. This re-emphasises the 'realness' and immediacy of television, as it allows us to follow characters as their lives progress day by day or week by week. Their experiences and routines thus reflect our own. The close relationship that we have with television characters also influences the way that the industry presents them to us. For example, Ellis (1982) argues that because television is a part of our home or family life the industry packages characters as personalities, rather than as stars. A good example of this is the weekly television schedule guide. These often profile individuals, usually characters from soaps or sitcoms, and ask questions about their favourite foods, their children or what they like to do when they are at home. They are thus presented to viewers as being 'like us', as ordinary folk rather than stars with rare and special qualities.

Another implication of the domestic context, noted by Ellis, is the reliance of television on sound rather than image. Because we watch in a distracted way, sound is used to entice us back to the events on the screen. Trailers, theme tunes, soundtracks and near-constant conversation are all devices employed to 'hook' us into the narrative. We might be reading a book and hear the signature tune to *EastEnders*, which will invite us to focus on the screen rather than the page. Old episodes of cop shows, like *Starsky and Hutch*, used very dramatic soundtracks to connote commotion, excitement and action in car chases. Quiz shows use audience applause, coupled with music that increases in tempo, to connote adrenaline and increasing anticipation as the game nears its end.

This reliance on sound is arguably another difference between television and film. If a film director used the quantity or style of sounds found in a television show, it would most likely sound very brash and overdone. In contrast, analysts have often proposed that film relies more heavily on image to create meaning. For example, in classic Alfred Hitchcock films such as *Rear Window* or *Psycho*, the camera is the main storytelling device. Often scenes can last for minutes with no sound or conversation, yet through 'pure' cinematic language we are still able to follow the story. By contrast, television rarely relies on detailed images to motivate narrative, partly because of the relatively poor quality of television reception compared to the movies. In our noisy homes, with all their distractions, a Hitchcock movie does not work as well as it does on the 'big screen'. Increasingly, however, this distinction between the two media is becoming blurred. Many young film directors, such as Quentin Tarantino, clearly owe a debt to television in constructing their style, and rely strongly on sound, music and conspicuous dialogue to create a mood in their films.

The result of these factors is that television is constructed as an ordinary medium that fits into the routine flow of everyday life. Modelled around family viewing and focusing on domestic or everyday concerns, it attempts to reach out to the viewer by presenting a reflection or mirror of their own lives. Ellis refers to this as a 'community of address' that binds together the interests of both television producers and consumers. Arguably, of course, this also has an *ideological* function, in that it presents family and domestic concerns as the 'norm' for both our real and our televisual lives. Moreover, when we look at what actually happens when families watch television together we see that patterns of domestic viewing reflect wider social power relations and conflicts. Indeed, families are usually contested sites of social bargaining, with each member struggling with others for control over cultural space and for a secure place in the family hierarchy. Which newspapers are delivered, which records are played, which radio stations are listened to and which television programmes are watched all become important micro-debates in this overall contest.

However, in this on-going game of family chess, some members are pawns, with limited power to influence the outcome, while others are knights, bishops, rooks or queens, with the king at the very top. More specifically, the cultural supremacy of the home is, according to authors such as Lull (1990), maintained by men over women. Lull observed how families come to make decisions about their viewing habits and discovered that men usually make the choices about what should and should not be watched, often without consulting other members of the family. The ability to dictate the terms of viewing has been made easier, according to Morley (1986), by the emergence of remote controls, which are usually possessed by men who interrupt the viewing of others by constantly hopping channels. In part, this control over the apparatus of viewing demonstrates how *technology* itself is strongly gendered. For example, Anne Gray (1987) has proposed that new technologies brought into the home find their place in a structure of family power that favours men. As a result, men appropriate certain technologies, such as the *video* recorder, in order to maintain cultural power, and in turn these technological apparatuses come to signify masculinity. As a result of this gendering process, women become less confident than men in using some technologies, including the video recorder. To bear this out, Gray asked women to imagine household technology as coloured either pink or blue and found that, unsurprisingly, the iron was always imagined pink and the drill imagined blue. The washing machine produced an interesting mixture of responses, being a pink object with a blue motor! Its function was therefore gendered feminine, with the expectation that women do the laundry, while its working mechanisms were gendered masculine.

We could argue that, in a 'common-sense' way, this locates the home as a place of woman's work that is supervised and maintained by men. If we extend the chess metaphor further, the home is rather like the chessboard, over which the queen (the housewife) has the greatest dominion, being able to move very freely around it, but ultimately her task is simply to protect the interests of the king. With respect to television, Gray found that certain parts of the video recorder (e.g. the rewind or play button) were neutral colours while others, such as the timer to programme recordings, was usually gendered male and imagined blue. The remote, in confirmation of Morley's findings, was a 'deep indigo' and was always in possession of the man. If we accept these views then the concept of family viewing takes on a political and ideological dimension, which locates the issue within wider critical debates emerging, in particular, from *feminist* scholarship.

See also: **Feminism, Ideology, Narrative, Scheduling**

Further reading: Abercrombie (1996); Ellis (1982); Gray (1987); Lull (1990); Morley (1986)

FANS

When we think about a 'fan', our minds are often drawn towards the margins of *culture*, particularly to those 'lonely obsessives' who idolise and even harass celebrities, or to eccentrics who dress up like characters from their favourite television programme, film or pop group. Paradoxically, we are both drawn towards and repelled by the excessive and passionate qualities of the dedicated fan. Fascinated, because they exist as the most visible expression of a devotee culture that, to a greater or lesser extent, we all embrace, even if that involves simply tuning in to our favourite soap opera, or going to watch the football every weekend. Repelled, because the obsessive fan appears to have been 'taken over' by the text in a way that 'we' have not, or has wilfully submitted to a zealousness that, in the extreme, can manifest itself in the pathological behaviour of the stalker. In focusing on those individuals or groups whose practices we, the 'non-fan' or 'ordinary' audience member, consider peculiar, we construct our own position as 'normal' set squarely against the activities of the fan as a deviant and dangerous 'other'. Despite the fact that we may enjoy the same *texts*, 'they' are somehow different to 'us' and we are content to keep the boundaries between us clearly demarcated.

Often, however, we draw our conclusions about fans without making any genuine attempt to understand the motives or experiences of those involved in particular acts of fandom, beyond a cursory caricaturing of their culture and their (lack of) *taste*. The media itself conspires in this process of labelling and *stereotyping*. Tales of celebrity stalkers are nowadays ten-a-penny in the news, while the activities of high-profile fan communities, such as the famous 'Trekkies' (fans of the long-running television series *Star Trek*), are discussed either for their humorous value or as being odd idiosyncrasies of culture. As Storey (1996) has argued, we do not need to look far before we find images of hysterical teenage girls screaming lustfully at pop stars whom dysfunctional boys or men fantasise about killing. The problem with these stereotypes, of course, is that they are very selective in the way in which they represent fans, with little effort made to engage in an empathetic way with members of fan communities. The practices and enthusiasms of fans are thus critiqued by people looking down on fan culture, rather than articulated from the point of view of fans themselves.

Jenson (1992) claims that many academics have contributed to this labelling process and that through this the dominant view of the fan as either an 'obsessed individual' or as part of an 'hysterical crowd' has been maintained and legitimated. Jenson proposes that these ways of explaining fandom position fans as being somehow 'deranged'. However, this says more about 'us' than 'them', as our desire to stigmatise fans is related to wider concerns about the modern world and its impact on societies and individuals. These concerns operate at two levels. First, there is a social/cultural distrust of fandom that locates fan behaviour as evidence of society's perceived decline. This is separate from, but related to, a second concern that is psychological in origin, which explains fandom in terms of the psychological 'lack' of individual fans.

The social/cultural position posits that the irrational behaviour of fans is symptomatic of a social and cultural disintegration in which established communities, traditions and patterns of social order have collapsed. This view is closely tied to broader analyses of *mass culture*. These have tended to discuss the culture and morality of the industrialised west in terms of its sacrifice of traditional values at the altar of material and technological progress. Pre-industrial societies, in which 'organic' communities bound people together through ritual and shared experience, are romantically remembered in contrast to the fragmentation of modern life. Many of these critiques, including those attributable to the *Marxist* Frankfurt School, have also generated debates about the role played by the media, including television, in 'dumbing down' culture and in manipulating audience attitudes. The fan of popular culture in the guise of the 'obsessed individual' thus serves as a parallel to the atomised, alienated and vulnerable 'mass man' created under the conditions of nineteenth- and twentieth-century industrial society. Likewise the 'hysterical crowd' is an equivalent of the subjects of propaganda, most visible in Nazi Germany in the 1930s and 1940s, who were incapable of resisting media domination.

At another level, Jenson discusses explanations of fan behaviour that construct fans as psychologically inept or lacking. Here, the argument goes that in a fragmented and uncertain modern world our sense of ourselves is ruptured, threatened and incomplete. The behaviour of the excessive fan is, therefore, a way of compensating for all that is absent in our 'real' lived existences. Fans, thus defined, are socially inadequate and ineffectual people who are enticed and deluded by a popular culture, in particular the media, which offer them synthetic fulfilment and escape from their pitiable lives. The emotional sustenance provided by popular culture, however, is both fleeting and shallow and is no compensation at all for a full and healthy 'real' life. Ultimately, excessive fandom can confuse the boundaries between fantasy and reality and, by implication, between normal and deviant behaviour. In this psychological model, being a fan is best avoided lest the trite excesses of popular culture corrupt us (Jenson, 1992).

Both of these explanations, Jenson rightly suggests, leave little room to consider the fan in anything but a negative way. Moreover, the explanations are theoretically flawed. There is little evidence, for example, to suggest that the majority of fans act in the manner ascribed to them by either the social or psychological stereotypes. In fact, many of these theories are forged from anecdotal evidence rather than rigorous analysis. As a result, the dominant representations of fandom as individual or group pathology are rudimentary and crude and tell us more about our broader concerns about urban life, popular culture and modernity than they do about the actual condition of being a fan.

Despite this, their continuing usage has real consequences for both fans and non-fans. For the non-fan, they act as reassurance that their behaviour is 'normal' and allow them to celebrate their ability to maintain a healthy distance between their 'real lives' and the objects of their 'fantasies'. For the fan, the consequence is a social stigmatisation that, Jenson argues, treats them like 'primitive tribes' whose behaviour is dissected, analysed and constructed as 'other' in order that the non-fan can assert a sense of social, cultural and psychological superiority. What Jenson's work shows us is that despite a difference in emphasis between the models that she discusses, their function is the same in that they reduce the debate to an unhelpful and theoretically untenable 'us and them' scenario (Jenson, 1992).

Jenson's concerns about the poor state of theorisation around fandom are replicated in the most influential work yet produced on television fans, Henry Jenkins' *Textual Poachers* (1992). Compared to other aspects of popular culture, particularly pop music, the literature on television fans is relatively sparse. As a result, Jenkins' book is an essential read. Like Jenson, his work challenges the conventional, public view of fandom. It opens with an account of an episode of the popular American show *Saturday Night Live*. Here 'obsessive' *Star Trek* fans, replete with fake rubberised Vulcan ears and an exhaustive knowledge of inconsequential trivia from the show (including the combination of Captain Kirk's safe), are parodied for their oddball behaviour and 'kookiness'. Even William Shatner, who participated in the sketch, urged them all to 'get a life' when they quizzed him about minutiae from the series. In doing so he contributed to the dominant classification of the fan as someone who exists outside of accepted boundaries of normal or sane behaviour.

Jenkins' work is an explicit attempt to circumvent both the popular *discourse* 'on' fans that this sketch revealed and the existing theoretical paradigms that have supported it. Instead, he articulates a view 'from' fans and explores their culture both as an academic and as a self-confessed fan. More broadly, his work also fits into a changing conception of media *audiences* as active rather than passive. His dual status as fan and critic, he contends, allows him to access relevant theories that are useful for interpreting fan behaviour, while affording him an 'inside' line on the knowledge and conduct that is peculiar to fan communities. In order to combine these objectives Jenkins undertook an ethnographic study of fans of British and American television series, including *Star Trek, Blake's 7, Alien Nation, Twin Peaks, The Professionals* and *Starsky and Hutch*. This methodology allowed him to construct the research as a collaboration between himself, the academic, and the fans that he was studying. In the spirit of co-operation that this engendered, fans were invited to comment on work in progress in an atmosphere of active dialogue (Jenkins, 1992).

Rather than consider fans as people who are the passive subjects of either social or psychological trauma, Jenkins articulated a position in which the fan is an active participant in the organisation of meaning. Each fan, he argues, makes a perfectly rational choice to construct an alternative 'reality' for themselves through their fan activity that, for them at least, is set against the mundanity and orderliness of everyday life. Rather than being a sign of misguided psychological compensation, their closeness to particular texts demonstrates a desire to negotiate with the media in an active and creative way, in order to make its products relevant to the material and cultural conditions in which the fan, or fan community, is located. This process is empowering rather than destructive, and at times the negotiation between fan and text can be very sophisticated and productive. For example, fans of *Star Trek* studied by Jenkins often created their own scripts or edited together shows in order to manipulate characterisation and narrative. Some gay fans rewrote the relationship between Spock and Kirk as being homoerotic in an effort to appropriate their own meanings from the 'official' text. These appropriations, Jenkins proposes, are a cultural equivalent of 'poaching', whereby fans steal or manipulate a text that was, initially at least, created for them by somebody else. They are efforts, as Jenkins neatly observes, to 'scribble in the margins' of the text, turning fans from being 'readers' to 'writers' of material that has been reinterpreted within the fan community (Jenkins, 1992).

The idea of textual poaching is a direct reference to the work of the French theoretician Michel de Certeau (1984), whose book *The Practice of Everyday Life* provided Jenkins with his broad theoretical framework. For de Certeau, all popular culture is a struggle between efforts to control that culture through imposing products and texts upon people, and efforts to contest that control through using and consuming those products in ways that may not have been intended. While Jenkins is cautious about the extent to which we can see all of the activity of the television fan as necessarily resistant, de Certeau's idea of poaching offered him a way of celebrating fan activity as an act of 'cultural bricolage', in which fans take apart and assemble television's artefacts according to their own wants and desires. Moreover, a lot of fan activity goes far beyond the text itself. For example, for many fans the act of reading and re-reading texts is not a solitary activity but occurs in liaison with other fans of the same programme or genre in a fan group or community. Many fans organise conventions, publish fanzines or create web-sites in an effort to share their passions with others. This 'organised fandom' allows for the negotiation with the text to recur and develop so that its meaning is subject to constant modification. Within the fan group this can produce a shared set of understandings about the aesthetics of the text and how it should be received and understood. Fan groups often set up an unofficial 'canon' or hierarchy of taste around their chosen text, in which they try to establish a 'cultural authority' over it. Acting as self-appointed critics, this allows fans to construct a 'correct' way of interpreting or reading a particular show. For example, Tulloch and Alvarado (1983) have argued that for fans of the long-running science fiction series *Doctor Who*, it became received wisdom that the early series (which, incidentally, were less popular) were superior to later series by virtue of being more 'authentic'. Similarly, Jenkins found that certain *Star Trek* episodes merited widespread recognition as exemplars of the show. Episodes including 'City on the Edge of Forever' and 'Yesterday's Man' were universally popular, while others, such as 'Spock's Brain', were widely mocked. For fans there is a power in being able to establish this hierarchy in the same way that a literary critic recommends great books. By showing a connoisseur's knowledge of the canon a sense of ownership of the text can thus be achieved.

While Jenson's and Jenkins' work has been useful in taking fan activity seriously, particularly by challenging accepted stereotypes, some questions about the usefulness of their analyses remain. For example, it is not made clear where the boundary between the ordinary audience member and the fan lies, or when a person turns from being one into the other. This raises questions about the usefulness of the term 'fan' as a conceptual category, as it is a moot point who is and who is not a fan. Moreover, implicit in much of the theorisation around fans is a sense that there is an 'active minority' (the fans) who can critically engage with a text and a 'passive majority' (the ordinary viewers) who cannot or do not. Unfortunately, this rehearses mass cultural theory that seeks to establish boundaries of taste between high art and its 'appreciators' and popular culture and its fans. This is a romanticised position that many theorists, such as Fiske (1992), have challenged by exploring the activity of all audience members rather than select groups.

See also: **Audiences, Marxism, Mass culture, Stereotypes, Taste**

Further reading: de Certeau (1984); Fiske (1992); Jenkins (1992); Jenson (1992); L. Lewis (1992); Storey (1996)

FEMINISM

There is little doubt that feminism has been one of the most significant influences in academic debates about *culture* in the past two or three decades. In a variety of senses, it has also been influential in television studies and in the television industry itself. However, its position has been difficult for a number of reasons. First, because it is an inherently political stance as well as an academic one and this means that it has demanded social change. Second, it has (successfully) mounted a critique of male-dominated practices in academia and within the media industries. Third, feminism has therefore been regarded as quite threatening to the status quo. To some extent, feminism has become a dirty word, and its ideas subject to a 'backlash'. This seems to have come about partly because it has been misrepresented by the media itself. Fourth, in recent times feminism has become fragmented and has found itself under new attacks, some of them perceived as 'from within'.

Feminism is a political and social movement which foregrounds gender as an important aspect of our social identity. *Gender* is regarded as a mechanism that structures our material and social world. Over time, there have been a number of different types of feminism (for example Marxist feminism, radical feminism, liberal/equal rights feminism) but all of them have argued that women as a group have been treated in a range of (unfavourable) ways by men as a group, in social and economic *institutions*. Most forms of feminism have argued the existence of 'patriarchy', which literally means the rule of the father or father-right, but more generally means male dominance. It is important to note that feminists have seen this not as a simple question of individual men being oppressive or discriminatory to individual women, but that patriarchy is embedded in our culture and institutions and this might well result in such behaviour and attitudes by individual men. So feminists have demanded changes ranging from political rights (such as the vote), to equal pay, to changes in the education system, etc. From early on, there has also been concern about the way women are represented in the media (see *Representation* and *Stereotypes*).

In different forms, feminism has been around on and off for centuries, but developed most visibly through the various suffragette movements in the late nineteenth and early twentieth centuries and then went through a 'second wave' in the late 1960s and 1970s. It is this second wave, and after, that is most relevant in terms of the study of the media and especially of television. After the upheavals of the 1960s, the time was ripe for a re-evaluation of sexual politics and gender roles and relationships. The 1960s foregrounded the problems of marginalised and oppressed groups via the Civil Rights movements, and saw the emergence of a new phase of feminism in the USA and in Europe. Through seminal works like Kate Millett's *Sexual Politics* (1970) and Germaine Greer's *The Female Eunuch* (1971) a critique began to form, not only of conventional patriarchy but also of patriarchal structures in the counter-culture. In other words, it was realised that women's place within groups fighting for equality was actually not that different from their place in 'straight' society.

The feminist critique of the media included a number of elements. Early concerns tended to focus on the relative absence of women in the powerful structures and positions within the media and art worlds. Moreover, it was clear that the policies and practices of the television industries actually prevented women from making headway since they were barred from many technical positions such as that of camera-person. Even today, while many changes have come about within television as an industry, women are concentrated into a narrower range of positions (with an emphasis on occupations such as make-up and wardrobe) than are men (see *Women in television*).

Second, 1970s feminists were concerned about the narrow range of representations of women offered in the media and argued that these were often 'negative' stereotypes. So, for instance, much *advertising* was taken to task for restricting representations of women to only a few stereotypes – the wife and mother, the housewife and the sex object, for example. This approach focused on the power of *ideology* as a force and a mechanism.

Third, the mid 1970s saw the beginning of what was to become an influential strand of thinking within academic studies: that is, a concern with how spectators are positioned to experience film and television as if through male eyes. This is called the 'male gaze' thesis (put forward by Laura Mulvey in 1975) and is based on *psychoanalysis* as a theoretical approach. Initially applied to the cinema, but with relevance for the *conventions* of television, the approach is based on the idea that conventional texts use a predominantly male camera gaze and that this gaze sexualises women and turns them into objects to be looked at. Because, in this perspective, looking is understood to involve desire and control (or the desire to control), the male gaze is tied up with issues of *power*. In conventional media, then, the gaze is 'owned' by men, which makes the concept of a 'female gaze' more or less impossible, at least in theory. In practice, changes in women's social position and the assertion of a female camera gaze have developed alongside each other. More recently, feminist writers such as Gamman and Marshment (1988) have debated the implications of these changes in relation to television and other forms of popular culture.

Initially, feminist studies of the media tended to try to put the above problems right by simply inverting male dominated studies to provide a focus on women. For instance, they shifted from the study of so-called 'male' texts like the *news*, current affairs and *sports* to look at so-called 'female' texts like *soaps*, romance novels, certain film genres, advertisements and magazines. Early feminist writings on these forms of media tended to look at how all of these texts encouraged domesticity and passivity in women through the articulation of a dominant ideology.

The approaches of the 1970s were limited in a number of important ways. For instance, the early critique was over-simplistic and reductionist. It tended to use *content analysis* or other fairly crude analytical methods to focus on the way women (and other minority groups) were stereotyped by television, especially in advertising. The assumption behind these studies was that women, as consumers, were adversely affected and limited by such representations. While some of this work was very useful as a starting point, it could not account for the complex *pleasure* that women often got from watching television and engaging with these products (see *Audiences, Family/domestic viewing*).

But this emphasis shifted in the 1980s, and feminist theory tended to be influenced by a range of other approaches such as *structuralism, semiology* and *psychoanalysis*. More recently, feminist theorists have been investigating the ways in which women gain pleasure from conventional, popular television texts, particularly those that are supposed to exploit women. Feminists have also looked again at gender in relation to audience research, and a range of feminist writers have moved the theoretical debates along as well as tackling the analysis of specific television forms such as the soap, the situation *comedy* and the *crime series* (Brunsdon *et al.*, 1997; Gamman and Marshment, 1988; Geraghty, 1991; hooks 1989 are examples).

These debates can usefully be seen in the context of changing practices both by feminist producers and by the 'mainstream' television industry. There has been some development of new styles and movements, including the growth of an independent sector, especially for *documentary*-making. Similarly, new directions within mainstream television have become evident. For example, more women in film and television production has meant a re-evaluation of gender stereotypes (of both genders). From the 1970s onwards, both male and female producers began to comment on, challenge and sometimes change these stereotypes by providing a greater diversity of roles and characters. An early example of this was in *Cagney and Lacey*, and more recent examples have included comedy roles such as *Roseanne* and dramatic series like the *Prime Suspect* cycle. We need to qualify this claim to greater parity, though, as critics such as Molly Haskell (1987) and Susan Faludi (1991) have identified a 'backlash' against feminism and the growing independence of women. This has been expressed not only in real social relations but also in increasingly violent screen images, focusing on women as victims. Haskell suggests that the more women try to assert their independence in real life, the more likely they are to be 'symbolically annihilated' on screen.

An important development or off-shoot of the debates about representations of femininity has been the more recent concern with representations of masculinity and of masculine *sexuality*. These debates have emerged very directly from feminist arguments around the representation of women. In television practice, too, there has been a growing tendency to re-evaluate traditional ways of signifying masculinity, for example through showing (some) male characters in softer, more 'caring' roles.

In the 1990s and beyond, there have been some important changes in feminist approaches to the media, and to television more specifically. According to a number of commentators, it is no longer accurate to talk of feminism but rather of feminisms. Feminist debate is now fragmented, exhibiting different emphases. An important shift has been to centre on the concept of 'experience' (as opposed to centring on the concepts of 'patriarchy' and 'ideology', as in the past). Many recent writers have discussed how women can and do differ in their experiences. For example, the place and experiences of black women within popular culture are very different to those of white women as well as to those of men (hooks, 1989, 1990). Similarly, the different experience of working-class and middle-class women has been commented on, and has included a discussion and critique of the role played by feminism itself in failing to represent the reality of working-*class* life. One accusation is that much feminism has been based on middle-class white women's experiences. Camille Paglia (1990) has argued that contemporary feminism has become stultified and reactionary. Thus, the collective term 'we', so cherished by feminists in the early days, and the notion of 'sisterhood' have been heavily questioned by these recent developments. Feminism has become fragmented.

See also: **Gender, Representation, Sexuality, Soaps, Stereotypes, Women in television**

Further reading: Brunsdon *et al.* (1997); Hollows (2000); van Zoonen (1994)

GAME SHOWS

The quiz or game show is an ever-present of modern television *scheduling*. Cheap to produce and popular with international audiences the *genre* is a boon for television networks keen to win high ratings. Tunstall (1993) suggests that these shows are judiciously placed throughout schedules in order to maximise their effectiveness in attracting viewers. Some cheap shows, aimed mainly at housewives and the retired, are placed in daytime slots and are run five days a week. Others are located in the afternoon schedule to appeal to older children returning from school, while the most elaborate and expensive are shown in the evenings during peak-time viewing. The latter tend to be fronted by high-profile hosts and sport the largest prizes.

Whannel (1992b) has suggested that, while sharing some similarities with fairground sideshows and Victorian parlour games, the quiz show or panel game is largely an innovation of radio and television broadcasting. McQueen (1998) identifies the earliest television show as the spelling quiz *Spelling Bee*, first aired by the BBC in 1938. This demonstrated that the potential of the genre was recognised early by schedulers. While the thrills of a quiz based on the ability to spell proved somewhat elusive, other formats rapidly became successful, particularly when big prizes were introduced in America during the 1950s (e.g. CBS' *$64,000 Question*). McQueen has proposed that, by 1957, half of the top ten programmes aired by American networks were quizzes. In 1987 Fiske estimated that American networks had broadcast in excess of 300 quiz shows, a figure that, more than ten years on, has no doubt increased substantially (Fiske, 1987). By 1993 Tunstall also claimed that the average British viewer watched roughly ninety minutes of quiz shows every week. These estimates provide some measure of the pre-eminence of the genre in viewing habits and scheduling on both sides of the Atlantic (Tunstall, 1993).

Despite their popularity – or perhaps because of it – many quiz shows, compared to other genres such as documentary and news, have tended to acquire a low cultural status. Whannel maintains that, in Britain, regulation to restrict the size of prizes and limit the number of shows aired is evidence of a deeply held cultural disdain for the genre. Regulatory action, once taken by the Independent Broadcasting Authority (IBA) but now rescinded, reflected a more general concern, particularly among the educated middle classes of society, that quiz shows were evidence of trivial or inferior programming. Given the cultural paternalism of the BBC and the ethos of *public service broadcasting* that it embraced, early quiz shows may have been worthy or high-minded, but the genre had to wait until the inception of *commercial television*, through the establishment of ITV in 1954, to come into its own as 'light entertainment'. By 1957, Whannel (1992b) suggests ITV was running eight quiz shows a week.

Reflecting the middle-class disdain for quiz and game shows, many academics have also been critical of the genre, particularly when identifying the *ideological* function that it plays in sustaining the values of competitiveness and social mobility that are central to the maintenance of capitalist societies. Fiske has identified elements of 'game' and 'ritual' within quiz shows that act to legitimate inequality and social hierarchies. Drawing on the work of the structural anthropologist Claude Lévi-Strauss, Fiske has argued that quiz shows create a myth of inequality and social mobility that presents them to viewers as if they were natural and inevitable occurrences (Fiske, 1987). They do this by taking the viewer through the *narrative* structure of 'ritual–game–ritual'. Lévi-Strauss proposed that a game starts off with participants on an equal footing but, as it unfolds, winners and losers with unequal aptitudes are revealed. In contrast, rituals take differentiated groups of people and provide a shared or communal experience in which those participants are 'equalised' and brought together, so that by the end they have a mutual group identity. In short, a game commences with the focus on similarities (e.g. two football teams of eleven players) and ends with difference (e.g. a winning and a losing team), whereas ritual practices start with difference (e.g. children of different ages, class, ethnicity or gender getting ready to go to school) and end up with similarity (e.g. as relatively undifferentiated 'pupils', identified by a common uniform, addressed as a group in an assembly hall).

The quiz show narrative usually starts with elements of ritual. For example, in most shows contestants are introduced to the audience and their differences are revealed. We may know their name, where they are from, or be informed of their occupation or even their hobbies. However, all are given identical treatment by the host so that, despite these differences, they are constructed as having identical status in the game and equal opportunity to progress within it. A sense of 'fair play' for everyone is also established as the host, for the benefit of all participants, recounts the rules of the game. Once this has been done the 'game' is initiated and the narrative switches to one in which competition between individuals or groups can occur, usually by enigmas being presented and resolved in the form of questions and answers, or problems and solutions. The resolution of the narrative materialises when participants are either successful or fail, by winning or losing the game. In this process, inequalities and differences are allowed to develop along the lines of 'natural' ability, with those possessing the requisite knowledge or skills rewarded materially. Fiske suggests that this replicates capitalist ideology in that people may come from different social and cultural contexts, but they are persuaded that they enjoy an equality of opportunity and can develop skills in exchange for material rewards. A myth of mobility is thus reinforced despite the realities of social inequality that may limit an individual's life-chances in the 'real' world, whatever their 'natural' talents may be (Fiske, 1987). At the end of the game show, however, the ritual element is re-established. It is common, for example, for losing contestants to return to the centre of the stage and wave at the audience with the winners and the host. This reinforces a sense of mutual identity and implies a full acceptance, by both winners and losers, of the competitive process that they have been through. The game may be tough on some, but with fair play allowing natural ability to prevail there are no hard feelings at its end.

However, despite this ideological function the popularity of quizzes suggests that audiences take some *pleasure* in the format, however harsh the conditions of the game. The BBC quiz show *The Weakest Link*, in which participants are encouraged to vote one another off the show on the basis of their ability to answer factual questions quickly, has taken the social Darwinism of the quiz show to new extremes. Even here, however, the narrative provides the audience with an initial sense of equality and cohesion, as all participants are allowed to introduce themselves as the game commences, so starting on an equal footing. Audiences also take pleasure in identifying with the winners of quiz shows, urging them on to achieve success. *Who Wants to Be a Millionaire?* secured its highest ratings in Britain when the first winner of £1 million was revealed. This represented something of a ratings coup, as it went head-to-head in the schedules with the final episode of a popular comedy, *One Foot in the Grave*, in which the principal character was being killed off. It is clear, therefore, that audiences enjoy revelling in the distilled *drama* that is carefully manufactured by the narrative of a quiz show. The higher the rewards to be won, the greater this pleasure becomes. It might be argued that the popularity of quiz shows thus demonstrates that audiences take enjoyment in the ideology of competitiveness that is promoted.

The popularity of the genre is also due to audience identification with people on screen, particularly the contestants and the studio audience. In many respects the success of an individual contestant stands in for the potential achievement of all 'ordinary' people. Quiz shows, along with talk shows, are one of the few formats where ordinary people and 'common-sense' knowledge are privileged. As a result, it is easy for the viewer to identify with individuals involved, as they are constructed as 'one of us'. Whannel (1990) has argued that during the 1980s quiz shows moved away from cultivating highbrow or intellectual knowledge, most evident in Britain in relatively 'academic' productions such as *Mastermind* and *University Challenge*, to focusing on common-sense or 'consensus' knowledge. For example, *The Price Is Right* celebrates the ability of contestants to estimate the price of household goods. Where intellectual shows test knowledge of 'objective facts' (e.g. 'Who was the second of Henry VIII's wives?'), populist game shows test knowledge of public opinion or common sense (e.g. 'We asked one hundred people the price of a lawnmower ...'). Audience pleasure is also increased in populist shows as we are symbolically invited to participate in the narrative. For example, in *Who Wants to Be a Millionaire?* contestants have the option to 'ask the audience' about a challenging question, or to 'phone a friend' if they are stuck. These rules bring the studio audience, who are there as representatives of all television viewers (i.e. us), directly into the game at crucial and often tense moments.

In one way we might see the shift to populist programming as culturally broad-minded and progressive, in that it undermines the authority of those educated classes, with high levels of cultural capital, who have traditionally patrolled the borders of knowledge (see *Taste*). It may also be seen as an overdue recognition of the social proficiencies of subordinate groups. As Whannel has suggested, this is true in terms of both working-class knowledge and *gendered* knowledge. Shows such as *The Price Is Right* or *Supermarket Sweep*, he argues, celebrate the skills of bargain-hunting, acquired by window-shopping or reading mail-order catalogues, that are traditionally perceived, at least within the dominant ideology, as 'inferior' women's knowledge. However, Whannel also suggests that the increasing predominance of common-sense shows has reflected a drift to political populism during the 1980s under conservative leaders such as Margaret Thatcher. Thatcherism sought a return to an ideology of economic liberalism centred on promoting individual achievement through self-help and material betterment. The logic of this ideology presented competition as being a good thing, while the promotion of an acquisitive, aspiring nature was seen as essential in regenerating an ailing economy. The competitive narrative of the quiz show thus fitted perfectly within this broader political ideology, with its emphasis on winning and individual achievement. But the move to common-sense shows also reflected a distrust of politicians like Thatcher for established expertise and intellectual orthodoxy, particularly that of the liberal left which had predominated in Britain in the post-war era. Thatcher's own populist style, reflected in her shopping at Marks and Spencer or likening government spending to a family budget, was warmly embraced by the tabloid press of the day and, Whannel implies, was evident within less obvious cultural forms such as the quiz or game show (Whannel, 1992b).

More recent trends in game and quiz shows are evidence of the *postmodern* blurring of genre boundaries that is occurring in much of contemporary popular culture. For example, the British game show *Families at War* and the celebrity panel quiz *Shooting Stars*, both hosted by alternative comedians Vic Reeves and Bob Mortimer, have combined the game show format with comic sketches and chat, while making playful references to other genres, television shows and personalities. They also parody the traditional skills and knowledge tested in other shows by asking absurd questions about women's nasal hair, or by inviting participants to demonstrate bizarre skills such as the ability to detect the temperature of warm air blown through a cardboard cut-out of Jack Nicholson's mouth. This demonstrates clearly how far the genre has moved since its rather cheerless origins at the BBC in the 1930s.

See also: **Commercial television, Genre, Ideology, Narrative**

Further reading: Fiske (1987); Fiske and Hartley (1978); Tunstall (1993); Whannel (1992b)

GENDER

'Sex' and 'gender' are closely related, but not synonymous, terms. 'Sex' has long been used as a term to denote biological differences (male and female) while 'gender' is generally acknowledged to refer to socially and culturally acquired roles and behaviours (masculine and feminine). However, even though these dimensions are often linked, the relationship between them is not straightforward. The biological basis of gender roles (and indeed, sexual preference; see *Sexuality*) has long been open to question, largely due to cross-cultural and historical study that has revealed great variability in patterns of behaviour along gender lines. Even physical characteristics like genitals and hormones are now regarded as not quite the clearly defined, stable entities they were previously thought to be. Transsexuality and gender realignment have given exposure to the syndrome of a 'woman trapped in a man's body' and vice versa. Recent and current debates around identity have re-defined sex and gender as existing along a continuum, rather than in terms of dichotomous polar opposites (male/female, masculine/ feminine). Whether or not this more fluid definition of gender is taken as a starting point, it soon becomes clear that the media may be powerful agents in constructing and representing gender and that television is an arena both for the construction of stable notions of gender (through *stereotyping* and generic *convention*) and where more contradictory, paradoxical versions of gender may be exhibited and discussed.

Since the development of a feminist critique of the media (see *Feminism*) gender issues have been of concern within the study of television. These concerns have primarily taken two forms. First, there has been the question of *representation*, which initially focused on how television (including *advertising* on television) stereotyped, under-represented or misrepresented women. Although both the debates on representation and some of the representations themselves have moved on, these concerns remain of interest.

Second, and in parallel, there has been an emphasis on the television industry and, in particular, on the potential and necessity to equalise gender opportunities in what has been, traditionally, a male-dominated domain (see *Institutions*). *Power* inequalities within televi-sion have been linked to the specific types of representations that have been made of women (and men). In other words, it is argued that male camera operators, directors and producers have objectified women's bodies and limited the range of roles in which women appear, whereas men have been represented more broadly (see *Women in television*).

Although 'gender' refers to concerns about both men and women, the majority of critical writing has, until quite recently, been about women's experiences and the representation of women. This can be explained as part of a broader concern by feminists about women as a 'minority', in terms of power if not numerically. However, recent critical debate has widened to encompass questions of cultural identity and the relationship between the media and the construction of identities. As these debates have developed, issues around the representation of men, discourses of masculinity and masculine sexualities have also come into the frame (see below).

Many investigations into representations of gender on television have suggested that the world as shown to us is a gender-skewed one (Tuchman, 1978; Gerbner and Signorielli, 1979; Communications Research Group, University of Aston, 1990). Comparing the television world with the 'real' world, it became apparent that the former is populated by many more men than women; men are more likely to be seen in jobs or careers, to inhabit a wider range of roles, occupational and otherwise, to be spread across a larger age range and to be seen in more body shapes. Many programmes and advertisements surveyed showed women as either overwhelmingly domestic creatures (house-wives, mothers) or as sexual prizes and accessories to men (bodies to sell products, assistants to male authority figures). The few older women represented on television tended to be figures of fun, while women from ethnic minorities, where visible at all, tended to be shown in highly stereotypical ways (see *Race*). So, on television, 'normal' femininity has been depicted, if only by default, as overwhelmingly young, slim, white and (hetero)sexual/domestic. In contrast, 'normal' masculinity has been seen as less restricted and more often associated with power, action and control, even in the traditionally 'feminine' domain of the home. In addition, conventional, restricted versions of femininity and womanhood have been idealised so that women who are shown as housewives or mothers are rarely shown actually carrying out domestic work, except in advertisements where such work is quickly and magically accomplished. Moreover, women (and, to a lesser extent, men) whose identities stray from the televisual norm have over-whelmingly been relegated to the margins. Eventually, the restrictive nature of such gender representations began to raise alarms not only among media theorists but within the general public, when they became linked to the spiralling number of eating disorders and other problems of low self-esteem being diagnosed among young women in the developed world.

But though these are serious concerns, some would argue that this way of analysing and understanding media images is itself problematic, since it assumes a relatively simple link between the 'false' or 'negative' representations of most television and the 'true' or 'positive' ones that might be substituted. The assumption that there are 'true' versions of femininity or masculinity 'out there somewhere', if only television producers were willing to show them, can be somewhat misleading. Femininity, like masculinity, is complex, varied and contradictory. Increasingly, television itself offers more complex images of men, women and their social roles (for instance, *Roseanne* – the programme and the character – Mulder and Scully in *The X-Files* and, more recently, the assorted members of *The Royle Family*).

One of the difficulties here concerns the methods that might be used to explore gender and media. Many of the early studies of gender representations used quantitative methods such as *content analysis*, which are useful as an initial mapping exercise but are limited in understanding the mechanisms used by television to 'naturalise' specific values or behaviours. What became more interesting then, for contemporary television studies, is the way in which television constructs its images, so that the constructions on offer seem like 'common sense.' Viewers may or may not internalise certain dominant values about gender roles embedded in television representations while being exposed to a wider range of ideas – some of them contradictory – than in the past. For instance, men bringing up children alone, women as heads of corporations, gay hosts on chat shows, all are still in the minority, but they are not absent from our screens and viewers can engage with and make sense of these representations and make judgements about their meanings. Qualitative research, such as *semiology*, can be helpful here in interrogating the range and limits of meanings in representations that might appear progressive on initial inspection. For instance, Williamson (1990) has argued that it is not necessarily progressive or 'positive' to see women as independent career women if they are also shown as spiteful and uncaring, nor if they can only be seen as 'successful' if they are also conventionally glamorous.

Television's link to *realist* conventions has, in the past, had a part to play in widening the types of roles in which women are seen. *Soaps, dramas* and *comedies* have been influential in pushing back some of the boundaries, offering a point of identification to strong, older, larger, ethnically or sexually diverse women. The British writer Lynda La Plante has consistently put women at the centre of her narratives and has refused to make them into passive victims or sex objects, while nonetheless dealing forthrightly with women's victimisation and sexuality. Television cop shows like *Cagney and Lacey* or *The X-Files* have also played a part in these changes, as have some *news* and current affairs programmes. Kirkham and Skeggs (1998), writing about the smash hit comedy series *Absolutely Fabulous*, have argued that it offers unruly and disruptive female characters and explodes conventions of 'proper' motherhood and femininity, while also poking fun at ideas of sisterhood and female friendship as espoused by feminism. Moreover, the series may operate differently in its appeal to working-class women than to the kind of middle-class women that form its central focus. *Absolutely Fabulous* succeeds on a number of planes, not least by articulating contradictory *discourses*. So, in terms of gender, the role of fantasy may be important, with an increasing awareness that television can offer not only 'mindless' escape but also a number of textual *pleasures* independent of their fidelity to reality.

In relation to masculinity and media, a body of work is now building up, although not very much of it is yet concerned specifically with televisual representations. Issues around theorising the 'gaze' (both female and homoerotic) (Easthope, 1986; Gamman and Marshment, 1988; Nixon, 1996), the 'spectacle' of men's bodies (Dyer, 1989; Tasker, 1993; Neale, 1993) and the notion of 'masculinity in crisis' (Faludi, 2000), have all contributed to, and moved forward, these debates.

It is true that certain representations and discourses still dominate our screens. Much daytime television positions women as domestic creatures and features traditional configurations such as male hosts alongside female assistants. The traditional association between men and sport, news and current affairs has hardly been shifted, and in Britain a clutch of 'new lads' programmes like *Never Mind the Buzzcocks*, *They Think It's All Over* and *Have I Got News for You?* have added a *postmodern*, knowing irony to what are, in effect, traditionally male-focused, male-dominated shows.

For both genders, prime-time television shows may seem more progressive than they really are. In programmes such as *Ally McBeal* and *Sex in the City*, there is an emphasis on independent career-women, but these characters are rarely seen focusing on work and they continue to be obsessed by body shape, beauty, youth and men.

So it is possible to argue that contemporary television is not a monolithic entity. Gender representations are neither simple nor always and only stereotypical, and we cannot therefore simply measure them against some external 'truth'. It cannot be assumed that unconventional representations will be automatically read as 'negative' or 'deviant' — indeed, they may offer a range of viewing pleasures. Television representations across the output of genres and programmes may now offer a greater range of socially acceptable gender identities and can act as a channel to critique the constricting nature of some gender roles. This means that early theorists' assertions and discoveries may lie uneasily with the way people experience television in the twenty-first century. There may be enough exceptions to the stereotypes for at least some viewers to feel comforted or even empowered. Gender on television remains a fascinating area of study with little settled in terms of debate. But on balance, while they may be stereotypical in various ways, it is certainly now too simplistic to claim that televised gender representations are one-dimensional.

See also: **Feminism, Representation, Stereotypes, Women in television**

Further reading: Dyer (1985b); Tuchman (1978); van Zoonen (1994); Williamson (1990)

GENRE

The genre approach within television studies is a way of theorising how television programmes are classified and organised. It includes a consideration of the *codes* and *conventions* within and between television programmes. Although the term 'genre' translates easily from the French as 'type' or 'kind', its meaning within media studies is both more complex and more far-reaching than this simple explanation suggests. Aristotle originally used the term as a way of classifying Greek literature into categories such as tragedy and comedy. It was later adopted by modern literary critics such as Northrop Frye, who wished to develop a more complex classification system capable of taking account of changes within literature. Thus, Aristotle's initial categories became extended into a range of sub-genres that used the actions of the hero as criteria for classification. Following this, genre classification in media studies was primarily used in relation to Hollywood films made within the specific historical and economic conditions of the studio system. The mass popularity of such films made them a significant cultural force, but initially critics (in opposition to *audiences*) were largely derisory in their appraisals, because of the films' tendency towards formula and repetition. The economic conditions of production – that is, the 'factory-like' arrangements whereby films were a product churned out as quickly and cheaply as possible – meant that once a studio hit upon a commercially successful idea, it would be repeated, with minor variations, for some time. These conditions militated against originality and the romantic idea of the individual author producing a unique piece of art. Interestingly, genre films became seen as worthy objects of study when a number of French critics (Bazin, Truffaut) took an interest in Hollywood cinema. These critics developed the idea of the director as primary auteur (author) of the film, and argued that certain directors, with their own unique capabilities and vision, could rise above the restrictions of the Hollywood studio system to produce films of great artistry. Thus the way was paved for a systematic and serious study of popular genre films. Writers such as Tom Ryall, Rick Altman and Steve Neale developed a more theoretical stance on the question of genre, seeing genres as systems of conventions and suggesting that they emerge by means of a symbiotic relationship between audience (the 'interpretive community') and industry. Thus, it is possible to study genres in a range of ways: as socio-historical actualities, as thematic and *ideological* constructions deriving from history, and in terms of their conventions in iconography, visual imagery, *narrative* patterns and archetypal characters. In 1980, Steve Neale defined genre as patterns, forms, styles or structures which transcend individual films, informing both their construction by the film-maker and their reading by an audience. He focused on generic conventions as well as audience expectations and he discussed the relationship between repetition and difference (the audience need to know what to expect, but they also want some surprises).

This and later work focused on the ways in which generically defined structures can help to build and maintain certain (conservative, patriarchal) ideologies and values which act as a form of reassurance to the audience. For example, feminists pointed to the *gendered* nature of genres (most genres are regarded as either 'masculine' or 'feminine' in their appeal) and to the gendered nature of much genre research (most work had been carried out by male researchers focusing on traditionally masculine genres such as the gangster and the Western). Subsequently, genres seen as traditionally 'feminine', notably the melodrama and the *soap opera*, were given critical attention (see *Feminism*).

A recurring problem within genre theory, whether applied to film, television or other media, is that of the genesis of classification into specific genres. For example, film genres were classified into familiar groups such as Westerns, crime films and musicals, but these categories were initially arrived at by watching a number of films with similar characteristics (such as settings, iconography, characters, etc.) and applying the label later. This then defined the genre, so that any subsequent example was seen to adhere to, or stray from, the 'classic' version. Genre classifications were thus historical accidents rather than theoretical constructs. In discussing this problem, Jane Feuer has pointed out that genre is an abstract notion rather than an empirically observable item (in Allen, 1992).

The problem of inconsistency of terminology may be partially explained by the fact that genres evolve, cross-cut and parody themselves, none more so than in the fast-changing world of television. In applying a genre approach to an understanding of television, then, it is necessary to exercise some caution. On one level, television genres can be fairly readily identified (see *Soaps, Science fiction, Comedy, News* and other entries for specific details of genre conventions), and much interesting research has been carried out on individual television genres (see, for example, Strinati and Wagg, 1992). Moreover, the television industry utilises genre classification as a shorthand means of *scheduling*, targeting and maintaining popularity. Television has long relied on regularity of programming to provide continuity, predictability and reassurance to its audiences, and to some extent these principles are still in evidence in the production of popular but generically recognisable programmes such as *Friends* or *Who Wants to Be a Millionaire?* But television is also primarily organised around time-slots and on a traditional division between 'fiction' and 'faction'. Thus, some important factors point to a second level where a simple genre classification proves inadequate for a full understanding of television. For instance, television genres differ from those in the cinema in their sheer variety, and can perhaps be better understood by the different kinds of relationships formed with their audiences. The cinema audience chooses a particular individual product. Television viewers engage in a range of viewing practices and strategies. They may watch a range of different genres as an evening's package on one channel, or they may pick out specific programmes or genres (including feature films previously shown in cinemas) across channels. They may 'channel-hop' more or less randomly, across genres and between fiction and faction. Moreover, television programmes are likely to combine across genres rather than commenting on earlier versions of the same genre (comedy sci-fi such as *Red Dwarf* or *Third Rock From the Sun* might be examples). Moreover, *postmodern* theorists might point out that genres need no longer make sense. The *intertextual* knowledge audiences display as skilled readers of media texts allows them to operate with an understanding that transcends and cuts across genres. Perhaps the other side of this partnership is that contemporary programme-makers are likely to knowingly engage in the playful disruption of generic conventions. An early example of this trend can be seen in *Moonlighting*, but it has been followed up in such programmes as *Twin Peaks* and the British spoof game show *Shooting Stars*.

Given the proliferation of television forms and channels, classification into recognisable genres is becoming increasingly difficult, even on a common-sense level. As an academic tool of analysis, the genre approach may be finally losing its relevance.

See also: **Audiences, Comedy, News, Postmodernism, Science fiction, Soaps**

Further reading: Allen (1987); Corner and Harvey (1996); Neale (1980)

GLOBALISATION

Globalisation has been an increasingly significant concept within cultural and media studies over the last decade. In essence, the concept refers to the historical development of global processes and structures emerging in the idea of the social world as 'one place' or what MacLuhan called 'the global village'. Previously, the argument goes, societies had experienced comparatively little dramatic social change, with populations tending to stay within the confines of their community of origin for their whole lives. The emergence of a world capitalist economy, however, unleashed significant social, economic and political changes which promoted an increasing global interdependence. At one level these generate a cultural homogeneity of process and product, but at the same time globalisation has a varying impact on different 'local' environments. It is experienced unevenly and leads to renewed cultural diversity, a process known as localisation. In particular, globalisation may be unsettling in its destruction of local certainties and can lead to a search for new sources of meaning within communities. For some theorists, globalisation is one of the definitive qualities of postmodernity, or what Giddens describes as 'late modernity'. The media, including television, are especially significant for globalisation theorists in that they have been historically constituted by processes of globalisation but are simultaneously seen as constituting a global order.

Theories of globalisation emerge, at least in part, from a critique of sociological approaches such as modernisation theory and dependency theory. The latter's attempts to explain the development of modern societies are criticised both for taking the nation-state or society as the unit of analysis and for conceptualising power relations between societies in uni-directional terms. The *cultural imperialism* thesis is similarly castigated for its core idea that one society's culture can neatly dominate another's. Sklair is one of those who argues that the analysis of social development must be transnational, recognising that social, economic and political processes now operate across national boundaries, and that power flows and operates in increasingly complex ways (Sklair, 1991).

Studies of globalisation have focused on various dimensions. Foremost is the emergence of a world capitalist economy which operates transnationally to the point where transnational corporations, or TNCs (relevant media examples might be CNN or News Corporation), have undermined the power of many nation-states. The transnationalisation of capital has resulted in an international division of labour with a transnational capitalist class and cheap productive labour concentrated in specific but constantly changing parts of the world. The system of nation-states is increasingly superseded by transnational political organisations, such as the UN and NATO, and movements like Islamic fundamentalism and environmentalism. Electronic communication and transport developments constitute technological globalisation and have enabled human mobility, both actual and virtual. Cultural globalisation, itself built on technological possibilities, is evident in mass tourism, networks of migration (what Appadurai, 1990, has called 'ethnoscapes'), McDonaldised consumerism (Ritzer, 1993) and the spread of popular cultural forms in music, film and television. New and logically confusing hybrid cultural forms and social movements – from fundamentalist Amerindian Christianity to Chinese smorgasbord – emerge and rearticulate existing social patterns. At a broader level, arguments for unidirectional cultural imperialism or *Americanisation* are replaced by an acknowledgement of a range of transnational social movements such as Islamicisation, Hispanicisation or Europeanisation, with the capacity to move and influence social life globally.

However, globalisation is also a profoundly *local* process and one that is experienced unevenly. It always 'enters' communities which have a history and a pre-existing social structure, so that the global and the local always interact to produce varying outcomes. Thus, the work practices of capitalism clearly have globalised features (payment, work-times, regulations) but work is organised very differently in, say, Japan, Italy and the United States. Alternatively, 'our' everyday lives are locally touched by disembedded globalisation in the origins of our shoes, the programmes we watch on television and the climatic change wrought by the use of refrigerators throughout the world. It is this interaction of the global and local which has stimulated the emphasis and re-emphasis of local identities. It has been argued (for example, by Hall, 1992) that globalisation is disturbing, and particularly with the decline of some existing 'certainties', such as religion and political ideology, there is a need for people to grasp and even create local identities and meanings.

Giddens argues, then, that late modernity sees fundamental shifts in the nature of social life. These include the shrinkage of space, with different conceptions of 'local' and 'distant', changes in the social organisation of time, and a 'disembedding of social systems' whereby social relations are increasingly shaped by abstract, global processes rather than just local circumstance (Giddens, 1990). But any semblance of unification is only half the story. Globalisation theory stresses the unevenness and uncertainty of globalisation as a process. It is unifying and diversifying, integrative and fragmentary, and homogenising and heterogeneous. This confusion and change, for some theorists, helps define the postmodern condition (see *Post-modernism*).

Globalisation theory has situated the media at the centre of its analysis of capitalist modernity. From one direction the global media as a technological development and economic opportunity is constituted by the globalising forces of capitalism with all 'nations' having access to the major media including television, radio and film. But from the other direction it acts to constitute globalisation in various ways, including heightening awareness of 'our' place in the global order, promoting the spread of *advertising* and consumerism, and offering the world mediated global events, from the Olympic Games to the death of Princess Diana. So, late modernity produces and is produced by the global ownership, distribution and experience of transnational television.

Macionis and Plummer (1998) distinguish three aspects of globalisation of the media: those of means, *ownership* and content. Globalisation of means is evident in the rapid spread of new *technologies* such as satellite, cable, digital and the internet, and the mushrooming of television channels and broadcasting hours. The costs inherent in developing new technologies can only be borne by TNCs who, as will be seen, are able to shape content supplying hotel rooms around the world with CNN. Opportunities for growth are more limited in North America and Europe, but there is plenty of scope for expansion in much of Asia, Africa and Latin America.

Globalisation of ownership has seen the apparent eclipse of *public service* communications agencies with their tradition of public accountability, regulation of content, and protection from competition.

113

This model, and the BBC for much of the twentieth century provides the clearest example, has increasingly been replaced by deregulated television which is privately owned, motivated by profit and largely funded by advertising. It also tends to be more popular in every sense of the word. Deregulated television is owned by TNCs such as News Corporation, who have pursued '*synergy*' across the globe: that is, the ownership of information providers, equipment manufacturers and transmitters across radio, film, publishing and computer games as well as television. In turn, this has provided a platform to undermine national and international regulating bodies (Barker, 1997).

A number of critics have followed Habermas in arguing that the power emanating from global media synergy threatens democracy in that 'the public sphere', where ideas may be discussed and formed, has been narrowed and constrained by the relationship between the media and commercial power. Paradoxically, the advent of communication technologies such as the internet, cable and *video* have also acted to democratise the media, enabling diverse individuals and groups to gain *access* to communications networks.

The globalisation of content is epitomised by global totemic festivals such as World Cups and Live Aid (Barker, 1997). But specific television *genres* have also become globalised. Barker points to the ubiquity of *soap operas*, noting the prevalence of particular textual qualities such as glossy visual style and archetypal Hollywood narratives – what Jack Lang, one-time French culture minister, has talked about as 'wall to wall Dallas' (Barker, 1997). Similarly, television *news* shares a set of common presentational *conventions* across societies.

However, within this there is unevenness and local diversity. In many parts of Asia, Africa and Latin America a significant number of programmes are imported from Europe and the US, but in Germany 80 per cent are German-made. Television news tends to originate from European and American sources and cover European and American 'stories'. But Barker, writing about soaps and the evidence of a globalising tendency in the widespread popularity of American, Australian and British examples of the genre, observes the significant success of Latin American telenovelas, produced most notably by TV-Globo in Brazil and Televisa in Mexico (Barker, 1997). These enjoy indigenous success – in fact they can contribute to the reassuring promotion of local identities – but are also exported to over a hundred countries. Even where a programme is globally distributed it will be consumed in a local context. Sklair (1991) points out that local cultures are always engaged in reinterpreting, mediating and possibly resisting transnational *texts*. Viewers use their own cultural competencies in *decoding* meaning, and these may well depart from any kind of dominant *ideology* were one even intended (e.g. critical viewings of *Dallas* by some Arab audiences). So the meaning of telenovelas and the impact they have on everyday life varies in different cultures, as does the significance of a football match for, say, African and European viewers.

Such an apparently chaotic pattern stresses the shift away from the unidirectional approach of cultural imperialism theory. Global communication cannot be reduced to Americanisation, with its flow of images and meanings from America to the rest of the world. Rather, there is also evidence of Latin Americanisation, Islamicisation and Europeanisation, with a flow of images and meaning from, perhaps, Latin America to Japan, Eastern Europe and the USA. In postmodern culture or whatever it is labelled, there is what Barker refers to as an increasingly complex *semiotic* environment with an explosive display of competing signs and meanings colliding in a postmodern bricolage (Barker, 1997).

The picture the analyst is left with, then, is one of confusion. Television is mainly owned by TNCs whose prime concern is profit, and it clearly has globalising tendencies with the capacity to communicate homogenous media products. It has given the world promotional culture in the form of advertising and it can do 'ideological work' – for instance, in seeking to define the Gulf War. But at the same time, television has the capacity to produce a virtual infinity of images and meanings in a multiplicity of contexts. It helps to constitute multiple selves for any one individual and results in a maelstrom of cultural flows. It is little wonder, therefore, that globalisation has been seen as a central feature of the chaos of postmodernity.

See also: **Americanisation, Cultural imperialism, Postmodernism**

Further reading: Barker (1997); Morley and Robbins (1995); Sreberny-Mohammadi *et al.* (1997)

HEGEMONY

The concept of hegemony, used extensively in media, cultural and communications studies has come to be of central theoretical importance. It is a concept linked to notions of *power* and *ideology* and to the complex ways in which power can operate in modern societies. The hegemonic model can be useful in arguing that television has the capacity to construct a limited range of views of the world. More specifically, hegemonic theorists argue that television promotes a set of views based on the ideas of a ruling bloc or alliance.

The term 'hegemony' was used long before television was invented. It goes back to the Greek *hegemonia* (leader) and *hegeisthai* ('to go before'). It is a complex term which can be broadly defined as leadership or control. In this definition, hegemony usually relates to control of one state over another. However, in the mid to late twentieth century, the word has come to acquire more specific, but still difficult, meaning, especially to Marxist historians and media theorists. It became a much-used term in media and cultural studies from the 1970s onwards, when these disciplines were still in their infancy and researchers were trying to find their feet over ways to understand and analyse familiar, contemporary culture and media. At that point, the notion of hegemony was seen as a major way out of a theoretical difficulty (see below); it then became so central that it formed a kind of new orthodoxy, but more recently has been somewhat overtaken by new ideas, for instance of *postmodernism*.

The term as used here was introduced by the Italian Marxist, Antonio Gramsci. He lived from 1891 to 1937 and wrote much of his most influential work in the latter ten years of his life while he was imprisoned by the Fascist leader, Mussolini. Gramsci was a major theoretician and founding member of the Italian Communist Party, locked up by Mussolini for having 'dangerous' ideas.

Gramsci's work was influential in Italy but only came to prominence in the UK and USA in the 1970s when his *Prison Notebooks* were translated into English and came to the attention of theorists in the field (Gramsci, 1971). In essence, this aspect of Gramsci's work is concerned with his belief that *culture* (and this of course includes television) is inseparable from politics and is inextricably bound up with leadership. To more fully understand Gramsci's perspective, it is necessary to know something of *Marxist* theory. Marxist analysis is based on the idea that society is divided into different economic classes and that the economically dominant *class* is also the class that rules in views and ideas. Marx saw the economic realm of society as its 'base'. Everything else (what we would broadly call its culture) sits upon, and flows from, this base; Marx called this the 'superstructure'. So, applied to television, the argument would go that people get the kind of television they do because of the economic system in which television is produced. The economic system is designed to be self-perpetuating, and in the case of capitalism

Marx argued that the ruling class could impose their values and ideas on the rest of the population because of their privileged economic and political position.

Marx also argued that this was a situation where ordinary people were exploited and that sooner or later they would realise this, get fed up with it and overthrow the system in revolution. However, by the mid twentieth century the capitalist system seemed to be becoming stronger and stronger. and it seemed that subordinate groups were becoming less and less likely to resort to revolutionary action. So it is important to realise that Gramsci developed the idea of hegemony because he was seeking to explain why socialist revolutions had not taken place (and he had plenty of time to consider this issue during his period of imprisonment).

Gramsci was interested in (and dismayed by) the fact that the working class had not risen up against capitalism, as predicted by Marx, but that it had somehow settled into an acceptance of capitalism despite the fact that there were still clear economic differences and opportunities between the working and the ruling classes. He saw that capitalism had been very successful in persuading people to identify their interests with the capitalist system (the idea that 'capitalism is good for all of us' rather than exploitative and beneficial to only a minority). The capitalist state had done this by offering a series of 'concessions' to the subordinate classes – in other words, 'buying them off' with, for example, a more affluent lifestyle.

However, unlike some other Marxist writers, Gramsci did not use the term 'false consciousness' to describe the process by which this had been achieved. Gramsci argued that if the advanced Western democracies are examined then there appears to be a high degree of consensus, and the power structure (the state, more generally) does not normally use coercion or obvious forms of control such as violence in order to rule. Rather, these are societies where subordinate classes seem to actively support (or at least 'put up with') the values and ideals of the powerful, dominant classes.

If these ideas are applied to an understanding of television, it can be seen that mainstream television *news* and current affairs programmes encourage us to regard the concerns and needs of capitalism as the needs and concerns of society as a whole. So, for example, the competing ideas and policies of different political parties are discussed on television as 'neutral' matters of the economy; share prices are announced on breakfast TV; political campaigns and elections are framed in terms of 'the people' deciding. The needs and concerns of a powerful section of society become 'universalised' as the interests of all. Gramscian theorists argue that the established position of capitalism has been internalised so fully that it is difficult to see any other way of comprehending things – capitalism is just there, just 'natural', even though in reality this relative stability and acceptance of capitalism is historically fairly recent (late nineteenth century). The role of the media in this is particularly important since most journalists, producers and programmers come from a similar, narrow, middle-class social background, and the majority are white and male. Therefore, journalism is dominated by a particular world view which effectively wipes out other ways of seeing and presenting things.

Gramsci's prime concern as a Marxist was with social class and *ownership*, but through the idea of hegemony he also points out that there is no one, identifiable 'capitalist class' – rather, there is an alliance, a ruling bloc, which combines certain interests. So *feminists* have argued that the ruling bloc is largely male, as well as middle-class, and theorists of *race* and ethnicity point to a white dominance within television. Moreover, Gramscians acknowledge that social formations within a ruling bloc are constantly shifting. They come together at certain points, for instance during moments of crisis, but these alliances are also liable to break up.

Although hegemony works by the appearance of consent and consensus, this does not mean that there is no conflict. On the contrary, conflict is liable to break out all the time so hegemony must be carefully preserved and monitored by those with vested interests. Hegemony is never fully fixed – and what is more, if it breaks down (this is a 'crisis of hegemony' or a 'rupture' in the hegemonic order), then it is quite likely that control and coercion will be brought in to maintain the status quo. How might this work out in practice? Some theorists have called attention to the way that the state can and will bring in measures (ranging from censorship of television and the press to actual force, such as using the armed forces to control strikes), in situations where capitalism is under threat.

But Gramsci's main point here is that it is much more effective for capitalism to 'win the consent' of the people (by persuading them through debate in the media that certain kinds of people are 'deviant' or undeserving, for instance) than to lose the struggle over ideas and have to resort to force. To take a different analogy: how much better for a parent to convince a child that it is only sensible to work hard at school to get on in life, than to beat them with a stick to make them do their homework. Parents could choose to do this (they are the 'dominant' group here, both physically and economically), but it is arguably much more effective to use persuasion to get children to see things in the same way as themselves (and parents who do not see the value of formal education can be just as 'successful' in persuading their children that there is no point in bothering with school work). In this example, hegemony can be seen as secured when parental (dominant) ideology becomes embedded in the consciousness of the children (the subordinate group). Similarly, *game shows* or televised national lotteries have been highly successful examples of the way ideologies around 'the big windfall' can become deeply entrenched into group consciousness.

So the concept of hegemony is a much more fluid one than that of coercion or social control. It is more akin to a process whereby the ideas of dominant and subordinate groups vie for ascendancy. This incorporates ideas of struggle and negotiation. Whoever is involved in cultural life is involved in a struggle to get their voice heard and their meanings seen as valid. Some groups have a greater opportunity to do this than other groups. Nevertheless, despite the unequal power relations, Gramsci argued that hegemony can sometimes be won by those who are not the economically dominant force and he was interested in ways in which relatively powerless groups might get their voices heard and win consent for their ideas. Thus, the notion of hegemony is a long way from simple ideological indoctrination. It can be conceptualised as an active (though largely unconscious) process of negotiation – from above and below – between groups, and it can also be seen as a process of resistance to dominant norms and practices. The implications of this kind of analysis are that culture and media are not just products of a dominant class, nor are they free-floating; rather, they are a shifting balance between competing interests at different times. Media and cultural products are redefined, understood and used in ways not originally intended by their producers. So the way we understand a television programme may not be that intended by its makers. Hegemony must then be regarded as rooted in contradiction and tension. Television is an important arena of popular culture where such contradictions are played out. Programmes must at one and the same time win the support of *audiences* and carry out the kind of ideological work which does not ultimately threaten the status quo. But the way programmes are understood and experienced cannot be entirely predicted, and there may be a number of possible meanings running alongside each other in any given programme. For example, a quiz programme such as *Have I Got News for You?* could be regarded as satirical, socially disruptive and disrespectful of the establishment, or alternatively as simply a harmless way of letting off steam. Equally, the programme could be regarded as very much a reflection of the status quo it appears to mock (its host and regular panellists are white, male and privileged; female or black panellists are few and far between and can be subjected to disparaging treatment). But on yet another level, *Have I Got News for You?* works by providing *pleasure* through humour; it is clever, funny and topical. Despite its often caustic tone, it provides a comforting (ideologically conservative?) reassurance through the predictability of its structure.

Hegemony theory has been very prominent in the last twenty years, as a means of explaining the relationship between the economy and the culture. It has the advantage of doing this in a way which does not over-simplify the connection between the two realms. Hegemonic relations might best be thought of as struggles from both above and below. It is also useful for helping us to see that much of what is produced in the media has an ideological dimension to it: that it tries to serve particular interests. However, some theorists have commented that because it stems from a Marxist analysis, hegemony theory is too limited. In particular, it will invariably come up with the kind of analysis that places great emphasis on ideology and exploitation rather than looking at other things that might be meaningful in under-standing television (such as the conventions of *genre*). Some theorists and historians argue that a fundamental problem with hegemony theory is that it began as an explanation of something that did not occur (socialist revolution) and this in itself makes it limited. Finally, postmodern theorists (see *Postmodernism*) have argued that it is no longer useful, or perhaps even possible, to explain the world by means of all-encompassing theories such as that of Marxism. If this view is taken then the notion of hegemony as an explanatory concept is thrown into some doubt.

See also: **Class, Culture, Ideology, Marxism**

Further reading: O' Shaughnessy (1990); Ransome (1992)

IDEOLOGY

In television studies, media studies and other social sciences, the term 'ideology' is generally understood to refer to a system of ideas, assumptions and beliefs. Since these are central to the process of mass communication, the notion of ideology has been particularly important in media studies. The use and development of theories of ideology has been most notable among more critical media scholars.

The concept of ideology has not always been defined so broadly. Early discussions of ideology often used the word in a pejorative sense:

ideology was counterposed to notions such as 'reality', 'truth' or scientific knowledge. In certain branches of *Marxist* theory, for example, ideology was linked to the notion of 'false consciousness' – a set of beliefs that obscured or distorted the truth that workers were being exploited by capitalists. Various forms of this dichotomy – between ideology and truth/science – still inform many popular definitions of ideology. The popular use of the term also carries another negative connotation, ideology being associated with particularly doctrinaire or inflexible sets of – usually political – beliefs. Thus one politician may accuse another of being 'too ideological' or an 'ideologue'.

The use of the term in media studies is neither value-laden nor limited. Ideology refers to any system of ideas or beliefs, regardless of their content or veracity. Ideology is therefore neither good nor bad, merely necessary. The politician that declares him or herself to be moderate, pragmatic and non-ideological is thus, in fact, stating an ideological position (i.e. the preference for a system of thought that values moderation and pragmatism).

Two theorists often associated with expanding the notion of ideology and stressing its importance in social life are Louis Althusser and Antonio Gramsci. Althusser insisted on the centrality of ideology and upon its inevitability, arguing that we are all ideological creatures and that, since we need ideas, beliefs and assumptions to function in the world, ideology is part of our cognitive existence. Althusser conceived the mass media – along with institutions like the schools and the Church – as ideological apparatuses, crucial to the maintenance of a society's support for one set of ideological beliefs over another.

Althusser's conception of ideology has been criticised for its monolithic quality – he described an overarching capitalist ideology operating like a vast orchestra on a single score. In Gramsci's work, ideology is a more flexible, dynamic concept – a vital arena in the struggle for power between different groups (see *Hegemony*). While repressive dictatorships can control the population by force, the struggle for power and dominance in democracies, he argued, takes place at the level of civil society through ideology. Ideology is therefore the conduit whereby ruling elites achieve – or fail to achieve – a form of popular consent.

In contemporary media studies, this notion of ideology is particularly useful for those working from a critical or *cultural studies* perspective, in which economic, social and cultural systems – such as capitalism, racism and patriarchy – are seen as distributing *power* and resources inequitably. Those with power and resources must use ideological means to persuade majorities that this situation is either fair, proper or inevitable.

In the United States, for example, recent decades have seen the stagnation of real wages for most middle- and lower-income Americans while corporate profits have soared. Although this upward redistribution of wealth would appear to be against most people's interests, there has been little organised protest in the form of political support or industrial action. This, critical media scholars have argued, is partly due to television's role in creating a form of ideological consent (or, at least, lack of resistance). The acceptance of growing inequities, it is argued, is sustained ideologically by notions like the 'American Dream', a belief – firmly inscribed within the *discourse* of television and popular culture – that wealth and power are potentially available to anyone who has the talent and desire to succeed. For both black and white people, the good life is readily available on American television, and most characters deserving of it appear to achieve it with little effort. The notion of exploitation – corporate profits coming at the expense of wages – is thereby erased and replaced by a discourse of opportunity.

Critical scholars have, in this vein, argued that the media tend to express the ideological positions of those with power, suggesting the notion of a 'dominant ideology' that serves the needs and interests of a powerful elite, thereby consolidating their economic and political power. Cultural studies scholars have tried to develop this framework by working with Gramsci's conception of society as an ideological battleground in which different interests struggle for dominance. In so doing, many felt that the notion of a single, unitary, dominant ideology was far too limited a concept to explain the many power relations that exist within society. *Feminists*, in particular, argued that these power relations not only cover different areas of social life – such as *class*, *race* and *gender* – but may cut across or conflict with one another. So, for example, as Andrea Press' (1991) study of women television viewers suggests, the interests and perceptions of working-class and middle-class women can be quite different.

Gramsci's theory of hegemony – developed by cultural studies – also stressed the contested nature of ideology. This allows us to conceive of ideological change, as well as the constancy of the battle for ideological dominance. Dominant groups do not simply 'win' ideological struggles and retire to enjoy the spoils – if a consensus is to be maintained, these battles need to be continually refought and rewon. The growth of feminism in the second half of the twentieth century is a good example of ideological dynamism and change. The struggle for women's equality represents a serious challenge to the ideology of patriarchy. The gradual acceptance of aspects of a more feminist ideology has not been a process of acceptance, but the outcome of a series of struggles between the ideologies of patriarchy and feminism. As many feminist scholars have argued, the media have been a constant site for this struggle.

Issues of *representation* are, in this sense, a key part of this ideological struggle. If we accept the *advertising* image of an attractive young woman in a bikini scrawled across an automobile as normal, yet raise our eyebrows if the young woman is substituted with an old woman, a fat woman or a man, then we have accepted a system of representation informed by patriarchy in which the objectification of women seems normal or natural.

Theories of ideology have also been informed by discussions of determination. Specifically, researchers have tried to understand what determines ideological change or the ideological positions of social groups. Early Marxist theory stressed the importance of economic determinations of ideological position (the notion that the 'infra-structure' or economic base determined the 'superstructure', or ideology). This notion of economic determinism would explain developments in literature, for example, by linking them to changes in a society's economic structure. Similarly, the nature of television output would be seen as determined by the ownership structure of the television company (so, for example, a private commercial television company would be expected to produce programmes reflecting a capitalist ideology).

In different ways, both Althusser and Gramsci challenged this traditional Marxist notion. In short, while there may be links between one's social or economic position and one's assumptions and beliefs, or between economic and ideological change, there was no inevitable or necessary correspondence between the two. Various scholars, such as Chantal Mouffe, Ernesto Laclau and Stuart Hall, have developed this idea with the theory of *articulation*, which allows us to trace the way things − such as social position and beliefs − may be linked, while understanding that these linkages are social constructions rather than fixed, permanent social relationships.

See also: **Class, Cultural studies, Discourse, Hegemony, Marxism**

Further reading: Althusser (1971); Hall (1988); Jhally and Lewis (1992)

INSTITUTIONS

Much work of a sociological or *political economy* bent has focused on television not primarily in terms of *texts* and viewers but as a set of institutions. Analyses of media institutions look at television as a set of social organisations with recognisable practices, rules, values and structures. Branston and Stafford (1996) suggest that institutions have the following characteristics: they have a history and are enduring; they regulate and structure activities; they have collective constraints and goals; they develop clear working practices; and public and staff are aware of their existence. Thus, unions of media workers, television networks, the BBC, production companies, news teams and the mass media as a whole are all, in some sense, institutions.

Many approaches to the study of institutions stress that they are shaped by a range of economic, political and cultural determinants. These relate respectively to the production and distribution of media 'goods', the exercise and regulation of power in media contexts, and the production and circulation of cultural meanings (O'Sullivan *et al.*, 1998). In terms of economic factors, most television institutions are capitalist, organised along commercial lines (see *Commercial television*). Television programmes are commodities, produced and distributed industrially with profitability as an operational imperative. This has meant that television companies have tended to tread a conservative path. They seek to replicate previous successes (for example, *game shows* and *crime series*), opt for programmes which are cheap and popular (e.g. chat shows, *reality television* such as *Jerry Springer*, and *The Benny Hill Show*, with its readily exportable form of visual humour) and show repeats of anything vaguely durable. Some analysts have argued that television is therefore an uneasy blend of what media institutions would ideally like to supply and what audiences demand.

The history of capitalist media corporations has seen a persistent concentration of *ownership*. This has involved institutions buying up rivals in a process of 'horizontal integration' (as has happened with Britain's regional independent television companies) and acquiring different parts of the production process in 'vertical integration' (e.g. News Corporation's global investment in digital technology). Media transnational corporations (TNCs) have become increasingly significant in expanding beyond the boundary of single societies to become active as agents of *cultural imperialism* and *globalisation*. Many commentators have become worried about concentration of ownership and the possibility of monopoly power for particular media institutions (Stokes and Reading, 1999). *Marxists* have argued that concentrated ownership gives power to a small number of huge institutions (e.g. News Corporation, Time Warner and Fox Television), allowing them to increase profit and propagate dominant ideology. *Pluralists* reject what they see as an overly determinist view of media institutions, arguing instead that audience demands, legal limits to monopoly control and widespread deregulation of media markets will ensure that a diversity of views are heard. They might point to the situation in the US where transmission of television programmes is controlled by the many local stations, most of which are technically independent of the major networks of ABC, CBS and NBC.

It does seem that there is an institutional resistance to allowing scope for alternative and independent voices. *Community* and *access* opportunities to provide programming for minority groups and space for experimentation have become available in the UK and US, but inevitably these have been at the margins of the broadcasting system. While the American networks do commission 'liberal' programmes such as *Hill Street Blues* or *Sex in the City*, the experience of *Lou Grant* (where the programme came under pressure for its sometimes radical storylines and for the politics of the star, Ed Asner), or *Ellen* (where the actress Ellen de Generes' declaration of her lesbianism was followed by the studio not renewing the series) highlight the power of advertisers, corporations and pressure groups to narrow the spectrum of cultural expression.

Public service broadcasting institutions have a rather different pedigree. State-owned, as in many African and Asian societies, or notionally independent like the BBC, these institutions are often shaped by the demands of state media *policy* rather than commercial goals. Thus, the history of the BBC reveals an attempt to develop a public service that would educate, inform and entertain the 'nation' and not direct itself to making a profit. Programme-makers have had some degree of 'authorial' independence but are subject to formal, statutory controls and engage in self-regulation, for instance in depictions of *sexuality* and during wartime. Critics have pointed out that the proclaimed independence of the BBC has in fact veiled an institution historically dominated by white middle-class males who have perpetuated wider patterns of social inequality. The institutional ethos of the BBC has been gradually altered by the challenges of commercial television, deregulation of British broadcasting and new technologies. These have resulted in a series of internal changes that have left the BBC more akin to a commercial institution.

As the case of the BBC reveals, institutions are subject to a range of external political constraints. This is most starkly evident in coverage of particular kinds of news stories. During the Gulf War, only a limited, selected band of international journalists were allowed near to the war zone and all copy was carefully vetted by the relevant authorities. In Britain, laws such as the Prevention of Terrorism Act, the Obscene Publications Act and the Official Secrets Act are accompanied by the more informal attentions of government departments, pressure groups and public relations consultants. Again, though, most television programme-makers monitor their own output so as not to provoke outright censorship and because British television channels are periodically licensed by regulatory authorities.

Some approaches to the study of media institutions have chosen to focus on their internal occupational culture to include consideration of the labour process, management practices and informal routines. Wider contextual issues, such as whether or not the organisation is commercially driven, are not ignored, but there is an acknowledgement that the 'local' process of television production is relevant in academic inquiry, not least because the norms and values of a media institution are often taken for granted and thus hidden. This emphasis on the workings of organisations rather than their structural determinants has resulted in some analytically rich qualitative accounts. Examples include Schlesinger's research on everyday work practices in a British newsroom (Schlesinger, 1978), Gitlin's *Inside Primetime* (Gitlin, 1985) and feminist analyses of the experience of women working in television production – for example, van Zoonen on *Cagney and Lacey* (van Zoonen, 1994). As this latter example suggests, analyses of media occupations have pointed to inequalities of race and gender within organisations and often related these to textual *representations* of social groups.

See also: **Commercial television, Marxism, News, Pluralism, Public service broadcasting**

Further reading: Comstock (1991); Curran and Seaton (1997); Gitlin (1985); Herman and Chomsky (1988); Stokes and Reading (1999)

INTERTEXTUALITY

Intertextuality is a concept that is commonly used in post-structuralist approaches to media and culture, and also informs debates around postmodernism and postmodernity. It refers to the 'connections' between texts and can be defined as the process by which texts communicate meaning to audiences through reference to other texts, *genres*, *discourses*, themes or media. The term derives its impetus from *semiology*, where it is mainly concerned with the connections between texts at the level of content, form and style. Intertextuality emphasises that texts do not exist in isolation – any one *text* is understood in terms of its relationship to other texts. Just as *signs* do not operate in isolation but generate meanings in relation to, and in combination with, other signs, intertextuality highlights the fact that texts (as signifying structures comprising of signs organised into *codes*) are interrelated. Texts are complex systems of signification, and the meaning(s) generated by any one text are the product of the combination of these systems of signification. A single text, then, constitutes an 'intertext' which is made up of references to other texts.

Fiske (1987) proposes that intertextuality operates both horizontally and vertically. In his view, intertextuality exists in the 'spaces between texts'. Horizontal connections exist between what he calls primary texts (the individual programme or series); these connections can be along the lines of genre, character or content, and can be either explicit or implicit. Vertical intertextuality works to establish links between primary texts, secondary texts and tertiary texts. Secondary texts make explicit references to primary texts and may take the form of reviews, publicity, *advertising* features and so on. Tertiary texts are the meanings produced at the level of the *audience* and can take a variety of forms, from conversation and gossip between family, friends and workmates to fan club membership, writing fan mail to (more recently) communication with other *fans* via the internet. So, for Fiske, intertextuality resides in the meaning potential that exists in the spaces between texts which are drawn from the culture's resource bank. *Culture* in this context, is a web of intertextual meanings. For example, *The X-Files* can be considered as being a hybrid text in that it refers across a range of media texts past and present. It borrows extensively from a range of genres such as *science fiction* (alien abduction and invasion), horror (mutants and monsters), detective and *crime* thrillers (missing persons, murder and government conspiracies), *soap opera* (narrative resolution is endlessly deferred) and romance (the relationship between Mulder and Scully). It is evident that various generic combinations, permutations and influences are at work within the structure of the programme.

The X-Files also draws on and combines competing and alternative discourses such as those of science, medicine, religion, folklore, mythology, UFOlogy, the paranormal and New Age beliefs in channelling and reincarnation. Texts connected to *The X-Files* are the recent film, made for video episodes, books, a soundtrack album, related print material (academic and popular) and various other fan club products. Dedicated fans of the series (known as X philes) actively participate in *X-Files* conventions – virtual and actual. The producer of the series, Chris Carter, also communicates with fans through the internet. David Duchovny (who plays the character of Mulder) and Gillian Anderson (Scully) have both appeared in various publications, modelling clothing as well as giving numerous interviews related to their roles in the programme. *The X-Files*, then, can be seen as being constructed out of, and in turn constructing, a complex web of intertextual layers of meaning.

Intertextuality demonstrates that our understanding of any one text will be informed, in part, by our experience of other texts. The reading of texts takes place in an intertextual landscape and is made possible by a wide range of cultural codes, social practices, discourses and expectations which facilitate the production, circulation and consumption of texts. Intertextuality, then, refers to the interconnection of meanings across different media texts, but it also refers to the connections between meanings across different media and other cultural experiences. As a tool for analysis, intertextuality is useful because it foregrounds the importance of text, context and audience in a postmodern milieu where we are all surrounded by an infinity of texts.

See also: **Fans, Genre, Postmodernism, Post-structuralism, Text**

Further reading: Fiske (1987); Sarup (1993); Thwaites *et al.* (1994)

MARXISM

All Marxist approaches to the study of television owe some debt of origin to Karl Marx's idea that the culture of a society is derived to a greater or lesser extent from the way in which production in that society is organised. More specifically, Marxists have argued that the mass media as an aspect of the cultural realm is, at the least, significantly influenced by the needs of the dominant *class* in capitalist society. However, this common ground veils significant theoretical differences reflecting debates inside and outside Marxism as well as a massively changing social context during the twentieth century. The traditions of Marxist approach to the media are generally divided into political economists, structuralists such as Althusser and a more culture-oriented approach associated with the work of Gramsci (see *Hegemony*).

Marxists who focus on the importance of *political economy* begin with Marx's base and superstructure distinction, arguing that a society's institutions – legal, educational, familial, political, cultural and so forth – work to reproduce the fundamental needs of the capitalist system. The ruling class is able to use its economic and political *power*, derived from ownership of the means of production, to organise the perpetuation of class inequality and its own dominance. In terms of the mass media, this class uses its control of material production to gain control over the cultural lives and ideologies of subordinate groups. Thus, the means of producing television lie in the hands of huge corporations such as Time Warner and individual 'moguls' such as Silvio Berlusconi and Rupert Murdoch, or (capitalist) state-regulated bodies such as the BBC. The media, then, is a superstructural *institution* owned and controlled by the ruling class functioning as an agency to disseminate what is, in effect, dominant ideology. Adherents of this approach point to increasing concentration of media ownership, a widening global *audience* and the marginalisation of critical viewpoints in support of its continuing relevance (Murdock and Golding, 1995). Television *news* is a commonly cited example, with ownership of news as a product and the means of its distribution enabling effective reproduction of capitalist *ideology*. Schiller widened the analytical horizon by focusing on the way in which capitalist media corporations have expanded internationally and used *advertising* to promote increased consumerism as an aspect of *cultural imperialism* (Schiller, 1995). From another direction Smythe (1981) has pointed to the way in which corporations are able to 'produce' audiences as commodities which can be sold to advertisers.

Political economy Marxists have been criticised for their conceptual over-reliance on political and economic power. Culture and its ideological meaning are not ignored, but there is an assumption that the ruling class's dominant position will enable the fairly unproblematic flow of ideology. This economic determinism – that is, that ideology and the superstructure (in this case, culture) will be determined by the class structure of society – has been countered from various positions within Marxism.

The Frankfurt School of Marxists, writing in Germany and America from the 1930s, share the foundational assumption that the mass media and other superstructural forms are propagated by a ruling class to help reproduce capitalist social relations. However, they stress the importance of the realm of *culture*, arguing that it can help explain the thriving persistence of modern capitalism and the absence of a proletarian revolution. 'Real' needs and 'real' culture are repressed in capitalist societies, to be replaced by a culture or consciousness industry producing standardised and 'vulgar' cultural commodities such as *soap operas* and *WhoWants to Be a Millionaire?* These not only promote a consumer lust – see the role of *MTV* in fetishising clothing – but also ideologically ensnare and hypnotise the masses. The subordinate classes are encouraged to pursue 'false needs' and 'false hopes' and in the process tie themselves materially and ideologically to the capitalist system. This was a powerful and appealing argument in the 1960s and 1970s, but a number of social and cultural theorists questioned the Frankfurt School's apparently elitist neglect of the audience, or subject. Any pleasures people might obtain from 'mass culture' tended to be ignored in their research, as did modes of resistance to dominant culture. A stress on class as the determinant of ideology rather than any other social forces also drew criticism.

The French Marxist, Louis Althusser, addressed some of these issues and reworked Marx's base and superstructure distinction. He argued that capitalist society is composed of at least three levels, the economic, the political and the ideological, and suggests that each level has relative autonomy from the others. The significant implication here is that the ideological, including the mass media, is able to act independently of the economic, or, more precisely, the demands of the ruling class. This helps explain the appearance in the schedules of 'liberal' television drama, such as *LA Law* in the USA, and more radical programmes in the UK, for instance realist drama from *Cathy Come Home* to *Cops*. Althusser, though, is clear. In the final instance the ideological, including the mass media, will maintain the economic relations of capitalist society; so, as an example, the BBC despite its nominal independence has always supported the British state during political crises.

In fact, Althusser lays particular emphasis on the role of the ideological in reproducing capitalism. He argues that capitalism is reproduced by powerful ideological institutions which he calls the ideological state apparatuses (ISAs). Education, religion and the mass media act to reproduce a capitalist 'frame of mind' in individuals. Ideology is effective because it represents our reality in an imaginary but familiar form. Television's depictions, for instance in news programmes, are never real but always a mediated but familiar version of our social world, encouraging us to accept and even embrace what are 'in reality' relations of domination. Here Althusser addresses the question of how we become subject to ideology. He argues that it operates by hailing, or interpellating, individuals, making them subjects within ideology. Thus an *advertisement* works ideologically by attracting individual viewers to the subject position of an avid consumer. For Althusser, the success of the ISAs means that the ruling class rarely has to rely on its repressive state apparatuses (RSAs) such as the police and military (Althusser, 1971).

Althusser's interest in the way in which ideology is constructed as natural and hence invisible relates to Roland Barthes' *semiological* writings (see, for example, Barthes, 1972). Barthes suggests that the mass media (and other cultural sites) produce ideological 'myths'. *Representations* hide the circumstances of *production* and consumption, and thus inequality and repression, within capitalist societies. This sort of approach has generated a number of fruitful ideological analyses; see, for instance, Whannel on *game shows* and *sport* (1990) or White on *Webster* (1987).

Criticisms of what was seen as Althusser's functionalist approach to ideology – that is, the suspicion that all culture is playing some role in the reproduction of capitalism – and of his neglect of resistance to ideological inculcation, saw many cultural and media theorists revisit the work of the Italian Marxist, Antonio Gramsci. The 'turn to Gramsci' during the 1970s owed much to his rejection of more determinist versions of Marxism. He placed popular culture and cultural *institutions* at the centre of his analysis, arguing that they are the site of 'cultural politics' with a struggle over ideological meaning taking place between dominant and subordinate groups. The ruling bloc seeks to use the ideological meaning of culture to persuade subordinate groups of the legitimacy of their rule. Where consent is attained – and to be successful, the ruling group will have needed to address, incorporate and accommodate the subordinate group's culture – the ruling group will have won *hegemony* and have had no need to resort to coercion. Hegemonic ideology which actually supports the system and the ruling class will then appear as 'normal' and 'natural' common sense. Gramsci is emphatic, however, that hegemony cannot be assumed but needs to be constantly won and re-won in the face of resistance from subordinate groups.

The mass media is one arena of cultural struggle. Thus, the majority of television programmes are produced by a dominant bloc, but alternative voices can be heard, for example via Channel 4 in the UK and, more distantly, in American television's coverage of the Vietnam War. This, in turn, ideologically organises a sense of media democracy. O'Shaughnessy (1990) discusses the complex ways in which television hegemonically masks, displaces and naturalises social contradictions, for example in constructing a 'national' rather than class-based or gendered audience for many British sporting and political events.

Jhally and Lewis observe that *The Cosby Show,* in departing from racial *stereotypes* by placing a black American family at the core of prime-time television, makes a claim for politically progressive representation. But they argue that this is a hegemonic myth because the programme inadvertently diverts attention from the difficult social reality of the majority of black Americans (Jhally and Lewis, 1992). The authors' very act of drawing attention to this promotes resistance to hegemonic ideology.

The Gramscian perspective in conjunction with other theoretical influences has been extremely influential, particularly in British cultural and media studies, where Stuart Hall among others has promoted wide-ranging ideological analyses of attempts to manufacture consent. However, more traditional Marxists have been uneasy with the focus on culture and a downgrading of significance for capitalist society's material arrangements. From the other direction, Gramscian analysis along with all other forms of Marxism has been attacked by *postmodernists*, who object to the assumption of such a coherent pattern of social relations and structures. They see Marxism as a 'metanarrative', imposing intellectual shape on what are, in actuality, infinitely complex social networks. Indeed, the burgeoning of television channels, technologies and texts, coupled with more heterogeneous ownership of the means of media production and a sense of the intricate and varying ways in which audiences relate to television, have all fuelled the critique of Marxist media theory.

See also: **Class, Cultural imperialism, Cultural studies, Hegemony, Ideology, Political economy**

Further reading: Boyd-Barrett and Newbold (1995); Curran and Gurevitch (1996); Strinati (1995)

MASS CULTURE

The idea of 'the public' as a single group – as in the classical assemblies of ancient Greece – was ruptured by the popular use of the printing press. The publication of books, periodicals, newspapers and journals allowed the dispersal of publics, connected by readership of a common text but no longer bound by place and space. For social and political elites in the eighteenth and nineteenth centuries, limits on the political franchise – which tended to restrict voting rights to property-owning men – made the public a comparatively safe and knowable entity. By the twentieth century, the extension of the political franchise, urbanisation and the mass production of goods created a greater distance between elites and the population to which they were obliged to pay attention. For many leading political and cultural figures, the public became a vaster and altogether less familiar formation – a 'mass society' of voters and consumers that was difficult to understand and impossible to ignore.

Raymond Williams (1963) argued that there were no masses, only ways of seeing people as masses. The idea of 'mass society' or a 'mass public' is, in this sense, an artificial construction that serves to conceptually bind people together into a single homogeneous, undifferentiated category. Nonetheless, in the first half of the twentieth century this notion of homogeneity was made more compelling by the growth of mass production and mass media – creating a society in which urban populations watched the same films, listened to the same radio programmes and bought the same consumer goods. From this confluence of economic, technological and social forces the notion of 'mass culture' emerged.

In the US, technocrats like George Gallup sought to turn mass society into a genuinely democratic force through the conduit of public opinion polls, thereby giving 'the masses' a form of expressing themselves other than through consumption. While mass society critics like Walter Lippmann saw the need for a professional/ managerial class to guide the inexpert masses towards informed democratic decisions, the work of media researchers at Columbia University suggested that this was already happening via 'opinion leaders' rising above the ignorant fray to point the masses in sensible directions. And yet the rise of Fascism and Stalinism in Europe prompted a more sinister set of associations: the automation of factory work and the propagandist possibilities of mass media suggested a mass public at the mercy of the forces of mass production and mass communication. This vision of witless ubiquity – expressed powerfully by films like *Metropolis* and *Modern Times* – was developed most famously by scholars of the Frankfurt School.

One of the best-known discussions of mass culture to emerge from the Frankfurt School was Walter Benjamin's essay 'Art in the age of mechanical reproduction', in which he reflected on the political and social consequences of an era when technology made works of art or culture into objects that could be reproduced, manufactured and widely distributed. Benjamin's essay is sometimes read as mourning the loss of 'aura' and 'authenticity' that comes from the reproducibility of art. In fact, Benjamin's position is much more optimistic, since he regards the aura that surrounds the unique work of art as a restraint on its potential meaning. Once stripped of this inhibition, cultural forms like film can begin to engage audiences in ways that allow for greater understanding of social processes, creating what Benjamin saw as possibilities for progressive social critique. But Benjamin also saw dangers in mass art forms combining aura and reproducibility in an essentially Fascist aesthetic (Benjamin, 1973).

While Benjamin died fleeing the Gestapo in 1940, other members of the Frankfurt School, such as Theodor Adorno and Max Horkheimer, moved to the United States, a context that prompted more pessimistic readings of mass culture (see *Americanisation*). The corporate control over mass culture, they argued, reduced culture to its most profitable form, mass produced to suit the lowest common denominator and thus typified by bland uniformity. Their critique of mass culture produced for commercial gain in a mass market provided a point of departure for many subsequent discussions.

Early studies of mass media were clearly influenced by the mass culture critique, particularly in terms of the ability of mass media to influence large numbers of people (see *Effects*). While studies from various traditions have suggested a number of ways in which the mass media are influential, it is clear the relationship between mass media and society is a complex one. Accordingly, the pessimistic view of mass culture has been criticised on a number of grounds:

- for oversimplifying the nature of mass media influence and neglecting the active role of viewers, readers and listeners in the construction of meaning (see *Audiences*);
- for neglecting moments of diversity, innovation and dynamism in the popular cultural industries;
- for adopting a somewhat elitist view of culture in which popular culture is assumed to be banal.

Nonetheless, the increasing concentration of ownership on a global scale and the dominance of a capitalist model of cultural production dedicated to the promotion of an ideology of consumerism gives the mass culture critique continued purchase.

In terms of its reach, concentration of *ownership* and domination of leisure time, television is, perhaps, the most prominent purveyor of mass culture, and research traditions like *cultivation analysis* and *agenda-setting* suggest television plays a role in producing common ways of understanding the world. The degree to which the proliferation of television channels – via satellite, cable and digital technology – has made the notion of mass culture less relevant is a matter of debate, particularly since the range of channels has not, on the whole, been accompanied by a diverse ownership or control structure. Similarly, while the growth of the internet has been celebrated by some for increasing cultural possibilities, others have argued that the internet has been placed increasingly under corporate control in ways that will produce homogeneity of content.

See also: **Audiences, Cultural imperialism, Effects, Ownership**

Further reading: Benjamin (1973); Boyd-Barrett and Newbold (1995); R. Williams (1963)

MEDIATION

In general terms, 'mediation' refers to the act of bringing together two parties (through third-party intervention) by the provision of some form of link in order to convey a message or provide agreement or reconciliation. In the context of media and communication studies, the term has developed a more analytically precise set of meanings in that it refers to the processes involved in the channelling of social knowledge and cultural values through an institutional agency to an audience (O'Sullivan *et al.*, 1994). Within this framework, mediation refers to more than the act of intervention: it is concerned with the form and nature of intervention and the ways in which it 'shapes' communication.

The centrality of television in public and private life means that, for most people, it is a primary source of *news*, information and entertainment. Television enables individuals to witness (hence experience) events which are often outside the realms of their everyday immediate experience, but it does so in ways which appear to be unmediated – its representations of social reality are held to be 'natural'. For Masterman (1992), it is this illusion of transparency that the study of television should take as its primary focus for analysis. Masterman suggests that television studies should be concerned with the formal characteristics of the medium, the continual flow of information communicated, and the *codes* and techniques of mediation. The main objective should be the fracturing of the seemingly natural connections between television, the information it conveys and the world it (re)presents. Once the techniques and processes of mediation have been foregrounded, the notion of television as a window on the world is undermined, the illusion of transparency is shattered and the ideological dimensions of the medium become exposed.

See also: **Discourse, Ideology, Realism, Representation, Rhetoric**

Further reading: McQuail (1994); Masterman (1992); Thwaites *et al.* (1994)

MUSIC VIDEO

Music video is a relatively recent cultural form. The first music videos were produced in the early 1980s and were designed, in industry terms, as promotional tools – hence the term 'pop-promos'. Music video can be described as a hybrid cultural form in that it is an industrial and commercial product combining visuals, music and a wide range of styles producing a very distinctive form of audio–visual textual flow.

Given the overtly commercial origins of music video, a good deal of the critical literature on it has focused on the notion of commercialisation and the commodification of *culture*. Theorists such as Fiske (1987) and Kaplan (1987) have pointed out the similarities (in terms of style and structure) between music videos and commercials. However, the idea that music video has in some way commercialised popular music needs to be considered within the wider context of post-war popular culture and the history of popular music. Popular music has long been subject to commodification (since the late nineteenth century, with the invention of the phonograph which enabled the recording and replaying of music) and has existed in a variety of mediated and marketable forms within the capitalist system of production, distribution and consumption – especially since the 1950s with the emergence of youth culture and youth-based industries.

Some critics have argued that the experience of music is degraded by the visual element of music video. Related to this criticism is the idea that the interpretative liberty of the listener is restricted, in that the meaning of the song has been predefined through the use of visuals. The main problem with these approaches is that the visual elements of music video are privileged over the aural. Prior to technological developments and advances (particularly in the latter half of the twentieth century), music was visual in the sense that the live performance was the main experiential form for popular music. Even with the invention of records, tapes, personal stereos and compact discs, music has always retained links with visual imagery through fashion, art and photography (album cover art), and, of course, the spectacle of the live performance.

A number of theorists have suggested that music videos are, characteristically, *postmodern* texts (Fiske, 1987; Kaplan, 1987). Music videos combine the *codes* and *conventions* of the spectacle of live performance (atmospheric lighting and locations, dry ice, coloured smoke, explosions, strobe lighting) with special effects, multi-media *technology* and post-production technical wizardry (exemplified in the extensive use of rapid editing techniques, extreme camera angles, slow-motion and freeze-frame devices). The eclectic and fragmented style of music video indicates a blurring of the cultural boundaries between past and present (all images seem contemporary) and between high art and popular culture. Music video borrows heavily from whatever cultural resources are available – old films, commercials, newsreels, avant garde and modernist art, fashion, animation, pornography and so on. This promiscuous *intertextuality* and mixing of styles results in pastiche, bricolage and parody as images are plundered from the culture's image bank, reassembled and juxtaposi-tioned with scant regard for narrative coherence. It is this abandonment of a linear *narrative* and of realist codes and conventions that gives rise to a non-linear pastiche of images (Shuker, 1994) and a schizophrenic viewing experience where no single viewing position (or preferred reading) can be established. Kaplan (1987) discusses MTV in terms of a series of looks (or glances) and the 'typical' MTV viewer as being fragmented and decentred. For postmodernists, music video (and MTV in particular) can be partly explained in terms of its mode of address to a fragmented youth culture.

Lewis' *feminist* approach to analysing music video work is useful in that she highlights how music video brings together two cultural forms which have a history of objectifying women – television and rock music (L. Lewis, 1993). She traces the elements of a predominantly male adolescent *discourse* running throughout most music videos constructed around male sexual fantasies, leisure activities and peer relationships. But she then goes on to show how female artists (such as Madonna) have been successful in reworking and rearticulating a female mode of address, thus appropriating the *pleasure* of the *text* for female viewers.

Music videos, however, cannot be explained simply in terms of their textual characteristics, and the links between postmodernism and music video are difficult to sustain (Shuker, 1994). Most approaches concerned with critically analysing music video have tended to privilege the visual dimensions of the form over the aural dimensions; in other words, the significance of the music itself is often overlooked. As a cultural form, music video must also be understood as a commercial and industrial tool and therefore needs to be considered within the context of the institutional practices of the music industry and of channels such as MTV. Most theorists have tended to treat music videos as self-contained texts, and have ignored the commercial and industrial dimensions of the form as well as the significance of the music and the lyrics, the star image of the performer(s), the relationship between television and popular music and the history of popular music in general. Additionally, the *polysemic* nature of music videos, the diversity of reception possibilities and the range of possible readings available to both *fans* and audiences also need to be taken into account.

See also: **Intertextuality, Postmodernism, Video**

Further reading: Frith *et al.* (1993); Kaplan (1987); Shuker (1994)

NARRATIVE

Media *texts* are not simply a cluster of words and images. Their content is structured and ordered in quite systematic ways. One of the most important organising principles for structuring texts is narrative. A narrative is integral to the process of storytelling. It structures content sequentially, so that words and images do not appear arbitrarily but in an order that makes sense to audiences. This structure allows ideas, themes or characters to develop or move forward in a coherent fashion.

Narrative is an extremely important part of popular *culture*. Most forms of entertainment are structured around narratives. It is narratives that draw us in, engage us and encourage us to keep reading, viewing or listening. The unfolding of narratives is one of the principal sources of *pleasure* in media, including television, film or popular fiction. The properties of a narrative can be identified by comparing a story with a list. A list may present information in no particular order – a shopping list, for example, may be a fairly arbitrary ordering of items, where tomatoes come before milk for no other reason than that we thought of tomatoes first – or it may be structured according to a system of categorisation, such as the alphabet or by type (vegetables first, then fruit, then dairy, etc.). Either way, the meaning of the items listed stands alone, unaffected by where they come on the list.

A system of categorisation like the alphabet has an order but no narrative: 'F' comes before 'G' on the basis of a fairly arbitrary designation – the alphabet would make just as much sense if we agreed to reverse the order. With a narrative, on the other hand, the order of appearance matters, it has a significance and a developmental logic. The alphabet *could* be incorporated into a narrative, but to do so the sequence of letters must fit into a storyline in which the ordering of letters becomes significant. A murder mystery, for example, may involve the villain who chooses their victims in alphabetical order: once Alicia Anderson and Bert Bertucci have been murdered, we may start to worry about the welfare of Christine Carter. On television, these narratives become quite routine: in the *genre* of mystery dramas, for example, we are introduced to the main characters, one of whom is then murdered, followed by an investigation and, finally, a successful arrest.

Integral to most forms of narrative are the notions of sequence and development. Stories are structured so that scenes relate to or build upon one another as we gradually learn more about a character, an idea or a plot. Narrative also incorporates a sequential logic so that the order of scenes or sequences makes sense to us. We might see two people introduced to one another, then we see them flirt, then we watch them fall in love. Each stage has a logical place in the sequence and the meaning of each stage is influenced by the order of its appearance. If the sequence is altered, then the narrative must give us another sequential logic with which to make sense of it. So, for example, we may see the couple fall in love before we flash back to their being introduced, because in the unfolding story the introduction is given a different kind of significance.

While most stories are structured chronologically, even an organising principle like time does not necessarily involve narrative. If we are told: 'At eight o'clock he scratched his nose, at nine o'clock he stretched his leg, at ten o'clock he went for a walk, at eleven o'clock he scratched his nose again', the information begins to seem lifeless, even pointless; the man's actions have no obvious sequential logic or significance beyond themselves. If a story were to begin this way, however, we may be intrigued by the oddity of such a flat, aimless description and read on so that we might make sense of it (who is this man, and why does he seem to be doing nothing?). This raises one of the most important aspects of narrative: the use of what Roland Barthes (1974) termed the 'hermeneutic code'.

The hermeneutic *code* consists of three stages:

1   The enigma: this involves something that prompts us to ask a question about the narrative's development. In the case of television mysteries or thrillers the enigma will often be fairly straightforward: who did it? how will they escape? who did we see moving furtively in the building that night? In the case of a *sports* event, we are engaged by the question of who will win, by what

score, and how certain players will perform. But the enigma may not be quite so dramatic. We may be asked to wonder how a character may react to a piece of news, or how a relationship between two characters may develop. What is important, at this stage, is that our interest is engaged by the narrative, so that we want to see how the enigma is resolved.

2   The delay: once our interest in an enigma is aroused, that interest can be magnified or sustained by a sequence that delays the moment of resolution. The delay sequence may refer us to the enigma and keep the enigma open. A scene in which characters speculate about an enigma (established earlier) reminds us of our own curiosity and allows us the pleasure of our own speculation, or else keeps us in suspense. While the delay sequence may appear to be a source of frustration, it is actually an important source of narrative *pleasure* – in short, we enjoy the speculation or the suspense. Indeed, an enigma that is quickly resolved loses its power as we have no time to dwell upon it.

3   The resolution: having experienced the curiosity of the enigma and the teasing of the delay, the resolution gives us the pleasure of having our curiosity satisfied. We know who did it, who won, who lived happily ever after, and so on. Although we tend to associate the resolution with the end of a story, most narratives will be structured around an intricate series of enigmas, delays and resolutions. In some instances, the resolution may create another enigma – we know who did it, now will they get caught? – thereby driving the narrative forward and sustaining our interest. *Soap operas*, with their extensive time-lines and evolution of character, provide a continuous interplay of resolution and enigma – few resolutions will be final, in order to keep a series of storylines open. Only the final resolution – one that closes a storyline or ends a film – will provide a final point of closure.

It is the hermeneutic code that will make most narratives absorbing or compelling. Without this narrative code, we need something else to sustain our interest – a piece of music, for example, which may use narrative but can hold our attention without it.

While we tend to associate narrative with forms of fiction or drama – such as movies, novels or sitcoms (see *Comedy*) – most forms of television use narrative. A non-celebrity quiz or *game show*, for example, will often engage us not simply by asking us to match our wits against the contestants, but by involving us in the contest so that we want to see the enigma 'who will win?' resolved. The US show

Jeopardy does this by introducing the contestants – brief exchanges that have little to do with the contest but which allow the audience to decide who they like and to give them some stake in the outcome. The British show *Big Brother* (and the series of European and American shows based on the same format) was popular not simply because it was a 'fly on the wall' view of a group of people interacting, but because of the tensions introduced by a narrative in which housemates would be gradually nominated and voted on to remove them from the house.

Similarly, the television coverage of sporting events relies a great deal upon the establishment of enigmas – who will win, who will play well, what tactics will be used, etc. – to keep us involved. The delay sequence is particularly important in the sporting narrative. Breaks in play or spells of inconclusive action ('lowlights') give spectators the opportunity to review the game thus far and speculate on its development. As a consequence, live coverage tends to be much more popular than edited highlights, not just because of the feeling of immediacy but because highlights (particularly if the outcome is known) deny the viewer the narrative pleasures of review and speculation.

Those televisual forms that rely less on narrative depend upon other forms of viewer engagement. Two notable examples are *news* and *music video*. While both occasionally use sustained forms of narrative, they are often less inclined to make use of developmental sequences or the hermeneutic code. Many music videos, for example, present a series of images whose ordering is much more arbitrary than in a conventional storyline. This is because *audience* interest needs to be sustained only briefly – usually for three or four minutes – something that can be achieved by striking images and musical enjoyment. If there is a loose, underlying narrative, it is in the use of images to build up or develop the persona – sexy, weird, moody, artistic, rebellious, etc. – of the artists.

In the case of news, the need to engage audiences is seen as less important. We watch, in many cases, not out of sustained interest but out of a sense that we need to be informed, or that something may happen that we should know about. If we find an item dull (and audience research suggests that many of us do most of the time), then there is always the next item, and if that bores us there is always the weather forecast (something that unlike most news stories directly implicates all of us). Despite the term we use to describe them, television news and newspapers often present us with lists rather than 'stories'. While television news often attempts to create interest by providing 'teasers' for upcoming stories, the information contained in news items is often structured in order of importance rather than in a clear narrative sequence. Indeed, newspaper journalists are taught to avoid narrative sequences so that an editor could cut the copy – at the end or halfway through – in the knowledge that the important information has already been given. Although the news will certainly use some narrative devices, its narrative thrust is present not in the news text but in the memory of an informed audience who can place the news item in a larger narrative context. Audience research suggests that this ability is, however, the exception rather than the rule.

See also: **Game shows, Music video, News, Pleasure, Semiotics, Text**

Further reading: Barthes (1974); Fiske (1987); Propp (1979)

NEWS

Television news is a genre of great significance for both television itself and researchers in media studies. Its general importance emerges from a range of factors. For instance, television news provides audiences with information about what are apparently matters of worldly consequence and certainly issues beyond 'our' immediate realm. It tends to be central to the identity of television networks, with news bulletins sometimes referred to as 'flagship programmes'. In both Britain and the United States, news programmes are often regarded by broadcasters as a 'public service'. News has also constituted part of a daily ritual for many people, with some commentators conjuring up images of families sitting down together to watch a scheduled bulletin. While this may seem a trifle nostalgic, the continuing public debate about timing of evening news programmes in Britain and the 'dumbing down' debate in the US would suggest that news is of continuing cultural and political relevance. The centrality of television news at key cultural moments, such as the death of Diana, Princess of Wales, or the Gulf War (which boosted news ratings in the US, especially for the news channel CNN) would add credence to this.

In media studies, however, the analysis of television news has centred on questions surrounding its supposed accuracy and the political implications of the version of the world generated by news bulletins. Historically, news journalists have set themselves up as a source of *objective* truth about events and issues (Cottle, 1993). In the case of public service and many other broadcasters, this has been a legal and political obligation, so that, for instance, the BBC's Royal Charter required that the Corporation refrained from expressing an opinion (see *Public service broadcasting*). Many analysts have argued, though, that the news cannot simply reflect reality as it occurs but must inevitably represent events and ideas in particular ways. This is because news, like any other text, is a social construction that produces versions of any reality rather than an unambiguous truth. Therefore, news items are not simply waiting to be discovered and gathered by scoop-hungry journalists. News is, in this sense, manufactured according to the rituals and routines of news production rather than a set of spontaneous events.

In terms of what is selected to reach a bulletin – where an item is placed (if it is), how long it is allocated and how it is presented – news is constructed by a number of related factors. First, sources shape news. Globally, because of television's cutbacks in expenditure on foreign correspondents, news is increasingly dependent on agencies such as Press Association and Reuters for its stories. Domestically, a news programme will follow other news sources, including newspapers and radio. News relies as well on 'official' sources, such as corporations, government agencies, pressure groups and the public relations profession. This is not only because news from these outlets seems more reliable, an assertion questioned by *Marxists* (see below), but also because such organisations ensure a steady supply for networks eager and even desperate to fill regular bulletins and, more recently, entire 24-hour channels such as *CNN* and *Sky News*. So the content of news, in the first instance, is derived not from 'the most important things happening', nor from stories hunted down by journalists, but simply from what is readily available. As budgets for news reporting decrease, reliance on a common set of 'official' news sources will inevitably increase.

Second, the news is constructed within professional and organisational contexts (see *Institutions*). For some analysts, the 'constructedness' of news can be traced to the role of gatekeepers, editors and other key personnel with the power and ability to make key decisions on what is included, and where, in a bulletin. However, the organisational context of news production is in reality somewhat more complicated. It is shaped by resource constraints and by bureaucratic rules and routine which encourage a need for predictable news. Schlesinger, in his study of the BBC, claimed that 70 per cent of news content derives from a 'news diary' known well in advance. It is also moulded by time constraints and the need to meet unalterable deadlines in what has been referred to as a stopwatch culture (Schlesinger, 1978), and the availability of raw news materials such as visual images. Tuchman found a similar set of constraints in her study of news in the United States (Tuchman 1978).

Third, the construction of news is strongly influenced by 'news values', the profession's informal principles which define what is newsworthy and which are deemed to shape selection, ordering and presentation of news. The concept of news values emerged in the work of Galtung and Ruge (1981) and has since been reworked by any number of media theorists (see, for instance, Watson, 1998; Branston and Stafford, 1996). In essence, they argue that whether or not events are reported will depend on their fit with a number of conditions which constitute 'a good story'. These include:

- Frequency – events which conform with the daily news schedule, say a celebrity death, are more likely to be included than long-term processes such as detailed comparative or longitudinal analyses of military budgets.
- Event-orientation – stories that can be packaged around an event are much more likely to be reported than on-going or long-term trends. When trends do get reported, it is usually in response to an event such as a press conference or the publication of a major report.
- Importance – stories need to be 'big' enough to cross a threshold of newsworthiness; for example, enough deaths in a rail accident.
- Familiarity – news needs to be familiar and relevant to people within a region or nation. This leads to 'ethnocentric' news which focuses on 'our' country and then perhaps countries in geographical or cultural proximity.
- Clarity – elections and wars provide examples of stories which, by being presentable in terms of direct competition and goals, can be delivered as unambiguous.
- Predictability – events which can be planned for, perhaps a presidential inauguration or a public demonstration, lend them-selves to inclusion. This condition also refers to events which can be reported in self-fulfilling ways – for instance, the expectation of violence at a public gathering will often involve reporters looking for incidents to fulfil this expectation.
- Untypicality – paradoxically, stories are also newsworthy if they disrupt normality, for example a gruesome murder. Thus it is that more typical kinds of violent crime – such as domestic violence – tend to be less 'newsworthy' than more unusual ones involving attacks by strangers.
- Continuity – events which run over a given amount of time (those

which 'have legs') may be amenable to organisation within an appealing *narrative*.

- Negativity – bad news is often good news. Similarly, conflict, between people, nations or viewpoints is valuable to news producers.
- Composition – stories may be included to provide a balanced bulletin, so that a cheery item often follows the normal run of 'bad' and serious news.
- 'Elite-orientation' – elite people, institutions and societies make good stories, partly because they may have wider symbolic value (the president or a member of the Royal Family representing 'us'). Rightly or wrongly, elite sources are also often regarded as more authoritative by journalists, who do not need to justify quoting an elite source. News teams will typically build visits to elite sources into their news-gathering routines – a process the elite source will usually be skilled in accommodating.
- Human interest – events are more likely to be included if they can be illustrated in terms of individuals.
- Availability of visual material – for example, footage of a plane crash will guarantee inclusion regardless of which country the plane crashed in.

This taxonomy does not infallibly predict whether or not an item will reach a bulletin. Nevertheless, it does give an indication of the extent to which news as an end product is the result of almost taken-for-granted practices developed within the professional training and organisational routines of news-makers.

Thus, television news emerges from complex processes of construction. A key debate has revolved around *what* exactly is constructed by television news. News producers and journalists tend to argue that, in line with political and legal constraints, television news provides audiences with the truth, and indeed a 'window on the world'. However, many media researchers counter that the news constructs a particular version of events, where that version is shaped by a wider context. This is plainly illustrated where the state explicitly controls news output and is able to disseminate what is, in effect, propaganda. However, news bears the hallmark of its social context just as obviously where the means of news production and presentation is in corporate or democratic state hands (see *Ownership*). Critics like Herman and Chomsky argue that business and government elites are able, through the structures of news reporting, to ensure that certain views prevail (Herman and Chomsky, 1988). This happens they argue, through structures of ownership, the pressures that come from *advertising*, the ability of elites to construct themselves as a news source, and from the power of elites to put pressure on news organisations. News thus becomes a means for the ruling group to control ideas in society to reproduce its pre-eminence – what Herman and Chomsky refer to as 'manufacturing consent'. Similarly, in a British series of studies, the Glasgow University Media Group (see, for instance, 1976) argued that British television news, in the way that it is collected, selected and presented, constitutes dominant *ideology* and thus serves ruling social and political interests. Their research, to take one example, suggested that coverage of British industrial disputes tended to take the management's side (and thus that of the ruling *class*). This was accomplished by techniques such as 'sandwiching' union views between those of management, filming from the police side of street demonstrations, and the use of language favouring government and employer. Selectivity, it is argued, emanates in the first place from more and less explicit state regulation, but long-term exposure to this eventually results in a notable degree of self-censorship among news personnel (Curtis, 1984). Even critics of the sometimes mechanistic Marxist position have acknowledged that television news, if nothing else, can set the agenda for what is thought and talked about (see *Agenda-setting*).

News has also been criticised for reproducing a white and male world view. A number of studies have shown that television news reporters continue to be predominantly male – especially for 'hard' news stories. Similarly, the development of international production of news in a global market is also seen as a form of *cultural imperialism*, since most news is produced by transnational corporations based in the United States and Europe and able, via new technologies, to rapidly transmit news to every part of the world (see also *Americanisation* and *Globalisation*).

It has been argued that the *conventions* and *semiotics* of news presentation heighten the idea of news as a transparent window on the world by making a claim to *objectivity*, immediacy and authority. Graphics and music at the start of bulletins often connote an air of being up-to-the-minute, allude to state-of the-art technology and reference significant icons such as Big Ben or the White House alongside images of the globe itself. Opening announcements are strident and heralding, while presenters tend to dress fairly formally (early BBC news presenters wore dress suits) and engage the viewer in a steady, serious gaze. Earlier accounts noticed that newsreaders tended to be male, reflecting and leading a social assumption that masculinity equates to authority. Even contemporarily, women newsreaders tend to be of a certain age and style which emphasises conventional 'attractiveness', with older women noticeable by their absence (van Zoonen, 1994). The ambience of television news, then, is one of formality, sincerity and neutrality, bolstering the ideological claim that television news is essentially truthful.

Pluralists (see *Pluralism*) are one group who reject the argument that news systematically favours elite perspectives, pointing out that power cannot be centrally located but is shared by a large number of groups all jostling and negotiating for position and influence. Television news reflects this plurality, being sensitive to audience interest and demand as well as constrained by the law and its own internal fidelity to democratic ideals. News organisations themselves have heterogeneous cultures which may be in conflict with each other. Other critics (see, for instance, Stevenson, 1995) have focused on the absence of an *audience* in the analysis, arguing that there is no guarantee of the news audience interpreting the news in a 'preferred' way. Examples are provided by Morley's seminal work (1980) on different interpretations among *Nationwide* viewers and Hartley's suggestion (1982) that women may ideologically reject the masculine genre of television news. Abercrombie (1996) discusses developments in news as a *genre*, noting an increased imperative to deliver an audience and hence to entertain as well as, or instead of, inform (*Eye Witness News* on ABC, for instance). This, too, could undermine any straightforward attempts at ideological inculcation.

Many writers in the field begin from the position that objectivity is unattainable and that no single definitive version of an event can exist. News, like any other text, is constructed from an infinite range of would-be versions in terms of potential stories, resources, modes of delivery and language. The result is that news stories and bulletins develop a particular narrative and meaning from multiple possibilities. But this is not to deny the significance of the debate, given the ideological implications inherent in being able to determine the content and structure of the news. Television news can and does set agendas, and the increasing globalisation of its production and transmission only emphasises the need for media studies to understand and monitor the genre.

See also: **Audiences, Globalisation, Ideology, Institutions, Marxism, Objectivity**

Further reading: Bell (1991); Curran and Seaton (1997); Eldridge (1995); Gans (1979); Hartley (1982); Tuchman (1978)

OBJECTIVITY

The concept of objectivity is rooted in the development of science, implying, as it does, the possibility of an external, knowable truth. In the world of television it has referred to the idea that the medium can remain separate and neutral with the ability to faithfully reflect contemporary and historical truths. In fact, 'objectivity' is often used alongside other concepts including 'impartiality', 'balance', 'neutrality' and their supposed opposite, 'bias'. The terms are by no means synonymous but they do reference a specific collection of debates within media studies. These cohere around the study of factual television, especially *news*, but have also been relevant to some genres of television *drama*, particularly those dealing with 'real' events and people.

At the core of the argument is the idea that the social world has an essential truth and that television, in its coverage of that world, should reflect it objectively. It has been suggested, though, that this concern for objectivity is of particular concern to only a few liberal democracies. Sceptics point to the capacity of American news anchors to editorialise, and to the explicit links between politicians and television stations all over the world – for example, in Italy, where Silvio Berlusconi makes little effort to suggest that the television station he owns will be neutral. However, in many countries, networks – particularly *public service broadcasters* – have been legally required to maintain an objective and arguably democratic stance. As it emerged, the BBC's avowed objectivity was intricately tied up with its reputation as a bastion of cultural authority and credibility. Even where objectivity is not a statutory requirement, for example in the US, it may be a political expectation, as witnessed by the furore when journalists are revealed as being 'economical with the truth'. Relatedly, in Britain there have been a number of controversies over television drama which has depicted a historical event in a radical or revised (and thus apparently subjective) version, as with, for instance, *The Monocled Mutineer*. Television professionals claim that for the most part they adopt a value-free stance, managing to reflect and represent each and every viewpoint. Equally, it would seem that audiences in democratic societies expect television networks to be impartial and are satisfied that they accomplish this, in marked contrast to their beliefs about newspapers.

In practice, a commitment to objectivity often emerges in efforts to maintain a balance between countervailing forces (Branston and Stafford, 1996). Thus, in the US, networks give equal weight to

Democratic and Republic positions while in Britain broadcasters have been concerned to provide equivalent space to Labour and Conservative Party voices. Where a programme is seen to depart from objectivity, whether deliberately or unintentionally, it is held to be biased and espousing a particular opinion. In recent years British political parties and television analysts alike have devoted considerable effort to exposing what they see as bias on the part of television stations. Famously, the Glasgow University Media Group (for example, 1985) has used a combination of *semiology* and *content analysis* to argue that British television news distorts reality in its representation of events and issues such as wars and industrial relations. Further, it suggests that news is told in such a way as to promulgate dominant *ideology*, so that strikes are 'a problem' but a state-supported conflict is 'necessary'. Objectivity from this perspective, then, can be seen as little more than adherence to not only a partial position but also a decidedly conservative one, focusing on mainstream cultural and political opinions. The BBC has frequently and proudly claimed that it knew it was 'getting it right' if it was receiving criticism from both sides of the conflict in Northern Ireland. But critics have argued that in actuality television news has tended to restrict coverage and airtime to a fairly limited and 'less extreme' range of opinion within the region (Curtis, 1984). Gans, looking at the US, has argued that the objectivity of news is, therefore, simply a political middle-ground articulating loosely democratic and liberal principles (Abercrombie, 1996).

The debate as it has developed has shifted away from a concern with the precise truth and bias of television texts and stations to focus on more theoretical and methodological questions. It has been argued that the pursuit of objectivity is pointless because all *texts* are constructed, embodying infinite social processes of production and articulating the point of view of whatever and whoever has produced the text. In television this is a particularly significant point because it employs conventions of *realism*, and the 'hand of the producer' is often invisible, bolstering the notion of objectivity (Abercrombie, 1996). Thus, television news is always the outcome of personal and organisational interpretations and perceptions about what will be interesting, significant and affordable. Equally, it has been suggested that the work of the Glasgow University Media Group betrays its political and operational foundation as a set of academics sympathetic to the political left (Harrison, 1985). Some *feminist* researchers have contended that television texts are essentially masculine and aimed at a male audience, reflecting the continuing influence of men in the television industry. Similar arguments have been put forward by researchers of race, nationality, class and age.

Certainly, British broadcasters have shown an awareness of these debates, seeking to tread a fine line between the democratic goal of impartiality and an understanding of a full breadth of perspectives. The BBC has claimed to pursue 'due impartiality', a recognition of the need to remain neutral but within a set of cultural boundaries about what is and is not acceptable.

Objectivity and bias, then, are viewed by many in media studies as myths with the pursuit of truthful representation being derided as impossible. Moreover, in some *postmodern* circles it is argued that audiences are increasingly sceptical, sophisticated and aware of the constructedness of the text.

See also: **Ideology, Marxism, News, Ownership, Public service broadcasting**

Further reading: Branston and Stafford (1996); Curran and Seaton (1997); Goodwin (1990)

OWNERSHIP

The questions of who owns and who does not own the mass media have been the subject of constant debate within media studies because of the relationship of ownership to *power*. Some accounts have tended to glibly couple the concept of ownership with that of control, but many media scholars are now more wary of making straightforward links between the two. The study of television, however, does emphasise the importance of understanding ownership and its implications for what programmes are produced and consumed, and indeed what is 'said' in those programmes.

In some European countries television as an *institution* has been in receipt of forms of public funding raised from taxes and licences. This sort of ownership has been associated historically with a sense of public service and, in the case of the BBC, a commitment to educating and informing as well as entertaining (see *Public service broadcasting*). In political terms, state or publicly owned corporations are accountable to governments, but in return they have been, until fairly recently, protected from commercial competition. Whether or not this has promoted freedom of expression or a narrowing of the range of public opinion has been a moot point. Since the 1970s, though, there has been a gradual process of deregulation, with an increasing amount of output being produced by commercially owned corporations on multiple channels.

Commercial television is owned by capitalist corporations, motivated by market, rather than cultural or ethical, considerations. It needs to accumulate profit and establish and maintain advertising audiences. What has been noticeable in the last third of the twentieth century is the steady concentration of ownership, with a decreasing number of corporations taking greater possession of the means of television production, distribution and consumption, and in the process devouring smaller companies. This has been driven by a variety of influences, including pressures of competition, the economies of scale deriving from cross-media ownership, the high capital needs involved in developing new technology (for example, digital) and, latterly, continuing deregulation (Abercrombie, 1996). All of this needs to be seen in a context in which the media in general and television in particular has grown in importance and economic potential. Britain, then, has seen mergers between commercial media corporations, links between terrestrial, satellite and cable companies, and synergistic (see *Synergy*) integration of complementary media interests such as those between television *sport*, magazine publishing and web-sites.

Debates around media ownership have focused on this increasing concentration of ownership in corporate hands. *Marxists*, as well as pointing to the implications of monopoly economic practices, have been particularly concerned by what they see as the ideological and undemocratic consequences emanating from corporate *power*. While they may differ over the degree to which *ideology* can be assumed to 'work', they agree that ruling groups, whether classes, corporations or individual entrepreneurs, need to own the means of television production and consumption in their efforts to reproduce the capitalist system using 'dominant ideology'. At the same time, alternative views are marginalised or silenced. So television corporations have the steadily increasing power to define 'news', limit *genres* and promote an *advertising* culture, and in so doing shape beliefs, ideas and values. Critics point to the Italian media 'magnate' Silvio Berlusconi to warn of the dangers emerging from concentrated ownership. Berlusconi, it is argued, has used his ownership of Fininvest to generate a political message and underpin his personal political career. These fears are echoed in Habermas' rather more general concern at ways in which 'the public sphere', in which opinion had previously been formed openly and democratically, has been annexed and thus stifled by the mass media (Macionis and Plummer, 1998). Relatedly, it has been argued that television as an institution reflects its overwhelmingly white, male and 'western' ownership.

For Marxists, then, television is a means of material and ideological production which ruling groups need to own monopolistically. *Pluralists* disagree, rejecting the evidence of limited ownership and the idea that ownership of the mass media bequeaths control. For them, media power is diluted by state regulation (television in many European societies is bound by legal and political constraints) and the influence of various advertisers and consumers who, it is argued, are ultimately uncontrollable and even sovereign.

This debate has become all the more significant in the light of concentrated ownership by transnational corporations (TNCs) within the context of *globalisation*. Mainly American- and European-based TNCs, such as Time Warner, Bertelsmann and News Corporation, have developed horizontally and vertically to take ownership of more and more parts of the global media industry. Time Warner, for instance, has holdings in global television channels such as CNN and Cartoon Network, but complements this with integrated interests in programme back-catalogues, publishing, film production, cinemas, video, theme parks and merchandise outlets (Macionis and Plummer, 1998). Global ownership of the means of television production and distribution is therefore perceived as a vehicle for a globalisation of content (television news) and consumption (the Olympic Games). The steady concentration of ownership in private hands is not, in this model, taken to assume the control implicit in other approaches, for instance *Americanisation* theory. Rather, television is owned in a complex *semiotic* environment in which a bombardment of *signs* and images denies the possibility of a single truth and the ideological ramifications feared by Marxists.

See also: **Globalisation, Institutions, Marxism, Pluralism**

Further reading: Abercrombie (1996); Comstock (1991); Tunstall and Palmer (1991)

PLEASURE

The use of the term 'pleasure' within television studies is far from unproblematic. Beginning with the assumption that viewers are not generally forced to watch television and that it is an activity freely entered into, it might then be assumed that television is consumed largely for pleasure. But this depends on how pleasure is understood. Dictionary definitions tend to focus on gratification (of body or mind) and on the agreeable, but pleasure is also sometimes conceptualised as the opposite of pain.

Both the concept itself and understanding its relationship to television are complex. Attempting to unravel the significance of pleasure thus raises questions and issues. For instance, one of the initial problems in discussing pleasure is that it is apparently an entirely subjective, individual phenomenon, outside the realm of the social and thus possibly beyond analysis. Nonetheless, attempts have been made to analyse pleasure, though, as Fiske (1987) points out, the term means different things in different discourses and to different theorists.

Historically, pleasure has, in fact, always been a matter of public concern, being bound up with questions of social order. The individual and his/her pleasures always become subject to moral regulation in that laws and moral imperatives do not allow individuals to do just what they please in pursuit of their own pleasure.

In an early attempt at understanding this, Plato wrote that the community (or the moral order) has to decide which pleasures are acceptable, so in this view the community has to take precedence over the individual. Much later, Freud (1922) wrote about what he called the 'pleasure principle': the notion that pleasure is the main purpose of our psychic life. Freud maintained that although we have a basic urge to find pleasure, the pleasure principle also acts as a regulator or a principle of constancy and stability. In other words, it balances our desires and outer constraints. He also suggests that pleasure has another dimension, which can constitute a threat to stability in the human ego: that is, a drive towards death (the 'death wish').

Marcuse (1964) attempted to understand pleasure by fusing the work of Marx and Freud. He argued that in bourgeois capitalist societies, people are allowed certain pleasures in exchange for labour, but these pleasures are restricted and many forms of pleasure become taboo or forbidden. For Marcuse, genuine pleasure is linked to liberation from the existing order. The social order has to be overthrown (negated) if genuine pleasure is to be gained. In this view, and to some extent in those noted above, pleasure is posed as an opposition or tension between the individual and society and between spontaneity and constraint. For Marcuse, pleasure can be understood by reference to power structures and notions of ideology. Some pleasures are socially approved, others are regarded as unacceptable, and much depends on which groups have the power to define the boundaries. Thus, while drinking champagne at an up-market affair may be socially approved, drinking cider in a city street is not.

Fiske (1987) provides a useful summary of recent attempts to theorise pleasure within media and cultural studies by grouping ideas under three headings: psychoanalytical, cultural/physical and social. Although these categories are not watertight, each of them can be utilised in understanding the pleasures of the television text. The first, which stems from Freud (see above) has been taken up, mainly in film and cinema studies, through the work of Laura Mulvey (1975) and others (see *Psychoanalysis* and *Feminism*). Conventional texts are seen to produce a certain kind of easy, comfortable pleasure by processes of identification (with a masculine hero) and voyeurism (through a 'male gaze'). This regime of visual pleasure is associated with a dominant, patriarchal *ideology*, which, Mulvey argues, comes to be experienced as 'natural' and 'normal'. She argues that such 'reactionary' pleasure needs to be broken down and replaced with more 'progressive' types, through new forms of cinema. Given the Freudian roots of this thesis, little space is afforded for resistance to the spectator position offered by the text, thereby rendering the spectator more or less passive.

While Mulvey's work has been hugely influential in the study of cinema, it can be only partially workable when applied to television. The main problem lies in the largely domestic conditions of television viewing, which are a far cry from the dream-like conditions of the cinema. In brief, the television viewer has been conceptualised as more active, and certainly less voyeuristic, if only through the constant disruption inherent in the television viewing experience, than a psychoanalytical perspective allows. Nonetheless, the approach gives some valuable insights into the pleasures of the television text when applied to specific ways in which women have been the object of a masculine gaze.

The French semiologist, Barthes (see *Semiology*) distinguished two forms of pleasure connected to bodily experience (the cultural/physical dimension in Fiske's typology). The first he called 'plaisir', a comforting pleasure found in ordinary and familiar or acceptable settings, such as watching most forms of television. This is a pleasure based on repetition, ritual and familiarity. And importantly, it is rooted in social patterns and conformity and thus linked to hegemonic relations (see *Hegemony*). The many pleasures connected with anticipating the *narrative* direction and textual *codes* of television (O'Sullivan *et al.*, 1998) can be seen as coming close to Barthes' notion of 'plaisir'.

The second kind is called 'jouissance' (joy or bliss). Here, Barthes is conceptualising thrills, ecstasy, danger, going to the limits, excess in various forms. Barthes likens this type of pleasure to orgasm: to the moment when culture breaks down into nature. It is linked to loss of self-control and loss of self, and ultimately loss of ideology. So jouissance is a pleasure which resists or evades social control and discipline. The strong connection to bodily functions in this concept has led to it being fruitfully applied to analyses of lived cultures, especially forms of resistant youth cultures. But it can also be helpful in understanding responses to some forms of television. For example, the intense emotions produced by some conventional television texts such as *soap operas* may be induced by both content (emphasis on the personal) and technique (use of the close-up shot).

The link between jouissance and the evasion of social control can be applied to popular television in a more general way, in that television has long been a battleground on which debates about 'high' and 'low' *culture* have been played out. Television is perceived as threatening by some moral guardians precisely because it is a site of pleasures that are not always or necessarily uplifting. This argument promises to persist with the proliferation of television channels and increasing deregulation (see *Commercial television*).

It is in this last sense that pleasure can be seen to encompass a more social interpretation. Pleasure in television can be many-faceted, even contradictory, with some texts offering comforting pleasure that could be seen as ideologically reactionary, and others allowing space for more challenging and oppositional positions. But it is also clear that viewers occupy variable positions in relation to television texts. In particular, there is potential to reject preferred meanings and produce alternative commentaries and knowledge. This is embedded in the process of contestation by which, according to Fiske, relatively powerless groups lay claim to cultural space. While a good deal of pleasure may be gained from this process of struggle for meaning, including a feeling of empowerment, such practices do not ultimately undermine the (economic or cultural) system and are rarely 'political' in any formal sense.

Pleasure, far from being so subjective that it is beyond analysis, can thus be understood as highly socially constructed and defined. It is also, arguably, one of the few areas where viewers can show resistance to the dominant order.

See also: **Audiences, Hegemony, Psychoanalysis**

Further reading: Fiske (1987); Geraghty and Lusted (1998)

PLURALISM

The word 'plural' means more than one. From this simple beginning, the term 'pluralism' has come to take on a range of definitions associated with the notion of more than one perspective or more than one power base. A pluralist society, similarly, is one in which more than one group has overall control and influence.

'Pluralism' is essentially a term widely used in political philosophy. Its assumptions have, however, come to form the basis of a theoretical approach within media and communication studies. Work undertaken from a pluralist perspective has been concerned with debates about the distribution of economic and cultural *power* and the means by which change can and does take place. It is also concerned with the relative influence of political pressure groups within societies. Within this general framework, a good deal of empirical research has been undertaken in media studies, mainly focusing on the *ownership* and control of media institutions and their relationship to wider economic structures. The ways in which ownership and control do, or do not, affect the content and potential bias of programming and editorials has also been a foremost concern of pluralists.

In philosophy, pluralists begin from the assertion of a multiplicity (plurality) of beliefs and phenomena. This position is set against a monistic type of philosophy such as materialism which asserts that everything, including the mental, is in fact physical, or idealism which asserts that everything including the physical is in fact mental. Although idealism and materialism are two positions in opposition, they are also similar since they rely on the belief in a single (monistic) system of explanation. In contrast, pluralism holds that there is more than one way of explaining phenomena and a multiplicity of positions and perspectives.

In political terms, the pluralist perspective stems from a liberal-democratic tradition based on the idea that in liberal democracies many interest groups compete, more or less freely, for power and influence. The basis of power is thus fragmented and diffuse. This perspective has become popular, especially in the US, since the end of World War II.

Theories and explanations about the ownership and control of the media are quite complex. In the twentieth century, they have been dominated by Marxist explanations, including a number of sub-types (such as determinist and hegemonic models of *Marxism*). The pluralist model, as put forward by such figures as J. Burnham, A.A. Berle and G.C. Means, stands in opposition to that of Marxism, as well as to classical elite theories. While Marxist explanations centre on the crucial importance of the concentration of ownership and control in the hands of a ruling class, and elite theorists argue that elites may not be economic but they will always exist, pluralism emphasises the distribution of power and influence among a wide range of competing groups. Such a multiplicity of groups, it is argued, ensures that no one political *ideology* or set of interests will dominate. Rather, the public will be exposed to a large number of views and perspectives from which they may form their own opinions.

One concern held by Marxist writers is the difficulty of avoiding bias in the media given the concentration of *ownership* in a very few hands. The pluralist model, on the contrary, suggests that media fairness is protected by a series of checks and balances. While one political view might predominate at a given point in time or in a given media outlet, in the long run a range of positions will be given an airing. Moreover, it is implied that short-term bias might well exist because of the vested interests of particular groups being given prominence, but if it does then this is because ideology and content are ultimately determined by audience choice. What audiences get is what they want, not what they are trained or conditioned to want. There is a plurality of media outlets and types, and all are capable of selectivity and bias, but since the bias is not all in the same direction it eventually balances itself out.

So, for instance, tabloid newspapers and some television news programmes tend to over-report sex crimes relative to their incidence as a proportion of crimes as a whole. They also emphasise stories about soap opera stars, royalty and other media celebrities, but that is because this is what their readers or viewers want. If they do not want it, so the argument goes, they can choose a different newspaper or switch to another channel. Such a view is in line with the *uses and gratifications* approach (see also *Audiences*). As far as television is concerned, its historical tradition and its codes of practice have been much more linked to the ideal of achieving a fair 'balance' in its coverage, whereas newspapers tend to have a more obvious editorial line. Either way, pluralists maintain that a wide range of views of the world will be on offer to the public in non-repressive regimes. So, although selectivity is clearly evident in the production of media stories, both fictional and factual, pluralists argue that this is so widespread that it inevitably covers all shades of opinion rather than that of a privileged minority. The argument here rests very much on the choices available to people: millions of people tune in to particular programmes on television or read popular tabloid newspapers because these reflect their views and *tastes*, not because they shape audience views and tastes.

Conversely, it is suggested that the reason that only a minority of people read politically radical publications, and the reason why there are few politically radical voices on television, is because these do not reflect most people's tastes or opinions. There are other programmes and other publications available for those whose tastes are different from that of the majority, and these are increasingly available in a more diversified market, where 'niches' can be identified. This explanation does not, however, take into account certain restrictive practices in distribution, nor does it account for the way marketing, advertising and publicity work to affect popular taste. For example, some retail chain outlets have sometimes refused to stock radical publications, and many working-class publications in the past have gone out of business, not from lack of readership but because of lack of advertisers. Television scheduling is similarly likely to relegate programmes reflecting 'minority' taste to the margins, particularly if they do not attract advertising revenue.

Thus, in both the UK and the US, the pluralist perspective has been criticised on the basis that most media products, such as newspapers, magazines and television stations, are owned by a very few major companies headed by a small number of people, most of whom have similar views (see *Globalisation*).

Pluralists argue that selectivity in television news is inevitable and based on largely technical constraints such as getting cameras quickly to remote places or unexpected events. They argue against the *Marxist* model by suggesting that although ownership is certainly concentrated in very few hands, this does not prove that content is affected. Editors and other managers determine the tone and line adopted in their publication or on their news bulletin, but they do this with marketing, not political principles, in mind. Moreover, there is, in the case of individual investigative journalists, a strong critical element in existence which suggests that it is possible for news reporting to challenge the status quo. There have been numerous examples where corruption in politics or business has been exposed in the media, and this has sometimes led to the downfall of influential people. This proves, according to pluralists, that there is free speech and a place for alternative views and voices to be heard. Similarly, despite concentration of *ownership*, there are still independent publications in the press and in broadcasting. Channel 4 in Britain was set up explicitly to provide for minority and under-represented tastes, and there has been an increase on both sides of the Atlantic in public *access* programmes.

As the media continue to fragment – further evidence, perhaps, of the postmodern condition – via multiple channels, digitalisation, interactive television and other new technologies, the possibility of a plurality of voices becomes stronger. Whether the possibility is exploited to become a reality, remains to be seen.

See also: **Access, Audiences, Globalisation, Marxism, News**

Further reading: Boyd-Barrett and Newbold (1995); Curran and Seaton (1997)

POLICY

The form and content of a country's media system will be significantly affected by the policy framework established by government agencies. Despite the centrality of the media's role in modern democracies – and its importance in our everyday lives – media or communications policy is rarely the subject of public discussion or debate.

Government policy towards media and mass communications generally encompasses two forms of intervention: regulation and funding. These can be used to shape a media system in order to promote ideals or objectives. We can, in broad terms, identify three types of media systems established by specific patterns of regulation and funding.

The first category is the *commercial* system. This involves government ceding publishing or the public airwaves to commercial interests. The costs of media production in a commercial system are covered either by direct payment for a service (such as a pay-per-view cable channel) or, more commonly, by *advertising* revenue. While media paid for by advertising are often regarded as 'free', the consumer usually pays for them indirectly, since the cost of advertising products will be passed on to them (one of the reasons why brand-named products are more expensive than generic brands).

Proponents of a commercial system argue that the free market will provide the best media products, and that a minimal level of government involvement will help protect this freedom. One area of disagreement among proponents concerns monopoly legislation: some argue that government intervention of any kind is counter-productive, while others see a need for government to pass anti-monopoly legislation to prevent a drift towards a concentration of ownership in order to keep the market 'free' (see *Ownership*).

The most notable example of a commercial system is the United States, where most media forms are run for profit and funded largely or wholly by advertising revenue. This has been the case since the growth of radio in the 1930s, although the regulatory frameworks – imposed by the Federal Radio Commission (FRC) and then the Federal Communications Commission (FCC) – have been lightened considerably since the 1980s, which began a process of deregulation of the media industries and declining levels of government support for the Corporation for Public Broadcasting (which helps fund a small network of public television stations). This period of deregulation included the loosening of restrictions on ownership, which has accelerated the trend towards concentration in the media industries.

Second, there is *public service broadcasting*. This broadcasting framework has heavily influenced the development of broadcasting systems – notably in Europe. Public service systems usually involve a publicly funded television/radio network existing alongside a regulated commercial system. The philosophy behind public service broadcasting maintains that the radio and television airwaves are public property and should therefore be used in the public interest. Proponents argue that the broadcast media have enormous cultural and educational significance, and that, as a consequence, they should be shaped by cultural or educational goals – such as a guarantee of diverse, informative or enlightening programming – rather than by the desire to maximise profit. Public broadcasting networks in this system are funded either directly by government or through quasi-independent public corporations, such as the BBC which raises revenue through a tax on television sets. In either case, the goal is to restrict direct government interference in public broadcasting and to maintain the integrity and independence of the public sector.

Commercial broadcasting in this system is mandated and regulated by a governmental framework designed to limit interference from media owners or commercial interests. The airwaves are leased to private companies who will be asked to fulfil certain criteria. This may involve, for example, a commitment to informative programming or educational programmes for children, a guarantee of fairness in the coverage of political and social issues, restrictions on the amount of advertising, or quotas on the amount of (usually cheap) foreign programming that may be shown.

Although some public service systems – such as the British Broadcasting Corporation – grew out of a fairly paternalistic notion of the public interest, some proponents of public service broadcasting argue that the public service ethos should also involve the provision of *access* to programme-making for *community* groups – whether community of interest or geographical. This can be done through publicly funded 'access' slots on public stations or through subsidised community or 'access' radio or television stations.

Even in countries with public service broadcasting systems, the ideals of a public service system are rarely replicated in non-broadcast media, such as the press. Regulations on publishing tend to be limited to legislation on the monopoly ownership of newspapers.

The third form is the government-run system. World-wide, government-run broadcasting or media systems are extremely common, particularly in the developing countries of Asia and Africa. In this model, the control of content and policy in general is handled directly by government. This system is clearly advantageous for totalitarian governments wishing to control information and create state-sanctioned forms of *culture*. In the third world, the popularity of government-run systems is not merely a function of a desire for information control. Broadcast systems like television are expensive: since the 'market' in many third-world countries is too poor to be of interest to advertisers they cannot be run commercially. The government is the only agency with the means to provide such a system.

These three systems will generally provide a framework for government policy. In the third system, the relationship between policy and media is fairly clear. In the first two, policy tends to be directed – through subsidy and regulation – towards creating a framework in which certain kinds of broadcasting may flourish.

The injection of public money into a system can enable the development of a number of policy goals. In its ideal form, the use of public subsidy allows broadcast media to fulfil public service goals without being concerned about the needs of sponsors or advertisers. This can be used to provide producers with freedoms that tend to be unavailable within a commercial system, such as:

- The chance to innovate, developing programme ideas that may be too risky in a commercial climate (where audiences must be guaranteed fairly quickly).
- The ability to make programmes for minority audiences – particularly those minorities without the disposable income to interest advertisers.
- The opportunity to promote *educational* rather than commercial value. So, for example, the most profitable form of *children's* programming in a commercial system involves content designed by

toy manufacturers (a common practice in the United States) –
without this pressure, it is easier to create children's entertainment
that educates for its own sake.

- The ability to provide information regardless of the interests of
corporate owners or advertisers. In a commercial system, corporate
pressures can come from the owners or the parent company or from
significant advertisers like the car industry.
- The freedom to make or broadcast programming without
commercial interruption. In a commercial system – particularly
one with few restrictions on the frequency of commercial breaks,
such as in the United States – programmes must be designed to be
able to incorporate commercial messages without disrupting the
flow or mood of the show. Programme forms where this is not
possible – such as serious *drama* or a soccer game – are therefore
difficult to broadcast.

Many of these goals can also be achieved by creating a regulatory
structure. So, for example, restrictions can be placed on the amount or
frequency of advertising (while this will place a limit on revenue, it
will also drive up the cost of advertising space, enabling programmers
to charge more for less). Used creatively, media regulations can be used
less as a system of constraints (such as anti-monopoly legislation) than
as a way to achieve certain public service goals. The creation of
Channel 4 in Britain is a good example: the channel was designed to
fulfil a range of public service functions within a commercial
framework. Because its remit was clearly not conducive to certain
commercial goals, other commercial channels were initially required
to cross-subsidise the new channel.

The enactment of policy through regulation will not take place in a
neutral environment. One of the main forces resisting regulation is the
commercial media industry itself. Regulations will often place limits
on a company's ability to maximise profits or to pursue a certain
political or social perspective. In the United States, and increasingly in
Europe and elsewhere, the trend towards deregulation has been partly
the result of intense pressure by the media industry.

See also: **Access, Advertising, Commercial television, Community
television, Political economy, Public service broadcasting**

Further reading: McChesney (2000); Streeter (1996); Tumber (2000)

POLITICAL ECONOMY

Research into the economic and *institutional* structures of media and broadcasting usually goes under the heading of political economy. This will involve looking at patterns of media *ownership*, revenue sources (such as *advertising*), technological changes and various economic or institutional factors that influence the way media companies operate and the content they provide.

While political economy might be seen as a fairly broad heading – one that might, for example, encompass celebrations as well as criticisms of the role of market forces in media production – research into political economy in media and television studies has generally taken a fairly critical perspective. Studies of the political economy of television have been strongly influenced by debates in Marxist theory. Most notably, these debates have revolved around the degree to which economic structures influence ideological or cultural outcomes (see *Marxism*). Those working from within a classical Marxist tradition tend to assume the importance of institutional or economic structures and therefore emphasise the determining influence of political economy, while others have argued that connections between economic structures and *ideology* are neither inevitable nor independent of certain conditions and contexts.

In media studies debates around political economy focus on the extent to which the ownership and revenue structure of a television company influences the content of its programming. The ownership structure of media, for example, may lead to certain ideological slants in programming content. In countries where media are controlled by government, we might expect programming – either subtly or overtly – to reflect the interests of those in power. Privately owned media, on the other hand, are more likely to be sympathetic towards a pro-business view of the world, which may or may not coincide with the interests of political leaders. *Public service broadcasters*, while generally created and sanctioned by government, have a more complex ownership structure and are therefore less predictable.

In terms of revenue, the notion that the one 'who pays the piper calls the tune' is palpably relevant to broadcasting. Since commercial broadcast media tend to generate the bulk of their revenue from advertising, programming is likely to be tailored to the needs and interests of advertisers, which involves not only delivering the kinds of audiences most likely to buy the products on display, but doing so in a way that keeps viewers or listeners receptive to commercial messages. This has both ideological and aesthetic consequences. In ideological terms, it is in the interests of advertising-based media to favour consumerist rather than citizenship approaches to problems, and to exclude negative messages about those businesses that advertise and the corporate world in general. On an aesthetic level, programmes will tend to be written or structured in ways that ensure a smooth transition to commercial breaks (something that is easier to do in light entertainment like *sitcoms* or *game shows* than hard-hitting *documentary*).

The political economy of media might therefore be said to identify frameworks and interests likely to promote certain kinds of messages or forms of *representation* at the expense of others. So, for example, the head of a private media corporation is likely to have political views commensurate with their position as a wealthy business owner. They are, in turn, likely to appoint senior executives broadly sympathetic to those views, thereby establishing a chain of command in which the owner's interests will be represented without the need for their direct intervention in programme-making. This produces textual tendencies rather than guarantees. Thus, while many would argue that media owner Rupert Murdoch's conservative views are broadly reflected in his Fox news network, one of the Fox network's first hit shows was *The Simpsons*, a programme regarded by many as somewhat left-leaning and occasionally subversive.

A show like *The Simpsons* also suggests a sometimes contradictory relationship between a profit motive – which may be best served by popular, left-leaning shows like *The Simpsons* or *Roseanne* – and the conservative ideological inclinations of media owners. Although we should note that these two pressures are often in sync rather than in conflict, these examples of ideological diversity indicate that the *production* process is not necessarily reducible to a set of economic origins. The political economy of broadcasting is therefore complicated by a range of professional and institutional ideologies which may work for or against dominant interests.

Research into the political economy of media has become increasingly concerned with four contemporary and interconnected trends:

- The increasing concentration of ownership in media industries, whereby huge companies like Disney or Time Warner have grown vertically and horizontally to establish media empires with widespread interests in television production and distribution, cable, film, publishing, music, retailing and other related cultural industries, while many independent or small-scale media companies have either been swallowed up or are unable to compete.

- The general move towards the deregulation and commercialisation of broadcast media. In commercial media systems like the United States, this has meant giving commercial broadcasters even greater freedom to expand vertically and horizontally, as well as reducing any public service obligations (such as limits on the volume of advertising, requiring some provision of balanced news programming or the obligation to show *educational children's* programming). In public service systems, it has involved public service broadcasters – like the BBC – playing a shrinking role. At the same time the expansion of media outlets via cable, satellite and digital *technology* has increasingly been put into commercial hands (hence, for example, public access to major *sporting* events has been limited as commercial broadcasters buy rights to them and then increase the cost of viewing).

- The *globalisation* of media production and distribution, as broadcasters become transnational corporations catering to a global market. This has created concerns about *cultural imperialism* (since production is generally based in rich western countries – notably the United States – and is chiefly designed to cater to the more profitable markets), and worries about the homogenisation of television culture as programming is required to appeal to large, transnational audiences. In a commercial environment, it also places national, public service systems at a disadvantage, as the market is increasingly flooded with cheaper US imports (cheap because they will have already made a profit in the lucrative US market and can thus be exported at a comparatively low cost).

- The expansion of media forms and outlets (although not necessarily media content) through internet and digital technologies. While this has led to increases in the number of television channels, critics have suggested that it has not necessarily meant a greater variety of content, merely a spectacle of global media companies using different channels to appeal to those demographic groups most favoured by advertisers. In the United States, for example, of the fifty or so channels available on cable, most are owned by a handful of large media conglomerates catering to lucrative markets. So, for example, there are a variety of business-oriented programmes or channels but none produced by or for organised labour, and a great deal of youth-oriented programming but very little designed for older viewers.

These concerns demonstrate the link between political economy and broadcasting *policy*. Governments, through regulation and funding, have the capacity to shape or influence the political economy of a broadcasting system, and hence influence the range and style of programmes available. In each case, these trends have been influenced by government's withdrawing from public service commitments and viewing broadcasting primarily in terms of economic development rather than as a cultural resource. This has been exacerbated by the rescinding of power over trade from national governments to international pro-business institutions like the World Trade Organisation. The political economy of broadcasting therefore has an increasingly international focus in response to the globalisation of production, markets and institutions.

See also: **Cultural imperialism, Globalisation, Marxism, Ownership**

Further reading: McChesney (2000); Mosco (1996); Murdock and Golding (1995)

POLYSEMY

Polysemy refers to words, images or *texts* that have many meanings. The notion of polysemy comes from *semiotics*, which begins with the assumption that the meaning of something is never permanently fixed. This is, for many, counter-intuitive: we are so used to assuming what familiar words, images or objects 'mean' that their meaning seems almost inevitable or natural.

In language, polysemy can refer to the realms of connotation and denotation, to the metaphorical or symbolic range of meanings as well as the literal, dictionary-style definitions. In language, for example, the word 'strike' can be defined in several different ways – as an industrial action by workers; the lighting of a match; a turn in baseball; to hit something or someone; to adopt an attitude (to 'strike a pose'); to instil (as in 'to strike fear'); or to occur to ('it strikes me that'). Words may also have a range of connotative meanings: the word 'rain', for example, might connote misery, refreshment, dreariness, cold winter nights or relief from summer heat. To a farmer it may connote food for crops, to the inhabitant of a damp, low-lying area it may connote danger.

Images and objects can also be polysemic. A picture of former President Kennedy might signify within a wide range of *discourses*, connoting: youth and vigour; the 1960s; the lost era of American innocence; America's royal family; a family of rich philanderers; a great twentieth-century leader; Boston Irish politics; and so on. While we tend to think of objects as being more straightforward, they are also polysemic: an apple tree, for example, may be regarded as a source of fruit or as a decorative plant in a garden.

The French semiologist Roland Barthes used the concept of polysemy in his distinction between what he described as 'open' or 'closed' texts. An open text is one in which the reader or audience is encouraged or able to construct a wide range of meanings. A poem or an abstract painting, for example, encourages the reader or viewer to 'play' with meaning, to search for symbols and metaphors which might add layers of significance to the text, to appreciate its polysemy. The 'open' text can be read in a variety of ways: audiences may interpret it, for example, within a *psychoanalytic* framework; a *Marxist* framework; an historical framework; a *postmodernist* framework; a religious framework; or an existentialist framework. The open text will resist attempts by a single discourse to narrow its meaning, to restrict its polysemy.

The 'closed' text – which applies to most television programmes – will be structured to limit the occurrence of polysemy, to restrict the number of meanings and prevent the possibility of ambiguity. A propaganda campaign, a television commercial, a polemical novel or a textbook, for example, will attempt to close meaning down and push the audience to adopt a particular interpretation. Barthes, writing from the perspective of literary criticism, saw open texts as much richer, more interesting and, ultimately, a more sublime form of pleasure than the closed text. In other, less artistic contexts we might see the ability to limit polysemy, to produce a closed text, as advantageous: a list of instructions or a policy document, for example, will attempt to limit the range of interpretations.

There is no such thing as a completely open or closed text – they are 'ideal types', two ends of a continuum in which most texts fall somewhere in between. The degree of polysemy or closure in a text will also depend upon more than the text itself: it will also be a function of the context and the *audience*. One of the functions of modern art, for example, is to create a context in which polysemy thrives. An artist may take a commonplace domestic object, such as a can of soup or a toilet bowl. By painting it or simply by removing it from a domestic context and exhibiting it in a gallery, the artist encourages the viewer to play with meaning, to consider the range of connotations that might give it meaning and significance. In a typing manual, the meaning of the sentence 'the quick brown fox jumps over the lazy dog' is closed – its significance is only that it requires the use of every letter of the alphabet. In a poem, the same line might become polysemic, the fox and the dog becoming metaphors with a range of possible meanings.

The degree of polysemy or closure will also depend upon the audience. What appears to be closed text in one cultural context may take on an entirely different meaning in another. Audience research suggests that television shows can be given new meanings in different cultural contexts. Research by Hodge and Tripp (1986), for example, found that Australian school children interpreted a popular prison drama (*Prisoner Cell Bloack H*) as an allegory of school life, while a study of *The Cosby Show* by Jhally and Lewis (1992) found that the show meant different things to black and white viewers.

Both polysemy and closure are therefore dependent upon the 'cultural competence' of the viewer, reader or listener. The scholar of Shakespearean criticism, having read a range of interpretations of *Hamlet* (psychoanalytic, Marxist, existentialist, etc.) will be in a better position than most to appreciate the polysemy of the text than someone who is struggling to make sense of the play. Conversely, someone well versed in current affairs might be more receptive to the reporter's attempts to 'close' the meaning of a story.

In the same vein, levels of polysemy also depend upon the notion of *intertextuality* (the way we understand one text in relation to another text). A show like *The Simpsons*, for example, often makes a number of comic references to other films and TV shows, creating another layer of meaning for those audience members who are aware of those references; a sequence in *The Simpsons* can therefore be read both in its own terms or as a parody.

See also: **Audiences, Intertextuality, Semiotics, Sign, Text**

Further reading: Barthes (1974); Eco (1979); Fiske (1987)

POSTMODERNISM

The term 'postmodernism' has become a buzzword in both popular argot and academic debate (Hebdige, 1988). It has been used to describe everything from the dawning of a new cultural or aesthetic era to the unusual mix-and-match concoction that is a chicken tikka pizza. Many of us, even if we are not attuned to the theoretical origins of the concept, may have heard it used or may tentatively make use of it ourselves when struggling to describe contemporary cultural formations. While the term has become increasingly familiar, debates around it have become more impassioned and more elusive, with diverse positions ranging from eager celebration through to suspicion or distaste not uncommon. These mixed reactions reflect the fact that defining postmodernism is problematic enough, before the scholar can have any confidence in using it as a way of explaining the world around them. However, it is precisely because the term is now so widely – and variously – used that an exploration of postmodernism, and its related term 'postmodernity', is essential, not least because of its intimate relevance to television as an *institution* and set of *texts*.

The varied definitions of postmodernism that have circulated reflect the different contexts of its usage and the diverse standpoints of the theorists doing the defining. The term has been in circulation throughout the twentieth century, but gained wider currency in the 1960s when artists and critics living and working in New York took it up. During the 1970s it was employed by European philosophers and social theorists such as Lyotard and Baudrillard, who have since become key figures within postmodern theory. Since the 1990s the term has also entered popular *discourse*, becoming something of a catch-all term that encompasses views on a wide variety of contemporary cultural phenomena – from television to architecture and from the philosophical to the popular. Despite its ubiquitous presence the term 'postmodernism' refuses to be pinned down to a precise or simple set of propositions. Some theorists have a confusing tendency to use the terms 'postmodernism' and 'postmodernity' interchangeably. In many ways this confusion is entirely in keeping with the postmodernist scheme of things, or what Lyotard calls the 'postmodern condition' (Storey, 2001). Put simply, 'postmodernism' refers both to a stylistic and aesthetic change in the arts and culture and to the body of theory that seeks to describe it. In contrast, 'postmodernity' refers to the contemporary era within which postmodern culture and experiences are produced. Here, prevailing socio-cultural and economic conditions are accounted for, along with the view that when 'living in postmodernity' the individual experiences the world in a new way.

As the prefix 'post' implies, postmodernism is viewed as a stage coming after modernity and modernism, and is seen by some as emerging in reaction to a crisis within modern societies. According to Sarup (1993), modernity developed from the eighteenth century onwards and denotes a cluster of economic, social and political changes specific to western culture and societies. 'Modernisation' refers to the stages of social development and changes associated with industrialisation, urbanisation and the rise of nation–states and fuelled by the expansion of modern capitalism. 'Modernism', on the other hand, is a term reserved for a set of cultural and aesthetic styles, associated with the arts and intellectual culture, which emerged in the early part of the twentieth century. The emphasis of this creative movement was very much on experimentation within the realm of art and literature and the quest for deeper truths beyond or below the 'surface' of representational devices (e.g. surrealism and expressionism in painting). These new expressive forms emphasised innovative ways of seeing and representing the world, along with a rejection of previous modes of *representation* such as romanticism and *realism*. Modernist thinking and cultural practices were driven by a desire to be progressive and indeed 'modern'. Postmodernism, in contrast, undermines these fundamental principles and thereby destabilises the whole 'modernist' project.

So, postmodernism can be described in terms of the replacement of modernity and modernism. Lyotard (1984) describes this cultural transition as a gradual fading of progressive modernity marked by key cultural, social and technological changes. These include the shift to a post-industrial economic sphere based more on consumption, information and services rather than production, and the development of *globalised* social life with transport and communications technologies enabling shrinkage of time and space and the transformation of global culture. At the same time, old political and ideological certainties (including socialism, Christianity and science) collapse or are 'debunked' as 'grand theories' or 'metanarratives' which cannot explain the complexities of the contemporary world nor locate 'truth'.

As an approach to contemporary culture and cultural theory, postmodernism reflects these shifting contexts, abandoning master narratives such as *Marxism* and privileging modes of thinking and representation which emphasise discontinuity, fragmentation and eclecticism. The loss of faith in established ways of explaining the world means that the postmodern subject looks to the past with no sense of comfort or reassurance and faces the future with uncertainty and pessimism. Implicit in much postmodern theorising is a view that society is not progressing but, in contrast, is in decline. One of the fundamental principles of modern industrial societies was a belief in social evolution, whether through stunning technological advances (from the steam train to the television set to the space race) or through innovatory, experimental culture and art. Nowadays, technological development in particular is more often seen as destructive rather than constructive and regressive rather than progressive, evident in common concerns about climate change, nuclear power or the cloning of genes. In the absence of grand metanarratives, it is also of little surprise that some people have turned elsewhere to furnish themselves with alternative ideas and philosophies, whether through Green politics, New Ageism, Paganism or the broad umbrella of anti-capitalism. All of these developments involve a changing mood or zeitgeist as people become less trusting and more knowing and cynical.

In the realm of culture, where modernism was concerned with questioning the relationship between reality and its representation, postmodernism focuses on surfaces, styles and appearances, and questions or ignores the very existence of a 'knowable', external reality outside of representation. Where modernism held on to a distinction between high and low culture, postmodernism has heralded and embraced the collapse of boundaries in the realm of popular culture, and especially television. In postmodernity we are surrounded by a mass media which increasingly comes to constitute what we know. For theorists such as Baudrillard (1983), the media – and particularly television – are at the core of postmodernity as they generate a blizzard of signs, postmodern texts and textual practices. Television is the dominant source of visual culture in contemporary western – and, increasingly, other – societies, making it central to public and private life. Its endless flow of sounds and images produces what Baudrillard calls a culture of simulation at the expense of originality. Media reality (and particularly televisual reality) becomes indistinguishable from social reality as what we see, hear and experience via the media is confused with the routine interactions we perform on a daily basis. Storey (2001) cites the example of the O.J. Simpson trial, which was neither a 'pure' legal event nor simply television drama. Baudrillard goes so far as to suggest that television and life dissolve into one another as free-floating *signs* and images come to constitute what we know and do in what he calls 'hyperreality'. This is an essentially negative development, giving rise to culture which is superficial and meaningless (Baudrillard, 1983).

Abercrombie (1996) summarises the relationship between television and postmodernity. First, he notes that contemporary television texts are seen to be over-concerned with style and image, of producing a certain 'look' or aesthetic, which has no deeper meaning beyond that which is represented textually. *Music videos* and *Miami Vice* are examples of texts in which form and potential *pleasure* are privileged over content. Second, he suggests that postmodernity is characterised by a blurring of boundaries between separate cultural domains, different historical periods and different styles. This can be witnessed in *advertisements* and in *Buffy the Vampire Slayer*, where the text borrows freely from fantasy, gothic horror, high-school genres and girls' adventure stories in a sometimes uncertain and fragmented historical period. Third, postmodern texts characteristically eschew the *codes* and *conventions* of realism and *narrative*. *Twin Peaks* is an oft-quoted example, but programmes like *Ally McBeal* and *The Sopranos* are notable for their less extensive but nonetheless significant tendency to tinker with television's earlier and more sacred *realist* traditions. Fourth, postmodern texts are held to be increasingly introverted, retrospective and self-referential, with a nostalgic yearning for past images and styles being recycled in contemporary formats. A good deal of television programming – for example, British shows such as *One Hundred Greatest TV Moments*, *Auntie's Bloomers* and *Tarrant On TV* – present audiences with little more than a cultural trawl through television's relatively short history. Some channels, such as UK Gold, by devoting complete schedules to past programming are founded on this self-referentiality. But just as importantly, television trades off *audience* familiarity with a myriad of texts by moving between and merging texts in ever more complex ways (see any episode of *The Simpsons* for a regular display of playful and *intertextual* pastiche).

Relatedly, the actual experience of watching television itself with the introduction of remote handsets, video and multi-channel programming has become a diverse and fragmented cultural experience (Strinati, 2000) where flow (see *Scheduling*) is disrupted as audiences take control of viewing. At the same time the blurring of reality sees viewers writing to *soap* stars or dressing up for *Star Trek* conventions in an active recycling of texts (see *Fans*).

Critics of postmodernism are not thin on the ground. As a cultural theory it has been accused of pessimistically abandoning a search for meaning and uncritically accepting culture as what exists only in the sphere of *mediation*, particularly on the television screen. Equally, the analysis of power has been deserted in a belief that 'anything goes' in the context of inevitable capitalism and 'the end of history' (Storey, 2001). In the specific context of television, some postmodernists point to the pleasure of the medium and the generation of audience 'bricoleurs' flitting between texts and excelling in a complex *semiotic* televisual language (Storey, 2001). But elsewhere in postmodernism, the agency of the viewer is lost as we drown in a sea of unoriginal images which we can neither resist nor fully understand. More mundanely, other writers have asked how far the bulk of television is postmodern. For every 'weird' episode of *The X-Files* there are plenty of other modernist or realist texts in circulation, from *Friends* to *Morse* to television *news*. This barrage of opposition has encouraged some opponents to suggest that postmodernism is nothing more than another 'master narrative' designed to keep academics and cultural commentators in work.

See also: **Intertextuality, Music video, Post-structuralism, Video**

Further reading: Abercrombie (1996); Fiske (1987); Sarup (1993); Strinati (2000)

POWER

Often erroneously thought of as referring solely to the formal arena of institutional politics, power as a concept suffuses media studies, referring to any social relations of difference and struggle over resources of a material or cultural character. Most obviously, only certain people, groups and institutions in general have the power to produce and distribute television programmes and therefore to shape *representations, narratives* and meanings.

Marxists argue that power is exercised by the mass media on behalf of ruling classes or blocs. States have the power to set regulatory and legal frameworks for broadcasting (see, for example, *Public service broadcasting*) and while these are rarely the vehicle for straight censorship in liberal democracies, times of war and other crises do see governments stepping in directly. In Britain, the Official Secrets Act and D-notices (defence-notices), whereby media organisations are prevented from publicising 'sensitive' military information, are codified examples of the power available to state bodies. Similarly, the corporations that own *commercial television* are seen as gigantic capitalist institutions able to reproduce political and economic power for themselves and for a ruling class. At the heart of their project is the goal of promulgating capitalist or dominant *ideology*, opinions, beliefs and values conducive to the perpetuation of inequality. In this model, television, with other media, is able to shape cultural experience, *set agendas* and define representations of phenomena unknown to people beyond this mediated experience. Moreover, the construction of the audience's 'reality' is veiled so that their views seem normal and natural rather than ideological or, in Barthes' phrase, mythical (Barthes, 1972). A concentration of *ownership* among a comparatively small number of corporations has understandably heightened concerns about the power of the media.

There is a spectrum within Marxism going from cruder approaches, which see media power as monolithic and virtually inescapable without societal revolution, to those which recognise political and ideological conflict as a struggle between a clutch of disparate and ever-changing interests, at the core of which are ruling blocs. Gramsci's concept of *hegemony* has been particularly influential in making sense both of the cultural and ideological politics being constantly played out in media contexts, and the tenacity of traditional capitalist groups in clinging on to power. But in the final analysis, all forms of Marxism are founded on the assumption that there is, if not a single source of power, at least a fundamental social and political formation, that of *class*. This has been the basis of criticism from feminist media researchers, who have revealed the extent to which male power pervades media industries, texts and even audiences (see *Gender* and *Women in television*), from those who point to racist practices throughout the television industry (see *Race*), and from researchers focusing on age and nationality.

Other approaches to the question of power have been uneasy with explanations which are over-reliant on one or even a few social dynamics. *Pluralists* hold that power is shared by a wide range of social groups and that the media industries, while owning the means of media production, are able to reflect what audiences want and think. While this liberal-democratic view is sometimes seen as naïve (and the marginalisation of *access* and *community television* could usefully illustrate this), power has been increasingly viewed as a more amorphous and multi-faceted concept. The explosion of innovative *audience* research has illustrated that while viewers watch television in a determined context, they take control of their viewing in unpredictable and active ways (Seiter *et al.*, 1991). Fiske has even argued that television viewing can provide active audiences with a *pleasure* from resisting the dominant ideology of, say, soap operas (Fiske, 1991).

Such studies gel with *post-structuralist* and *postmodern* analyses that stress the complexity, fragmentation and 'decentred' character of contemporary political environments. They reject the idea of universal loci of repressive power organised around collective identities (such as class), arguing that power is diffuse, transient and apparent in infinite contexts of daily life. The idea that power is harnessed to hoodwink viewers is dropped in the belief that the division between reality and ideology has dissolved amid a barrage of signs and texts. In their uncertainty over meaning, audiences concern themselves with more superficial consumption and pleasure.

Related to this, *globalisation* theorists have criticised the one-dimensional perspective embodied in the notion of *Americanisation*, where power is seen to be located in US corporations responsible for exporting American culture and ideology all over the world. Globalisation theory acknowledges the capabilities of American-based transnationals, but locates the global mass media in a complex semiotic environment in which cultural products and ideas flow in multiple directions, untrammelled by national boundaries. Thus, power is enjoyed by programme-makers all over the world and by local audiences interpreting texts within their own social contexts.

On the one hand, then, postmodernists abandon traditional ideas of politics while, on the other, political rebellions the world over head for the television station before the presidential palace. Everywhere in media studies, though. power is a central issue, whether it be the power of media institutions, the power of texts or the power of audiences.

See also: **Class, Gender, Globalisation, Marxism, Ownership, Pluralism, Postmodernism, Race**

Further reading: McChesney (2000); Scannell et al. (1992); Seiter et al. (1991)

PRODUCTION

Like every form of popular culture, such as pop music, magazines or film, television is located within two, often conflicting, spheres: the cultural and the economic/financial. Fiske (1987) refers to these as the 'two economies'. This means that, on the one hand, television texts are a site of pleasure and meaning. which audiences actively exploit to forge their identities. On the other, they are goods produced for their exchange value on the marketplace and to generate profit for those that produce and distribute them. However, for a television programme to be successful as an economic commodity by winning high ratings or attracting advertisers, it has to function effectively as a cultural 'good' that offers pleasure to viewers. To achieve this it must be relevant to their lives and cultural needs. This means that the two economies are, in Fiske's view, contingent upon one another. The fact that audiences discriminate between different texts, so exercising influence in the cultural economy, has a direct impact on the exchange value of those texts in the economic or financial one. Fiske thus argues that we should think about audiences, as well as programme-makers and broadcasters, as 'producers', in that they are responsible for assembling the meanings and pleasures of television within the cultural sphere.

As a result of the unpredictable relationship between production and consumption, producing television is a hazardous business prone to failure. Many programmes. even if they adhere to tried-and-tested *genre* conventions, fail to make an impact on audiences who, for whatever reason, make a cultural choice not to watch them. In Britain, for example, the BBC invested considerable sums during the early 1990s in a *soap opera*, set in Spain, called *Eldorado*. Although some audience research had been conducted prior to running the show, it flopped and was quickly dropped from the schedules. In a highly competitive industry the disposal of a failing show like *Eldorado*, particularly from an organisation protected by a licence fee, ably demonstrates that the television market is very responsive to the laws of supply and demand.

Like other industries, therefore, television production is organised as an efficient industrial process that seeks to minimise uncertainty. In many respects, this approach is similar to the production of more obvious industrial commodities, such as cars or canned food. Abercrombie (1996) has argued that television production is separated into distinct stages within which there is a division of labour, with workers performing specialist functions. This is rather like a factory 'production line', and in order for these different aspects to work together effectively the whole operation is overseen and co-ordinated by managers who are placed at the top of a hierarchical management structure. This production-line process is well suited to television which, instead of making 'one-off' shows, often produces programmes in the series or serial format that are genre oriented (Ellis, 1982). The need for an efficient procedure that can be repeated time and again is therefore essential if organisations are to deliver programmes in the volume required.

Television production is also characterised by high fixed costs, such as studios and technical equipment. Compared to other media it is expensive to produce, with one hour of network television costing roughly ten times as much as ten hours of radio. If audiences choose not to watch a show a good deal of money is therefore at risk. Television thus requires substantial investment on behalf of broadcasters, while any programme that is commissioned is done so with fingers tightly crossed. The significant cost of new production may also disadvantage genres that have traditionally been associated with 'high-quality' programming. Tunstall (1993) has estimated that the cost of one hour of drama in Britain ranges between £400,000 and £800,000. In contrast, a soap opera, organised along the 'production-line' system discussed earlier, might cost between £100,000 and £150,000 per hour. An hour of *sports* programming is even better news for television's financiers, costing the relatively paltry amount of £40,000. While *drama* might win out in terms of acquiring status, it is unsurprising that soap and sport, with high ratings, usually win out in commercial *scheduling* decisions.

To an extent, the television industry can offset the high costs of new production and eliminate some of its inherent uncertainties by repeating successful shows, producing spin-offs from them, or importing programmes that have already been proven elsewhere. Even these strategies, however, cannot guarantee the delivery of audiences. While some individual shows, formats or genres may have proven staying power, a substantial proportion of television production is devoted to new programmes with innovative content in a bid to tap into the cultural zeitgeist. Garnham (1992) has argued that all cultural industries are led by a demand for novelty and difference, which drives them continually to produce 'prototype' material. The fashion for *reality television* shows (e.g. *Big Brother, Survivor* and *Castaway*) is evidence of the current 'flavour of the month' in television taste. In a similar vein, Garnham has also argued that uncertainties about audience demand make it necessary for a 'repertoire' of programmes to be produced, in the hope that while some will surely miss the mark, others will be more fortunate and will hit (Garnham, 1987).

While television functions as a financial or economic product at a 'macro' level, the production of texts also depends upon the creativity and craft of individuals at a 'micro' level. Marrying the organisational goals of the broadcaster with the needs of individual workers is one of the main challenges of television production. This is often resolved by keeping some occupational roles loosely defined, particularly the role of 'the producer', which allows for a flexible approach to the needs of industrial production on the one hand and creativity on the other. It has also been suggested that television production, although overseen by a hierarchical management structure, provides a degree of autonomy for specialists working within it, whether they be editors, camera operators or vision mixers. No individual can thus exercise absolute control over production, as they will not know enough about each specialised area to manage everything. In a study of management at the BBC, Burns (1977) argued that this specialisation created a 'pluralistic' rather than 'autocratic' organisational culture characterised by many 'centres' of control.

In his investigation of British television, however, Tunstall (1993) has argued that production is, in fact, 'producer driven'. Likewise, Newcomb and Alley (1983), in research on American production and producers, have also argued that television is a 'producer's medium'. In both cases the multi-skilled producer is seen as having major responsibility for making the complex job of production function efficiently. Most importantly, the television producer plays a vital role in mediating between the business of production and the creative process itself. This is very different to the role of the film producer, who is usually concerned with the provision of budgets and the allocation of resources and has little if any creative input (this is left to the director). The producer is also responsible for ensuring that television provides the required degree of novelty by having its finger on the cultural pulse. Newcomb and Alley (1983) suggest that this places producers in a delicate position. On the one hand they recognise the need to redefine genre boundaries by developing innovative programmes according to prevailing social and cultural trends. On the other, they cannot throw caution to the wind or be too cavalier in their approach, particularly given the adverse financial implications of a failed new show. The role of the producer thus demonstrates very well the conflicts that exist between activities in the economic and cultural economies.

The power of the producer thus derives from his/her supervisory role over both creative direction and the allocation of resources and budgets. As the television industry requires an increasingly high and quick turnover of new shows, delivered within tight budgets and with due regard given to genre uniformity, this supervisory role becomes all the more vital (Abercrombie, 1996). In his exploration of the history of television production in Britain, Tunstall has indicated that the supervisory role conferred on the producer was, in part, rooted in the origins of television within the civil service. After all, the BBC was originally a part of the Post Office and developed when a generation of people had sharpened their skills in organising and administrating 'centralised' utilities in wartime (e.g. coal, health, food rationing, etc.). As Williams (1997) has suggested, it was within this corporatist context that the BBC was born. During the 1920s and 1930s, therefore, the values of experts within the BBC, including producers, tended to reflect the concerns of civil administration. The personnel who filled those positions also reflected the 'elite' demographic make-up of the civil service. When job vacancies at the BBC were filled, one of the board members assessing candidates was always a civil servant, whose role it was to check that the standard of appointees was 'first class'. Stuart Hood (1987), one-time controller of the BBC, suggests that the interviewing process often centred around enquiries about which public school the hopeful candidate had attended, what sports he liked (for it was usually a he) and what his house master was called. More recently, and particularly with the advent of *commercial television*, the social and cultural credentials of television producers, including their *gender*, have become more varied, a pattern mirrored in other countries including the US.

By the 1970s, Tunstall argued (1993), British television broadcasting, both at the BBC and at ITV, had an established hierarchical infrastructure. At the top of the ladder were managers, many of whom were either active producers or ex-producers. In the middle were a cohort of skilled workers (e.g. the operators of studios, editors), while at the lowest level were clerical and administrative workers. In general, it was men who were more commonly found in the first two categories, particularly within the managerial elite, while women dominated within the clerical sphere. Producers, therefore, enjoyed privileged access to powerful positions within the major television networks, particular at the managerial level. As a result, many have stayed in the same occupation and institution for the duration of their careers. Tunstall has estimated that 86 per cent of BBC producers in 1989 had spent their entire career with 'Auntie'.

The model of production exemplified by the BBC has, however, changed irrevocably. Tunstall points out that with the emergence of Channel 4 in 1982, British broadcasting increasingly moved towards a 'publishing' system. Channel 4 stimulated independent television production as it had to commission, acquire and 'publish' programmes rather than produce them 'in house'. The intention here was to give *access* to a range of 'minority' voices that had previously been ill served by the BBC and ITV, assisted, no doubt, by the culturally conservative regime of recruiting producers that had previously existed. Later, the 1990 Broadcasting Act meant that both the BBC and ITV were also required to contract out at least 25 per cent of productions to independents. This meant that producers, who had previously led a privileged life with audiences conveniently shared between ITV and the BBC, were now subject to competition from other sources. This new competitive context has developed further with increased channel choice due to the availability of satellite and cable *technologies*. The impact of these changes has been a greater 'casualisation' of labour within the television industry and an increase in short-term contracts. Tunstall has estimated that the BBC, who found themselves with huge overcapacity in terms of studio space and technical equipment, initiated a 40 per cent cut in production capacity in 1991. By the 1990s, therefore, the television producer's position was far from being invulnerable.

See also: **Commercial television, Genre, Institutions, Policy, Political economy**

Further reading: Abercrombie (1996); Burns (1977); Newcomb and Alley (1983); Tunstall (1993)

PSYCHOANALYSIS

At first glance, the connection between television studies and psychoanalysis may not be at all obvious, but this theoretical and methodological approach, stemming initially from Freud, can provide a valuable tool for the analysis of visual texts. It has also proved useful in extending debates around the reception of media texts. Used extensively in film theory, especially feminist film theory, the psychoanalytical perspective can also be applied to the analysis of television so long as it is utilised with caution. The conditions of television viewing are quite different from those of cinema–going, and therefore as a tool of analysis this approach cannot simply be transferred wholesale from film to television. Psychoanalysis has had both its passionate adherents and its vehement critics, and its use within television studies is still highly contentious.

Psychoanalysis stems from the work of Sigmund Freud (1856–1939) who developed it as a way of understanding and treating psychologically disturbed patients in Vienna, but its basic assumptions have been developed and applied to the study of a range of cultural products such as literature, film and television.

The perspective has been used as a method for analysing literary texts since the 1930s and 1940s, and the application of psychoanalysis to film theory has become influential since the 1970s, partly as a response to *structuralism*. Much of this work has been associated with the influence of Jacques Lacan and was taken up by Christian Metz (Hayward, 1996) and developed by the feminist scholar Laura Mulvey (1975, 1979) and others. More recently, it has been applied to broader cultural areas, especially in attempts to theorise *pleasure*.

Psychoanalytical film theory now comprises an extensive and complex body of literature. Its general application to film will be outlined before assessing its use in the study of television. Freud is seen as having 'invented' psychoanalysis, as the science of mental life. He argued for the existence of an unconscious as well as a conscious mind, and his work is very much based on this initial premise. Freud made a number of assumptions: there is a link between childhood sexuality and adult mentality; adult *sexuality* results from a series of tensions created in childhood and a child's tensions with its parents; all of these tensions are universal and are found both in adult sexuality and in the adult mind.

He made the distinction between three parts of the unconscious – the id (our instinctual drives), the super-ego (the constraints of parental authority and/or society) and the ego. The conflict/tension between the id and the super-ego could be brought together in the ego – as the social, integrated individual. All this can be conceptualised as drives (often sexual or aggressive) fighting to gain precedence over socially imposed rules, and coming together in an acceptable form, though some elements will become repressed.

For Freud, the 'subject' can be unified as we mature, but this involves repressing (and thus consciously forgetting) our childhood. The unfulfilled desires and fears that we repress can, however, be subject to 'slippage': that is, they sometimes 'pop out' accidentally from our unconscious. This can occur in the form of dreams or also in what we call a Freudian slip in language (for instance, using a word that 'gives away' what we are really feeling). The analysis of dreams was what Freud called 'dreamwork'; he argued that such analysis should examine symbols rather than the overt story, which Freud regarded as only a disguise for the true underlying meanings (Marshall, 1994). This means that in dreams our repressed wishes and desires emerge from our unconscious but in a non–literal way. We may dream of an object to represent something or someone else. The analysis of dreams has become important in Freudian work, and it is through making a connection between dreams and films that psychoanalysis came to be used as a tool for analysing media texts.

Hayward (1996) outlines three related areas in which film theory has developed using this perspective: the analysis of film texts, the relationship between text and spectator, and an understanding of the mechanisms of fantasy.

Reading texts as if they were dreams and utilising Freudian and post-Freudian terminology has become a commonly accepted mode of analysis, not only for film texts but also for television and *advertisements*. For example, horror texts can be analysed in keeping with Freud's ideas on the fear of castration. Most horror films include the fear of punishment (often linked with being sexually active) and although horror films rarely show scenes in which a penis is cut off, it is not unusual for such texts to deal with the idea of castration through some form of harm, mutilation or symbolic de-masculinisation. Similarly, Bruno Bettelheim (1969) undertook Freudian readings of children's fairy tales, finding that all of them had an Oedipal theme where the young hero or heroine was pitted against an older, evil character who tried to inflict harm on them. Films such as the *Star Wars* series can be subjected to this kind of reading.

Additionally, and in a connected way, psychoanalysis has been utilised to explore text–spectator relationships. We can see that the conditions of watching a film have some similarities to dreaming, and indeed, cinema has long been regarded as a 'dream factory'. From the early days of cinema it was observed that the medium affects not so much our heads or hearts as our sexual instincts (Kuhn and Radstone, 1990). This dreamlike, eroticised experience begins from the actual social (and then psychic) experience of film-going. We generally watch films in a dark cinema, and this involves a reduction in motor activity alongside a heightened visual perception. Spectators become part of a 'regime of belief' in that dreaming and (film) reality appear to be similar states engulfing the viewer and creating the 'spectator position' (Flitterman-Lewis, 1987). It is this similarity between dreaming and cinema-going that has led cultural critics to utilise the insights of psychoanalysis. We can analyse film texts in the same kind of ways as we might analyse dreams because the state/experience is similar, and this throws some light on the relationship between the spectator and the text itself.

In considering the text–spectator relationship, the question is: if the film is like a dream, what does this imply about spectators watching the film? Again, caution must be exercised here in that the notion of the spectator in film theory is quite different from the notion of the viewer or *audience* in television theory. In the former, the spectator is an artificial construct, a position or space produced by the film text. In the latter, the viewer or member of the audience is conceptualised as a real live person, a more 'active' conceptualisation (which has become further confirmed with the development of *video* technology and games and interactive television). Thus in psychoanalytical theory, spectatorship is a state induced by the film text itself. Flitterman-Lewis (1987) suggests that we are experiencing a kind of hallucination when we watch a film and thus we are acted upon by the text. It is a passive conception of how we respond to the text – it is as if we do not have much choice as to how to respond because everything happens *to* us, not *by* us. We are positioned by the mechanisms of the film we are watching, and these mechanisms mobilise the structures of unconscious fantasy. This position on spectatorship has been much criticised by those who see it as reductionist. But it has also been highly influential, especially in aiding an understanding of how visual pleasure (and voyeurism) works.

Lacan used structuralist linguistics and a reworking of Freud to focus on the importance of language in the development of 'subjectivity' (and thus spectatorship). He argued that the unconscious is 'structured like a language', and that the subject is inevitably split and incoherent (that is, it cannot be unified). Importantly, Lacan says that our subjectivity is constructed through language, which is the realm of the social. As he puts it, we are spoken by our culture; we enter the 'symbolic order'. Lacan focuses on the 'mirror phase' of the child's development, when the child recognises itself in the mirror and sees itself as both 'perfect' and as separate from the mother, for the first time. But what it sees is a perfect, coherent self, and the child has not until this time experienced itself in this way. So the child identifies with the image, but also sees it as 'other'. This is internalised in what Lacan calls an 'ego ideal'. The moment when this happens incorporates both narcissism (love of self) and the child's entry into the 'symbolic order' (through language). The concept of the mirror phase has also been appropriated by film theory to explore a parallel experience in cinema-going when we identify with characters on the screen – a more perfect vision of ourselves.

Film theory has appropriated Freudian and Lacanian analysis to explore the relationship between text and spectator. This has involved questioning the role of the text in producing a 'spectator position' and since the 1970s has been very much bound up with the notion of a gendered spectator through the writings of Laura Mulvey and others. Mulvey's (1975) 'male gaze' thesis has been highly influential and much cited. Its influence on feminist film theory cannot be underestimated (see *Feminism*). Mulvey reworks Lacan to argue that the pleasure induced by conventional cinema is essentially a reactionary and patriarchal one that needs to be destroyed in order to release us from oppression and build a more liberated form of pleasure. Her analysis centres specifically on the pleasures of voyeurism (or scopophilia) borrowed from Freud. Although in a sense we are all inevitably voyeurs when we experience a film, Mulvey argues that conventional (classic Hollywood) cinema offers us the chance to exploit a tendency towards a 'controlling gaze'. Importantly, she links this to an explanation of the power imbalance in gender relations. In brief, she argues that, in cinema, men are coded as active and women as passive. Men are the protagonists or heroes, women are there as spectacle, as the reason for men acting or the prize for their success. Mulvey uses the term 'to-be-looked-at-ness' to describe the relation of woman to film. This is the main function of woman in film and it is accomplished by the way the camera is used. In effect the 'gaze' of the camera, far from being neutral, is a male gaze. It is a camera 'as if through male eyes'. Thus, in this view, the mechanisms of the text inevitably position the spectator as a 'male' voyeur with the female body as its object. Mulvey's feminist project aimed to destroy the conventional patriarchal pleasure induced by the conventions of cinema, and indeed, Mulvey herself co-produced a number of avant-garde films that broke entirely with scopophilia and the objectification of the female body. However, her films and her theoretical position came to be criticised as elitist and puritanical, too successfully destroying the pleasures of looking.

Critical debate, along with the revision and extension of Mulvey's thesis, has followed (Byars, 1991; Doane, 1990; Mulvey, 1979) with some doubt being cast on the use of psychoanalysis as a methodological framework (Arbuthnot and Seneca, 1990; Pribram, 1988; Stacey, 1990). For a while the approach seemed to hold out great hope for feminist analysis of a range of media texts. But many feminists have argued that psychoanalysis is inherently sexist, since it is founded on the theories of Freud, which are phallocentric (centred on the symbolic power of the penis). Simultaneously, a lively debate has developed around the possibility of a female gaze (Gamman and Marshment, 1988) and texts that address a female spectator, offering a female subject position and its associated pleasures (Modleski, 1991, 1997). For example, many popular *soaps*, and certain *crime series* (*Cagney and Lacey, Prime Suspect*) have been said to offer both a female gaze and a female subject position. Other dimensions of the debate have included the spectator positions offered to gay or lesbian spectators, and the theoretical problems (and actual pleasures) associated with the eroticisation of the male body (Dyer, 1989; Easthope, 1986; Neale, 1993).

Given the overwhelming emphasis on film, and the dimensions and trajectory of the scholarly arguments, the potential for a psycho-analytical approach within television studies is debatable and perhaps limited. Nonetheless, attempts have been made; Kubek (1996), for instance, effectively draws on Lacanian psychoanalysis to investigate father/son relations and the symbolic order in *The X-Files*. None-theless, a major problem is in considering the social (and therefore psychic) conditions of viewing, since watching television, unlike cinema-going, is a fragmented experience, subject to interruption and distinctive for its 'immediacy' and its impression of being 'live'. Thus, as Ellis (1982) has suggested, television viewers 'glance' rather than 'gaze' in a sustained way. Moreover, the largely domestic conditions of viewing mean that the 'dreamlike' qualities of the cinema are not necessarily reproduced (even when watching televised films) and this clearly throws doubt on the logic of the text–spectator relationship in psychoanalytic film theory when applied to television (Flitterman-

Lewis, 1987). Fiske (1987) has suggested that the problem resides in the different subject positions created by film and television. In particular, television constructs a range of social subjects, as opposed to the individual subject conceptualised in relation to the cinema. Television viewing, especially in the context of *family viewing*, is far more easily explained by reference to social, rather than psychological, subjectivities.

On the other hand, some aspects of the psychoanalytical approach seem to transfer more easily. The gendered, voyeuristic characteristics of the camera are evident in much television output, with examples easy to find. But this may say as much about power relations within the television industries (and therefore about masculine *hegemony*) as about the workings of the unconscious. Equally, recent debates about the pleasures of television viewing experienced by real women owe much to the theoretical convolutions of psychoanalytical approaches to spectatorship, if only as a reaction against them.

See also: **Feminism, Gender, Pleasure, Sexuality**

Further reading: Flitterman-Lewis (1987); Gamman and Marshment (1988); Hayward (1996); Mulvey (1975, 1979); van Zoonen (1994)

PUBLIC SERVICE BROADCASTING

It may seem an obvious statement, but the nature and structure of media *institutions* affects what is and is not made available to the audience. One important distinction which can be made is that between public and private forms of media. The aims, objectives and means of financing public and private media can generally be based on quite dissimilar assumptions and motivations. A useful starting point in understanding the nature of public service broadcasting, therefore, is an examination of the history, in Britain, of the BBC. Before television, the BBC was initially the British Broadcasting Company (a private body) which in 1927 became the British Broadcasting Corporation (a public body). Radio broadcasts by the BBC became the most significant medium of mass information, news and debate until the introduction of television.

Public service broadcasting can be defined as a system that operates, or is meant to operate, primarily in the public interest. Historically, 'the public' in this sense was conceived as a national body of people, only differentiated by region. This was reflected in radio stations operating as a national service and a set of regional services. Lord

Reith, the first Director-General of the BBC, wanted to bring *culture* to ordinary people. He saw broadcasting as an educational tool and one that would aid democratic principles of participation. For Reith, broadcasting could – and should – bring the best and highest of cultural offerings to the greatest number of people. Reith was against the idea of broadcasting as purely for entertainment purposes. He envisaged the listening audience as family or work groups who would listen to debates, *news*, serious music or *drama*, and who would then be given the opportunity, through pauses in transmission, to reflect upon and discuss what they had heard. But Reith's notion of culture was very much defined in upper-class terms, and his enthusiasm for the educational function of broadcasting was matched by his distaste for popular, mass entertainment. It was Reith's view, too, that broadcasters should lead, rather than follow, public taste.

During World War II, radio listeners showed a certain amount of resistance to the Reithian notion of public service broadcasting when they were able to perceive some of the more obvious propaganda produced for the war effort. *Audiences* were also exposed at this time to commercially produced American radio stations broadcasting in Europe. Such stations were much 'lighter' and more populist in tone and content. Listeners, impressed by the differences in style and programming, began to demand changes within public service broadcasting. Lord Reith resisted the pressures towards commercialisation, arguing for freedom both from commercial interests and from state intervention. He was wholly in favour of maintaining a monopoly and an independence of expression. Scannell (1990) argues that these structural arrangements were far more important to the development of broadcasting in the long term than the content or the style of programmes.

After the war, television emerged as an increasingly popular medium on both sides of the Atlantic. Attitudes had altered during the war years, and the BBC world of 'high culture' was threatened by the emergence in the 1950s of *commercial television*, after the BBC's monopoly was ended. The aim of commercial television was to maximise revenue via advertising, and therefore it has always been more likely to produce programmes on the grounds of the potential size of the audience rather than to encourage sophistication. Thus, public service broadcasting has had to adapt to keep its place. Nonetheless, commercial television need not be seen necessarily as an alternative or opposite to public service broadcasting. Initially at least, it was intended as an extension to it. Scannell (1990) certainly argues this point on the basis that commercial TV in Britain was established as

an aspect of public service broadcasting, through the creation by Act of
Parliament of the Independent Television Authority, whose brief it
was to inform, educate and entertain. However, in reality, the means
by which revenue is raised in commercial television influences policy
and programming at least as much as the government influences public
service broadcasting. This relationship is complex. In Britain, the
setting up of Channel 4 in the early 1980s illuminates the growing
recognition of the need for television that would more fully reflect the
interests of minority groups within the audience. Thus Channel 4 has
aimed to cater for diverse and previously under-represented tastes. It is
a commercial channel that has nonetheless been willing to take risks
with its programming, appealing not to the 'lowest common
denominator' but to tastes sometimes edging towards the margins of
the viewing public. As a result, commercial interest was initially slow
and cautious, although it has picked up latterly and Channel 4 is now
well established as a commercial channel operating within a modern
interpretation of public service.

A number of other constraints exist on the operation and funding of
television: political control, state and legal controls, and the constraints
of the *technology* itself. For example, the BBC, unlike the commercial
companies, has been funded through the mechanism of the TV licence
and by a special Charter from the government, so its relationship with
the state is interesting and complex. The degree to which it is
controlled is arguable, but there are examples where the state has quite
openly intervened to suppress information or to force the BBC to use
its information in particular ways. This is generally done in times of
war or other crisis.

While Britain has generally been taken as the prime example of
public service broadcasting, this does not mean that it has never
existed elsewhere. Indeed, other countries have operated along similar
lines (CBC in Canada and ABC in Australia, for instance). In the
USA, though, the dominant model has undoubtedly been a
commercial one. Public service broadcasting existed mainly in the
form of *educational television* until the late 1960s, when the Public
Broadcasting Act provided for networking of educational channels and
the setting up of the Corporation for Public Broadcasting. Soon
afterwards, the Public Broadcasting Service was established, and this
eventually took control of creative management. The most noteworthy example of innovative programming by the PBS was the
creation of the Children's Television Workshop, who made *Sesame
Street*. For many years, public service broadcasting in the USA relied
heavily on programmes bought from the BBC, but – perhaps ironically

– in 1980 the BBC entered an agreement to sell to a cable network, thus undermining the provision of 'quality' programming for public service television in America. In any case, the commercial basis of US television had never provided a fruitful seed-bed for the growth of this form of television.

In recent years on both sides of the Atlantic, there has been a massive increase in available channels through the introduction and development of cable and satellite technology. This, and the widespread use of *video*, has meant that the role and power of the audience have changed dramatically. Current debates have shifted away from issues of public service towards issues regarding deregulation and the changing relationship between providers of media and their consumers. Other developments, such as pay-as-you-view TV, may mean a greater differential within already fragmented audiences. Although the viewing public currently has a great deal of choice in terms of television channels, it can be argued that much of what is available in fact falls within a limited cultural range. It remains to be seen whether the trend towards pay-as-you-view and interactive television exacerbates this tendency or provides a liberation from established patterns. What seems likely, however, is that the viewing public of the future, far from fulfilling Reith's ideals of high culture and exposure to educational material across the social spectrum, may be accessing television according to their ability to pay.

See also: **Commercial television, Pluralism, Policy**

Further reading: Abercrombie (1996); Goodwin and Whannel (1990); Hiebert *et al.* (1991)

RACE

Much has been written in the social sciences about racial and ethnic difference and attempts have been made to theorise these terms by looking at the position of ethnically distinct groups within the wider social structure and system of power relations (Miles, 1989). In media studies, a body of literature is building up, although research specifically on television and race, particularly in the UK, has been slower to accumulate (Daniels, 1998). For our purposes, it is useful to look initially at some definitional problems.

It has been commonplace since the nineteenth century to refer to race as a set of biological features, such as bone structure or hair type, which distinguishes one human group from another. Ethnicity, on the other hand, has been viewed as a set of *cultural* features including religion, language and customs which are characteristic of a particular group.

However, categorising race in the above way has been discredited, on a number of grounds. First, no reliable scientific basis has been finally established for the sub-division of humans into 'races'. Second, for a variety of reasons, including colonisation, slavery, war and economic or political migration (as well as more friendly intermingling such as that afforded by mass tourism), recent centuries have witnessed a much greater mixing of ethnic groups within the world than was the case previously. The existence of diasporas (dispersal) of various kinds means that 'race' and 'ethnicity' are often intertwined, and the concept of 'hybridity' (Bhaba, 1994) to describe contemporary cultures is becoming more accurate. Ultimately, it can be argued that the old categorisations of 'race', which asserted and emphasised biological difference (and sometimes, by extension, the notion of racial 'purity'), have served primarily ideological purposes, particularly those of white Europeans during a period of imperialist expansionism and nationalism (Allen and Kaur, 1993).

Marshall (1994), in general terms, and Ferguson (1998), in discussing ethnic identity and the media, have argued that the term 'race' should always appear in inverted commas, partly because of the unreliable scientific status of the term, but also because in the real world issues of 'race' continue to have substantive and sometimes deadly consequences, through prejudice and discrimination. Globally, issues of racial and ethnic difference and 'otherness', whatever their scientific status, can carry important meanings for people. For Ferguson, then, it is important to resist any temptation to 'normalise' the term 'race'.

An investigation of how television or any other medium treats racial or ethnic difference might logically focus on any number of dimensions of distinctiveness. It has been observed, however (Daniels, 1998) that most public debate, as well as the bulk of the academic research on racial and ethnic identity, including that on 'race and television', has actually focused on differences of skin colour, and particularly on African-Caribbean and Asian people (mainly those originating from the Indian sub-continent) and mainly on men. In the USA, the major focus has been on relationships (and major differences of economic position and social status) between black and white sections of the population. While the terms 'black' or 'people of colour' are themselves open to doubt and dispute, conflating as they do widely varying groups and cultures, there may nevertheless be a number of reasons for this channelling of research interest. First, skin colour is the most obvious marker of 'difference' and one that continues beyond one generation. It is therefore the signifier that may have the greatest consequences for people in terms of patterns of prejudice and discrimination. Second, the most prominent recent writers in the field of ethnic identity and *representation* theory have been black male academics (Henry Louis Gates, Herman Grey, Stuart Hall, Kobena Mercer, for instance) who have been concerned to research an area previously neglected. Third, black *feminists* (bell hooks, Michelle Wallace, Jacqueline Bobo) have been significant in challenging not only white feminists but black male academics who, they say, have neglected issues of *gender* and *sexuality* in their work.

Notions of 'difference' and 'otherness' are complex and do not always imply negativity. Hall (1997b) has outlined a number of paradigms within which 'difference' has been conceptualised (linguistic, social, anthropological and psychoanalytical). He argues that while all cultures mark difference in order to stigmatise and to close ranks, difference is also, paradoxically, powerfully attractive for the very reason that it symbolises taboo and the potential unsettling of the social and cultural order.

As well as identifying these broad models of explanation, Hall locates western ideas about 'race' and the origins of media images of racial difference in a number of key historical moments, from the sixteenth century onwards, when 'difference' was racialised in the popular images produced. Hall argues that such encounters profoundly shaped ideas about racial difference.

Given these historical precursors, it is hardly surprising that *stereotypes* of ethnic and racial difference have been common in popular media and culture. Bogle's study of Hollywood cinema (1973) identified five main stereotypes, modernised and adapted but originating from, and owing much to, the racist heritage of slavery, while Hall (1981) showed how racist ideologies are constructed across a range of media, including television.

Scholarly academic debate on this subject developed alongside some significant social changes, and these in turn connected with and undoubtedly contributed to shifts in media production and practice, including toning down the crudest forms of racial stereotyping. From the 1950s onwards, it became possible to discuss race as a social issue within popular media and cultural forms. A few films such as *Guess Who's Coming to Dinner?* took a liberal, integrationist position on race relations, and a similar trajectory soon became apparent within television programmes. On both sides of the Atlantic, a slow move away from rigid stereotypes (as in *It Ain't Half Hot, Mum* or *Amos and Andy*) towards a greater variety of representations has been evident in popular television. The case of *The Cosby Show* is particularly significant in that, for the first time, US television networks were persuaded that a show featuring non-stereotypical black characters could reach a large white audience.

But the history of popular television representations is complex. The emergence of the civil rights movements and black power movements of the 1960s and 1970s helped open up debates and pushed for a more radical set of alternatives in popular media representations. While this radicalism emerged to some extent in popular film (through a series later condemned as 'blaxploitation' movies), it was hardly evident in popular television, where a more common strategy was to replace 'negative' representations with 'positive' ones. Nonetheless, these texts achieved something that had rarely been done in the popular culture of any western country, by placing black characters at centre-stage. Echoes of both the integrationist strategy and its more radical response are widely evident today in popular television programmes on both sides of the Atlantic (*The Fresh Prince of Bel Air, Sister Sister, Da Ali G Show, Goodness Gracious Me*). However, examples of racial and ethnic stereotyping persist on television screens, not least in *news* programming where members of minority ethnic groups are frequently linked to crime and drugs.

This persistence may be linked to the relative lack of minority ethnic workers in the television industry, since one of the problems in fighting stereotypes of any kind is in gaining access to the machinery that produces the images. This has been a slow process for ethnic minorities, and when a degree of access is gained there are further difficulties in deciding what kinds of representations to produce. Early attempts at rectifying black invisibility on television tended to accept non-black conventions and standards. For instance, 'assimilationism' (or 'universalism') underplays cultural or economic differences between black and white people; 'homogenisation' tends to lump people of colour together, obliterating ethnic, class or gender differences.

Mercer (1994), reflecting on developments in the politics of ethnic representation, suggests that two common strategies have emerged from these early struggles. The first, 'social engineering', is based on the argument that, given the overwhelming predominance of 'negative' stereotypes within popular media, and since any form of representation is selective, then black representation should offer 'positive' images to counter negative stereotypes ('Black is Beautiful'). In this way of thinking, black workers within the media industries bear a particularly heavy responsibility to represent their cultural roots. A second response is a reflectionist approach, which rejects the idea of 'positive' representations in favour of an attempt to fight racial stereotyping by reflecting the whole of the black community, rather than just certain aspects of it. Mercer takes issue with both of these strategies (what is the 'real black community'? what is a 'positive representation'?) and looks to *postmodern* theories of the cultural politics of difference which highlight new complexities of identity, based not only on skin colour but on a range of other factors. He argues for the need to re-write the language of representation: not to ghettoise 'otherness', but to value it.

On a slightly different tack, Daniels' (1998) work on race and television in the UK is instructive in shedding light on the inadequacy of much quantitative and qualitative research to date. She notes how the partial nature of survey data, itself often a result of lack of adequate or systematic funding, has led to a potentially skewed interpretation of televisual representations of black people in Britain. The majority of research suggests both under-representation and misrepresentation of these groups. Moreover, the findings of such work have been couched, familiarly, in terms of 'negative' representations and stereotypes, thus implying that the solution is to campaign for more 'positive' representations in future. Like Mercer, Daniels recognises a host of conceptual problems around the 'negative'/'positive' dichotomy. She also points to more prosaic issues such as the emphasis within much research on popular light entertainment programmes, especially sitcoms (see *Comedy*), the very programmes that have been most likely to produce stereotypes of any number of social groups. Citing Stuart Hall's ideas on how racist ideologies work, Daniels argues that scholars in this field need to move beyond a blanket condemnation of all television output as racist and engage with the relationship between real social and economic subordination of minority ethnic groups and the specific forms of television representation. In the USA this more specific approach has been taken by Jhally and Lewis (1992) in their study of *The Cosby Show*, where they found that what appeared to be 'positive' representations, and therefore an important leap forward in popular programming, in fact could be read as a form of 'enlightened racism', a way of underplaying the real social and economic disadvantages of many black people in the USA.

Despite a regime of negative stereotyping, it is possible to see how challenging stereotypes, and campaigning for more black workers in television and other media industries, has begun to bring about some change. Black music and style has long been accepted as 'cool', there are more black characters on television, sometimes in interesting roles, and there are an increasing number of 'authority figures' (such as newsreaders) who are black. Additionally, issues of race and ethnicity are now more likely to be openly discussed, and there is a greater acceptance that there are no homogeneous communities but a large number of different groups of people with diverse experiences and traditions. But while the representation of black people has become an important issue, other minority ethnic groups, such as Latins and Asians of Oriental origin (Chinese, Japanese, Vietnamese, for instance) remain largely excluded from mainstream television and from the academic agenda. So, as most commentators would argue, there is no room for complacency – the developments outlined here have not yet heralded the end of racism, either on or off the television screen.

See also: **Comedy, News, Objectivity, Representation, Stereotypes**

Further reading: Daniels (1998); Ferguson (1998); Hall (1997b); Mercer (1994)

REALISM

'Realism' refers to a set of codes and conventions that have been particularly significant throughout the history and development of television. The term has had a very central role within the history of visual media forms, initially because of developments in *technology*. The camera – beginning with the still camera and later the moving camera – allowed for the first time a more direct access to recording what was in the world. Earlier forms, such as landscape or portrait painting, were always patently 'artificial', allowing for symbolism and artistic licence. In terms of their relationship to 'reality', such forms were considered, at best, copies or interpretations of observable 'reality'. Thus, when the camera was invented, it was thought that it was primarily and simply a device for capturing reality (although this term is in itself problematic – see below), but it became clear very early on that the camera is a tool for interpreting reality and that it could be used to re-present and reconstruct reality in a myriad of ways. Prior to the introduction of television, from early in the history of cinema, the camera was used to picture and create fantasy as well as reality – to present, through various tricks, imagined and constructed worlds. We see this very clearly nowadays in the sophisticated special effects that are possible in the cinema and on television, but the potential for creating fantasy as well as for being 'realistic' has been there since the birth of the camera.

The crucial point is that from the outset the relationship between the 'real world' and its recording, has been complex (see *Representation*), but the assumption has been made that 'analogical' media such as photography are inherently more 'realist' than other forms.

Maltby and Craven (1995) suggest that 'realism' is a complex term with a multiplicity of meanings. They suggest that by our everyday use of the term 'realistic' we try to judge how far a media representation is like some reality that we understand or have experienced. However, realism, just like other approaches to art or the media, is heavily reliant on a system of *conventions* of representation. Similarly, it can be argued that our judgement of whether a text is realistic or not relies on the quality of the text, even if it is fictional. In other words, we can evaluate the extent of a text's truthfulness or lifelike qualities, whether or not the story is based on a real event.

So realism can be regarded as a system of conventions which represents the world to us through a series of devices. For example, television presents the viewer with *narrative* structures that are tightly patterned ways of organising reality. Television narratives tend to be recognisable, reassuring and comforting. The *soap*, for instance features regular characters, plot lines centring on domestic and personal experiences, and resolutions to the problems faced by the regular characters. Equally, while much of the content of television *news* might not appear comforting or reassuring, on closer examination it is clear that the news too is presented as a series of structured narratives. 'Real' people, 'real' events, 'real' places are used, but edited and reorganised to fit a specific time slot and to make a rounded news story. The regularity and patterning of the form can thus be seen as providing both comfort and reassurance to viewers. Similarly, television programmes, both fictional and factual, commonly give the audience a central hero or other figure with whom to identify.

In relation to television, there has been an expectation from the early days that television could, and should, 'bring the world into our homes'. An emphasis on news and other actuality reporting like current affairs, as well as a developing tradition of *documentary* on television, has deepened that link. Television news generally claims to be 'telling the truth', and there are numerous mechanisms in the regulatory frameworks of the television industries to ensure that 'balance' can be checked and 'bias' eliminated (see *Objectivity*). This is the case despite the fact that some journalists clearly recognise the selection process in which news, like any other television programme, is not reality but a realist representation. The very immediacy of much television news, the notion of reporting events as they happen, enhances the impression of fidelity to reality.

Similarly, documentary, a form which is overwhelmingly concerned with depictions of the real, is a useful genre to study when looking at how the world is actually 're-presented', but even the most seemingly basic, simple and objective documentaries (such as those using 'fly-on-the-wall' techniques) are still complex constructions. The selection of subject matter, the manner of filming, who is filming, choices over where the camera(s) should be placed, over how sound is used and over editing the raw material, all indicate that the relationship between 'reality' and the finished product is extremely complex.

Much television *drama*, though fictional (*soaps* and sitcoms, for instance) works through the conventions of realism, and recent moves into the televising of courtroom proceedings, public *access*, vox-pop and '*reality TV*', such as *Video Diaries* and *Big Brother*, have meant that the conventions of realism are to a great extent masked by what appears to be a direct, raw access to reality. The ideological implication of this point was recognised in Britain by the Marxist-influenced writer Colin McCabe in the 1970s. McCabe outlined the existence and function of what he termed the Classic Realist Text (CRT), arguing that the widespread use of realist conventions in television and film severely limited the possibilities for producing radical and politically challenging ideas. In essence, the CRT produces a hierarchy of discourses, defined in terms of an empirical notion of truth. Within this hierarchy, the narrative is given an unquestioned dominant place, which sets up 'reality' as unproblematic. This is achieved by the camera appearing simply to show the viewer what is there, and by giving the spectator a privileged position and point of view: what McCabe refers to as 'dominant specularity'. For McCabe, the CRT is a highly problematic form because it cannot, by virtue of its formal properties, show the contradictions inherent in reality. McCabe's position was challenged, particularly by Colin McArthur in relation to the British television drama series *Days of Hope* (see Bennett, Boyd-Bowman *et al.*, 1981).

Today, some television, in a bid for new styles and innovation, has moved away from the older established forms and conventions (see *Genre* and *Postmodernism*). Equally, it needs to be recognised that audiences have become more aware of – and possibly sceptical about – television realism. Nonetheless, debates about realism continue to be highly relevant to studies of both historical and contemporary television.

See also: **Convention, Documentary, Drama, News, Postmodernism, Representation, Soap opera**

Further reading: Bennett, Boyd-Bowman *et al.* (1981); Lacey (1998); Maltby and Craven (1995)

REALITY TELEVISION

The term 'reality television' is used to describe a variety of programming from *crime* and emergency-style shows (such as *Police Camera Action, Rescue 911, 999, America's Most Wanted*) to talk shows (*Kilroy, Ricki Lake*), docusoaps (*Airport, Lakesiders*) and some forms of access-style programming (*Video Nation, Video Diaries*). Reality television is generally thought to have emerged in the late 1980s in America and very quickly established itself within mainstream popular programming by the mid 1990s. The label 'reality TV' encompasses a wide range of texts which take as their subject matter real lives, real-life situations and events, and the first-person accounts of ordinary people (non-media professionals). Within this context, the personal, emotional and often intimate revelations of the first-person accounts are the driving force behind the *narrative* structure of these programmes, supported with actual footage (or dramatic reconstructions) of the events concerned. The people who participate in these programmes have usually been the victims of crime or some kind of disaster, have a life-threatening illness or have had a near-death experience, or, more simply, may have a vocation or lifestyle that can provide for interesting and entertaining viewing. One of the key elements of reality programming is the juxtaposing of the 'everyday' and the banal with the unexpected and the bizarre. Given the overtly voyeuristic, dramatic, emotive and sensationalist tendencies of such programming, the (somewhat pejorative) term 'tabloid television' is often used to describe television's current fascination with the mundane – and, more often than not, the less mundane – aspects of social reality.

However, while the recent trend for reality programming has undoubtedly contributed to new areas in factual programming the idea that television can in some way bring us closer to reality is not, in itself, new. Gripsrud (1998) states that immediacy and liveness have always been key aesthetic values of television, and that television established itself from the outset on the premise that it is *the* medium that is closest to 'the real'. Gripsrud goes on to point out that the 'everydayness' of television (in terms of its situation in the domestic context of the home) functions to convey a sense of contemporaneity about the medium, along with its (perceived) capacity for the transmission of reality in the raw. Coupled with this, according to Gripsrud, is the apparently insatiable demand for 'reality' in modern societies – an observation which has a certain resonance considering the significantly high ratings for reality programming. Dovey (2000) advances a similar argument, claiming that reality TV is the perfect form for the times in which we live, in that it provides a cultural space where contemporary anxieties are played out within a dramatic structure and in an entertaining format.

Reality television is a hybrid form, drawing on (and reworking) *generic* codes and *conventions* derived from a variety of sources such as fly-on-the-wall *documentary*, investigative and tabloid journalism, camcorder activism, social action broadcasting and docudrama. More recently, the influences of *soap operas* and *game shows* have also filtered into the genre with programmes such as *Big Brother* and *Survivor*. What is significant about reality television is the way in which it utilises new technologies (camcorders, CCTV footage and webcams) to convey a sense of authenticity and immediacy to viewers. Conversely, the poorer the quality of the footage used, the more 'real' the images and sounds presented appear to be. Hence, camera wobble, poor lighting, sound distortion, off-centre framing and disjointed editing can often operate as indexes of authenticity – as cultural markers of spontaneity which serve to bolster the 'reality effect' of these *texts*.

Critical approaches to reality television can be broadly divided into two main positions. First, a considerable body of literature (popular and academic) has concerned itself with the shock value of these programmes, criticising television producers for pandering to the lowest common denominator in parading the less pleasant side of contemporary life as voyeuristic spectacle. Second, an oppositional position has emerged wherein theorists and pundits have been keen to cite these programmes as examples of 'democratainment'. Within this approach, the emphasis is placed on the participatory nature of reality programming, which, it is claimed, represents a break with traditional forms of factual television. The fact that these programmes use real people, their lives and real-life experiences as the raw material for their content suggests that they are a more democratic form of television. Other issues relating to reality TV are concerned with ethics and social responsibility, and focus on the content of programmes which take genuine human suffering and distress as their subject matter and turn them into spectacle for mass audiences. Finally, some critics of the genre have argued that reality television presents a chaotic model of society: a decentred, ahistorical and futureless reality (Nichols, 1994) which denies real socio-historical, political and economic contexts.

See also: **Access, Documentary, Realism, Representation, Video**

Further reading: Kilborn and Izod (1997); Langer (1998); Nichols (1991, 1994); Renov (1993)

REPRESENTATION

The concept of 'representation' is central to the study of all media forms as well as more specifically to television. It is closely linked to issues of depicting reality because, although not all media texts set out to be 'realistic', many of them (*news, documentary*, much *drama*, for instance) do set out to do so, and there is a historic and specific connection between television and the idea of 'reflecting reality' (see *Realism*). However, whether a television programme sets out to be realistic or not, it always engages in a process of representation.

A good deal of research has been carried out around the way representations make meaning. Much of it has centred on the notion of stereotypes and the way they work (see *Stereotypes*). Understanding representation also takes us into an exploration of *power* and *ideology*.

It is possible to understand the term 'representation', as used in media studies, in a number of ways. First, 'to represent' can mean 'to present or depict something'. In this kind of understanding, it is useful to hold on to the idea of representation as, in fact, the 're-presentation' of the world because it emphasises the process of construction within any media *text*. In essence, this means that by virtue of the very process of making a television programme, what we see can never provide the viewer with a simple, unmediated access to the 'real world'. No matter how 'realistic' the presentation might be, what we see on screen will be a construction, involving decisions about what to select for recording, where to place the camera, how to edit the material, and so on.

A second way in which the term 'representation' is used is in the sense that one might talk of a statesperson or politician as a 'representative' of the people. Thinking of it this way, media images can be seen to represent or 'stand in for' us, the consumers. This understanding of the term can lead to thinking about how social groups are shown on television, and in particular how stereotypical representations may come about.

This way of conceptualising representation implies a good deal about the relationship of representation to reality. It implies that media representations are a reflection or maybe a distortion of something 'true' or 'real'. It is the idea that something 'real' is or was there already, and, through television or another medium, has been reflected or distorted. By implication, we can all understand and grasp what is real, and we can measure how far media images are true to that reality or how far they distort that reality.

If, in studying television, one is engaged in measuring the gap between the 'true reality' and the media representation, it could be said that 'distorted' representations of specific groups of people are those which attribute certain characteristics to the group as a whole, rather than examining the variety of attributes within that group. This could equally be applied to specific events as well as groups of people. Such representation could be seen as narrowly, and damagingly, stereotypical. Moreover, this line of argument, put forward by the Glasgow University Media Group among others, has led to the idea (and examination) of 'negative' representations (of, for instance, trade unionists) on television. By extension, the converse of negative representations would be 'positive' representations. One strategy that television programme-makers have undertaken to counter criticisms of stereotyping and negative representations has been to offer a wider range of 'positive' representations to the viewer. For example, social groups such as *women* or specific ethnic groups, seen mainly in a limited range of roles (as housewives, girlfriends and secretaries in the case of women, or criminals and servants in the case of black people) have begun to be seen in roles signifying status and authority. Such representations are seen to resist stereotypes. However, some writers argue that simply reversing the stereotype is not sufficient in itself. This is because the relationship between representations and reality is a complex one: we cannot easily understand or know what is 'real' in the first place; our social identity and position may lead to different understandings and interpretations of the same event.

A useful starting point in outlining this debate is the work of media theorist Richard Dyer (1985a) who outlined an approach to help readers understand how representations work. He noted a number of questions that could be posed regarding the sense that representations make of the world, about who, typically, represents whom and in what ways. He suggested ways in which students of media might analyse specific examples of stereotypical representations.

At the same time, Dyer also examined the question of *pleasure* – in other words, what pleasures are offered by a text and to whom? Dyer links this with a sense of self and the process of identification that is encouraged by a given television text. Put another way, he talks about how, when we watch a TV programme, we become absorbed into a character's role or position in the *narrative*, understanding their thoughts and feelings. In order to engage interest, in order to involve the viewer, media representations must provide something pleasurable. But the question is: from whose point of view is a scene, line of dialogue or image shown? Do audience members all get pleasure from something in the same way? This assumes that all can share equally in the enjoyment, which might not in fact be the case. Given social differences such as ethnicity, *class*, *gender*, age and sexual orientation, it is unlikely that all viewers would be equally at ease with the range of representations shown on television.

This issue of point of view and identification also links back to questions of power and therefore ideology. It raises the question: who has the right to speak? And who is silenced in these representations? The important point here is that representations are produced and circulate within a context of meanings (such as 'common sense') but this is governed by a system of power, offering legitimacy to some meanings and marginalising others. So some ideas and meanings come to dominate while others are left out. The predominance of white middle-class males within the media industries could lead to certain values, ideas and views of the world being over-represented on television and being put forward as 'normal' or 'common sense'. In other words, what is being represented is not 'the truth' but a representation of the truth as seen by (in this case) white middle-class males. It is in this sense that it is possible to see representations as 'ideological' (see *Hegemony*).

Dyer's approach led to a great deal of research on such things as the way stereotypes work and the part they play in limiting our ideas about people. But some recent theorists have moved on from this position. Stuart Hall (1997a) argues that although much good work has been done using the above assumption – that representations are a reflection or distortion of something real – we need to go beyond this, to see representations as constitutive. By this he means that the 'old' view is now regarded as too literal and too straightforward. We need to ask the question whether events in the world really do have one essential fixed or true meaning against which distortion could be measured. For example, if one were to take a current event such as talks between heads of state from around the world, it would be possible to agree that the talks are going on, but what they mean constitutes different things to the different participants. To even begin to understand the range of meanings you would first have to know about the history leading up to the talks, something which, in turn, is likely to be contentious in meaning. There will, even when the talks are over, never be any final fixed meaning, according to Hall's perspective. So this means that representation cannot capture the real event because what is being re-presented – that is, the initial event – is dubious in the first place. Reality is slippery, not fixed or known at all.

In a sense, then, reality has no fixed meaning until it has been represented, and the representations and the various meanings attached to them will change over time and according to whose point of view is being put forward. Hall thus argues that reality does not exist meaningfully until it has been represented. Representation does not occur after the event but becomes part of (constitutive of) the event itself. What we call 'reality' does not exist outside of the process of representation. This does not mean that there is no real material world – of course there is – but simply that the real material world has to be given meaning. Hall says that nothing meaningful exists outside of *discourse* (1997a). A fundamental point in this is that language is pivotal to the way meaning is produced (1997b).

This is a long way from where this debate started, because it implies that the task of television studies is not simply to try to measure the gap between reality and representation but to try to understand how meanings are produced through practices. To do this, we have to learn to unpick the images, get inside them and interrogate them. In outlining strategies for dealing with these issues, Hall discusses the way we communicate meanings through systems of representation (language). We classify the world and then communicate these classifications to each other. In so doing, we make and re-make the world through its representation, sometimes with serious conse-quences for those who are without a voice in this process. A random sample of any mainstream television programme or the *advertising* around it would be likely to reveal an over-abundance of certain ideas and images at the expense of others. For instance, television tends to represent developing nations and their citizens with images of poverty, starvation, ignorance and dependence, while developed nations such as the US and Britain are more usually represented as urban, educated, often rich and glamorous, even though this may not be the experience of many citizens in such societies.

So, generally, the study of how representations work is essential to an understanding of television. Although complex, such study has commonly been approached by thinking about the part played by all kinds of shared, recognisable media *codes* and *conventions* (including visual images) in actively constructing meanings.

Further reading: Dyer (1985a); Hall (1997a, 1997b); Lacey (1998)

RHETORIC

Rhetoric as a concept, with its origins in the development of political oratory in the classical traditions of ancient Greece, preceded the mass media. It came to comprise a formal branch of learning as one of the seven liberal arts in medieval Europe, and Barthes is able to describe a tradition stretching from Aristotle to the advent of modern social psychology (Barthes, 1988). In the United States, the study of rhetoric is a well-established sub-discipline of communication studies, focusing mainly (although not exclusively) on political rhetoric. This focus has been increasingly influenced by other forms of *discourse analysis*, as well as the need to concentrate on images along with speech in the analysis of contemporary political communication.

The term as employed in media studies, though used in many forms, refers primarily to persuasion or influence through a variety of formal and informal structures and processes of signification. Thus, it is argued that television producers are able to provoke an emotional response through systematic use of devices such as editing and music. An explicit example might be the way rhetoric is used in party political broadcasts to persuade viewers of the need to vote for a particular political party. Understanding these techniques and their specific usage allows consideration of the essential complexity and 'constructedness' of viewing.

The use of rhetoric in relation to media texts has been particularly profound as analysis of visual codes and signs has grown in importance. For some theorists, for instance Masterman, an awareness of rhetoric is vital because attention to the organisation of a *text*, the effects it achieves and how those effects are produced allows the analyst to escape subservience to, and in fact achieve critical liberation from, the text. Masterman argues that it is especially important to be able to deconstruct television because the processes by which it uses rhetoric are more hidden than in other cultural forms. That is, when we are at the theatre we are aware that what we are seeing is only a *representation* of reality, whereas television can make a claim to truth in its representations. This argument sees nothing sinister in the media concealing the processes by which meaning is made – indeed, some of these processes are 'inevitable' – but suspicions are voiced where television professionals are less than honest and open about the techniques they employ (Masterman, 1985). Thus newscasters who claim objectivity rather than acknowledging their rhetorical stance might be criticised on these grounds (see *News*). Some analysts working in the field of media education have advocated education of the *audience* from an early age with the objective of developing a 'more critical eye'.

Masterman offers us a list of rhetorical techniques including selection, the combination of image and linguistic text, suppression of the existence or effect of camera, crew and reporter, film and sound editing and *narrative* (Masterman, 1985).

Using television news as an example, consideration could be given to what stories were selected, what order they were shown in, the tone of the reporter, the way violence might seem to be emanating from only one side, the way the reporters' tones matched the imagery, the way in which the audience is given a particular visual point of view ('in there' with the reporter, experiencing the problems at first hand, or maybe external to the action with an uninvolved and less caring overview). An understanding of rhetoric might allow the viewer to question the actual truth or validity of the situation. So, the selection of two 'balanced' viewpoints to illustrate a political conflict might be critically assessed as setting up a limited spectrum of debate (see *Objectivity*).

Some critics have perceived a tendency in Masterman's work to identify a single meaning in a text and to tie this to the workings of a dominant *ideology*. However, the resurrection of rhetoric as a concept has been helpful in provoking a debate on the methods and meanings of various television *genres*, including *documentary* and television news.

See also: **Educational television, News, Semiology**

Further reading: Barthes (1988); Emerson (1993); Masterman (1985)

SCHEDULING

A television schedule is the running order in which programmes are placed during a day. As Ellis (2000) observes, while individual programmes may be the 'building blocks' of television, the schedule is the 'architecture', giving structure and meaning to 'blocks' of programmes on a given channel. A familiarity with the schedule allows the *audience* member to order their viewing around particular programmes, perhaps the *news* or a favourite sitcom or *soap*. This familiarity makes viewing a very habitual activity, allowing broadcasters to make concrete assumptions about who is watching and when. Predictability is important, as one of the core aims of scheduling is to assist broadcasters in capturing the biggest audience possible, thus maximising *advertising* revenues. The careful scheduling of programmes in particular slots may also allow a broadcaster to win viewers away from other television channels. As a result, scheduling has become increasingly important as an aspect of competitive 'ratings wars'. For example, by placing popular programmes either at peak viewing time or when a competitor's programming is poor, or by hiding weaker programmes at quieter times in the schedule, a broadcaster can increase the number of people tuning in to their station. Often, less popular or newer programmes are squeezed between two established programmes in the schedule, a process called 'hammocking', in the hope that viewers already tuned in will keep watching. A consequence of these activities is that the scheduler is effectively responsible for creating a *'narrative'* of viewing in which different programmes, old and new, are blended together into an enticing package (Ellis, 2000).

With increasing competition in the television market, due largely to the availability of more channels via satellite, cable and digital *technologies*, it has become harder for broadcasters to ensure viewer loyalty to their channel. In this context, efficient scheduling pays an even greater dividend. Abercrombie (1996) argues that broadcasters used to make their programmes first and then decided when to schedule them. Now their foremost concern is about ratings and capturing particular audiences, so they decide the schedule and then commission programme-makers to produce shows for specific slots. As a result, scheduling is crucial to the strategic planning of television companies and is more often than not the responsibility of senior managers.

However, broadcasters do not always have the freedom to schedule programmes when they see fit. Sometimes they are restricted by laws and mandates telling them what kind of programming they can show and, on occasion, when they can show it. As a result, scheduling strategies vary from place to place. For example, in post-war Britain successive governments have placed restrictions on the content of terrestrial television channels, including the BBC, ITV and more recently Channel 4 and Channel 5. This is because British television has developed within a model of *public service broadcasting*, which dictates not only the mix of programmes that have to be shown (which must include news, educational programmes and 'minority' programming) but also, on occasion, where in the schedule some of those programmes should come. Paterson (1990) has suggested that, in comparison, American television has developed along a more *commercial* model, with fewer legal restrictions on scheduling or content. In this climate American broadcasters have been able to pursue an aggressive 'jugular' approach to scheduling, where each broadcaster simply tries to maximise their ratings and take viewers away from other stations.

Perhaps the most important skill of the scheduler is to match programmes to audiences watching at different times of the day. For example, *children's television* usually starts in the middle of the afternoon, when children come home from school. Major news bulletins are also reserved for times in the schedule when adults come home from work. *Soap operas* are an example of a carefully scheduled *genre*. Viewed by many theorists as a genre for *women*, they are traditionally screened during the daytime when, supposedly, many women are (or were) working in the home. In its infancy during the 1930s, the soap opera developed as a radio serial sponsored by soap manufacturers, such as Proctor and Gamble. Here, the genre developed to meet both the needs of broadcasters who wanted to win high daytime ratings, and the needs of advertisers who wanted to capture the mind and money of the person controlling home finances. In their view this was the housewife, who would be most likely to watch daytime television in gaps between household jobs.

Clearly, this approach to scheduling assumes that people, particularly families, watch television in very predictable ways. Indeed, Paterson has argued that schedules are carefully constructed around models of *family* behaviour. These assume, for example, that people eat meals throughout the evening or do household chores while the television is on. In response, schedulers commission many pro-grammes, such as soaps, that can be watched without the viewer paying full attention to the television set. The break-up of a soap into small narrative segments, lasting only a few minutes, means that we can easily 'lock back on' to the story, even if we have missed the preceding segment. However, schedulers not only have to respond to chaotic household conditions, but they must also tailor their schedules to accommodate *when* different family members are watching. It is commonly accepted by broadcasters that children dictate viewing in the early evening, until 7.30 p.m., while women will take over control for the next ninety minutes, with men directing programme choice after 9 p.m. This *gendered* behaviour affects the content of the schedule, with 'serious' current affairs or documentary programming coming later in the night. This decision clearly carries with it a 'common-sense' view of male and female viewing preferences that reveals disparities in cultural power between men and women. Many *feminist* scholars have taken this as evidence that television plays a role in upholding patriarchy. For 'serious' programming is gendered 'masculine', and brings with it a high cultural status that is borne out in the practice and content of late-night schedules, when full attention can be paid to the television set. Women's interests, on the other hand, are perceived to be located in the personal rather than the public sphere and are represented in programmes like soaps, which suffer low cultural status despite high viewing figures. This lower status relegates these shows to a time when the home is often dominated by noisy distractions. Although schedulers are clearly working with an archaic perception of *family viewing* behaviour, based around very conservative stereotypes, the idea of the 'typical' family viewing unit remains very influential on their decisions.

Scheduling also has an important role in regulating our *experience* of television viewing. Raymond Williams (1974) has argued that television is not received as a set of discrete and distinct programmes, but as a flow or sequence of images and feelings that we absorb over a whole day or evening. Most programmes are broken up by adverts or by trailers for other items, which are not directly related to the narrative of the show being watched. For Williams, this leads to a disjointed and uneasy experience that diminishes the quality and experience of viewing. However, for a commercial broadcaster, maintaining the flow of viewing is crucial. It is hoped, for example, that popular programmes will 'hook' people into the sequence of items offered on a particular channel, while trailers will remind viewers of upcoming pleasures so that they do not hop across to another station. The scheduler's art, then, is not in placing individual programmes into the itinerary, but in creating a seamless televisual flow that secures channel loyalty. When we look at a television schedule it gives the illusion that we are watching a set of distinct events when, in actuality, we are not.

Nowadays, however, this seamless flow of viewing is increasingly difficult to maintain. Many people own video recorders (in 1994, 77 per cent of British homes had a video) and do not watch programmes when they are aired. This makes it hard for schedulers to dictate or predict television consumption. Similarly, many of us now enjoy a range of channel choices due to the emergence of satellite, cable and digital technologies. The audience fragmentation that this creates makes it more challenging for broadcasters to pitch their schedules

SCIENCE FICTION

against those of competitors, as it is unclear who is watching what and when.

See also: **Audiences, Advertising, Commercial television, Family viewing, Public service broadcasting**

Further reading: Abercrombie (1996); Ellis (2000); Paterson (1990); R. Williams (1974)

SCIENCE FICTION

Science fiction is a complex *genre*, found on television as well as in other forms of media. While it might be possible to take a *drama* programme about space travel and state unambiguously that it fitted within the category of science fiction, there are many films and television programmes which share the *conventions* of other genres, such as *comedy* or *crime*. Moreover, science fiction has a couple of close relatives in the horror and fantasy genres. Thus there is scope for overlap and generic confusion, and increasingly television programmes mix or play with the conventions of different genres. In these cases, it is sometimes argued that such texts are examples of *postmodern* television. A good example of this tendency is *The X-Files*, which mixes science fiction with the crime/FBI detective genre, and in some episodes also incorporates parody or horror. Science fiction has been successfully combined with comedy in such series as *Red Dwarf* and *Third Rock from the Sun*.

Televised science fiction has a long history, but as a literary and then radio and cinematic genre its roots are even deeper. Around 160 AD, the Greek storyteller Lucian formulated a science-fiction story about getting to the moon. In more recent times, the genre, especially in literature, has flourished, mainly since the Industrial Revolution, when machinery and science became far more central in people's lives.

As well as existing in the popular literature of the nineteenth century (*Frankenstein*, for instance), science fiction developed at this time in magazines, and later in radio and the cinema, before it was taken up and adapted for television. The genre has been popular with audiences and programme-makers alike and has proved a resilient and adaptable genre over time. While in its cinematic form the genre has grown to rely heavily on expensive special effects (examples include the *Star Wars* series and *Independence Day*), in its television variant science fiction has more often existed in the long-running-series format (*Dr Who, Star Trek*). This can mean relatively low budgets

207

through the establishment of regular characters and the repetition of sets. Generally, science fiction on television has taken the form of the half-hour self-contained episode, although the more serious drama versions might last for an hour per episode. Much television science fiction has been aimed at a young audience, although its popularity seems to suggest an appeal to a wider, though largely male, group (Leman, 1991). Some series have attained cult status, and many of the more popular ones have developed huge devoted fan followings complete with clubs, conventions and symposia (see *Fans*).

Science fiction tends to deal in metaphors, and it has the advantage that it can escape the confines of naturalistic and realistic conventions (see *Realism*). Its content and even its form are very often symbolic representations of something other than what is manifest, and it has consistently been a genre within which alternative views of social, cultural and political arrangements can be explored and debated. In recent years, it has been a particularly fruitful genre for feminist and other women writers, for example (Doris Lessing and Margaret Atwood, to name but two). Thus, where readers or viewers might be presented with a narrative about distance (in time and/or space), often the meaning of the text can be read as signifying something much closer to home, such as fear of changing social roles or, more optimistically, the imaginary exploration of the possibilities of social change. The television series *Dark Skies* is a good example of this phenomenon in that it seemed to take a sidelong glance at issues such as changing gender roles.

Although science fiction is generically complex, it is distinguished by a number of familiar themes and characteristics. First, science fiction takes its departure point as real scientific and technological development. Many science-fiction texts extrapolate from an actual invention to the possible ways in which it might be used or abused (weaponry, computers and biological experimentation are common examples). Therefore, although it is fiction, it begins with 'fact' and can be seen as based in the rational and the explicable. Second, science-fiction texts are based on the present or look ahead to the future. They have narratives centred around travel to other dimensions (time, space) and form a debate about what might happen to human society, for better or for worse, under changing conditions. Science fiction could thus be described as dealing in prophecy and unease. For example, a frequently occurring theme centres on invasion by 'other', usually alien, beings from elsewhere (one example from early British TV is *Quatermass*, and a recent US example is *Dark Skies*). Thus a third characteristic of the genre is that future societies tend to be viewed in either a dystopian (gloomy, pessimistic, apocalyptic) or a utopian (positive, optimistic, progressive) light. Within such visions, key figures such as scientists, military leaders and politicians may feature as representatives of repressive or potentially liberating ideologies and practices (*Dr Who*, *The X-Files*). Likewise, beings from other times or places may be viewed as benign visitors, bringing hope, peace or enlightenment to the world, or alternatively as aliens who, in contrast, are by definition malign, destructive and potentially permanent forces.

All these features distinguish the genre from that of horror, which frequently looks back at the past and attempts to deal with the non-rational, the supernatural or the inexplicable. Since World War II (and the atomic bomb) there has been an increasing tendency to combine elements within the science-fiction and horror genres (as in the *Alien* trilogy and, once again, *The X-Files*), possibly because the growing potentials to destroy the world and to travel to other planets are both real creations of science. Totalitarianism versus democracy, ecological disaster versus conservation of the earth's resources, changing *class* and gender identities and relationships, fears about over-population, international warfare, the *globalisation* of communications, have all been real debates and real issues in the latter half of the twentieth century, and all of these have been represented in fictional form through the science-fiction and horror genres.

Cultural critics have long regarded science fiction as a low-status, somewhat disreputable form, frequently regarded as 'pulp' fiction. Its cult status and the phenomenon of fandom associated with the genre have, if anything, only increased this tendency, although serious academic consideration has been given to some televisual versions of the genre recently (see Lavery *et al.*, 1996). Despite its status, science fiction remains an intriguing and significant area of consideration for the student of television. It is one of the only popular television genres which allows a framework for difficult philosophical and political debate. The articulation of questions based on 'What if this were to happen?' provides a way of considering collective hopes and fears and may work as symbolic manifestations of a shared unconscious. Seemingly lightweight popular texts can thus function as collective catharsis by representing mythically the fears and concerns that are commonly shared.

See also: **Convention, Drama, Genre, Postmodernism, Realism**

Further reading: Lavery *et al.* (1996); Leman (1991)

SEMIOLOGY/SEMIOTICS

Semiology – or semiotics – is usually defined as the science of *signs*. For those unfamiliar with semiotic terms this definition can be a little misleading. Although we are used to thinking of signs as particular kinds of symbols – like a traffic signal or the wave of a hand to mean 'goodbye' – the word 'sign' in semiotics has a much more pervasive meaning. A more straightforward definition of semiotics or semiology would be to call it the study of meaning.

The origins of semiotics/semiology go back to the early twentieth century. In the United States the logician C.S. Peirce developed a semiotic theory of signs, and in Europe the linguist Ferdinand de Saussure posited semiology as a broad field of which linguistics was a part. However, it was not until the 1970s that semiology began to be widely used and developed, most notably through the work of Roland Barthes in France and Umberto Eco in Italy. Semiotics has, since then, exerted a considerable influence on the study of media and *culture*.

The semiotic approach begins with the assumption that the meaning of words, images or objects is neither natural nor inevitable. Meanings do not come with mental labels attached to them, they are socially constructed. So, for example, we understand that a chair is something to sit on and that a banana is a fruit because we are taught that this is so. The meaning of things is inscribed within *discourses* (we are told that a chair is something to sit on and that a banana is in the same category as apples, pears and so on) and social practices (we see people sitting on chairs and see bananas in fruit bowls). The meaning of things is therefore fixed by culture, not by nature.

The central unit of meaning is the sign. A sign refers to anything that has a meaning, be it an object, a word, an image or a symbol. Like a mechanic who takes something apart in order to see how it works, semiology deconstructs meaning to see how it is constructed. The sign is therefore broken down into its component parts. The sign is made up of a signifier – which is the object, word, image or symbol before it has been given a meaning – and the signified – which is the meaning we associate with it. The equation at the heart of a semiotic approach is therefore:

signifier + the signified = the sign

The signifier and the signified exist in very different realms. The signifier exists outside our heads in the material world: we relate to it by using our senses (we hear, see, touch, taste or smell it). The signified, on the other hand, has no material presence. It is what we think of or feel in response to the signifier, and it therefore exists purely in our minds. Because these two realms are separate, they can never be permanently attached to one another. The relation between the signifier and the signified is therefore something we construct.

It is for this reason that communication – whether interpersonal or mass communication – can never be perfect. For us to communicate what we are thinking (the realm of the signified), we cannot pluck the thoughts out of our brains and put them in someone else's head. We must transform them into the material form of a signifier – a written or spoken word, a picture, a gesture, etc. These signifiers then represent what we are thinking, but because they are interpreted by someone else to become meaningful (or, in other words, to become signs) we cannot guarantee that what the other person is thinking is an exact reproduction of our thoughts. Communication, in this sense, is a process of *representation* and interpretation. This is, perhaps, a more precarious process in mass communication than in interpersonal communication: in mass communication the producer will not know who their audience is or be able to interact with them to ensure certain meanings are understood.

The distinction between the signifier and the signified is, of course, a theoretical one. The moment we encounter a signifier – even if it is an object or word that is unfamiliar to us – we give it some kind of meaning. So, for example, an English-speaking person coming across a new word – perhaps an uncommon word like 'ziggurat' – will try to make some sense of it, even if only to assign it to a category like 'foreign-sounding word, probably a noun'.

Once we make the distinction between signifier and signified, the nature and source of meaning becomes clearer. Meanings are formed by a process of association and difference. Many infants will learn, for example, to associate mother with breast-milk. We also learn to differentiate between mother and creatures like mother, between mother and objects unlike mother (or what we could call 'systems of difference'). Or, as adults, we might learn to associate a French accent with sophistication and charm, an association that works within a system of difference (the accents that are not French, such as German, Cockney, etc.).

A sign's meaning is thereby dependent upon the context in which it appears. The meaning of a car, for example, may change from one context to another. Advertisements generally show cars gliding through pristine empty landscapes, a context in which the car may signify notions like speed, freedom, *power* and adventure. However, for someone sitting in traffic in a smog-infested city the car may signify a very different set of meanings, such as pollution, congestion and inefficiency. Semiotics draws our attention to the cultural or symbolic environment – the set of semiotic structures that establish or encourage meaning in our society. The fact that people within a culture inhabit similar cultural or symbolic environments – in families, schools or through mass media – explains why people can communicate successfully and agree about the meaning of things. Umberto Eco (1981) refers to these semiotic structures as frames (so we might have the 'supermarket frame', the 'office frame' or the 'classroom frame').

The distinction between the signifier and the signified also enables us to distinguish between different types of sign. In the case of language, for example, before it has been 'fixed' by social convention the relationship between the signifier and signified is usually completely arbitrary. The word/signifier 'apple' – a set of five digits or a two-syllable sound – has no relation to the thought/signified that we associate with it, which is likely to be a visual representation of an apple or our memory of what an apple tastes like. The word is a symbol: it stands for something else, in the case of language something with which it has nothing in common. We generally use language to refer something to the realm of objects, and it is those objects – rather than the words themselves – we tend to think of when we speak, listen, read or write. There are exceptions to this rule: words like 'splash' or 'cluck' refer us to sounds not unlike splash or cluck, while words like 'and' or 'but' have no deliberate reference outside language, hence the objects they signify might be the words themselves. In general, however, language consists of what semioticians refer to as symbolic or unmotivated signs. Other examples of symbolic signs systems might be Morse code or the system of semaphore.

Non-linguistic signs, such as images or objects, tend to involve a less arbitrary relation between signifier and signified. A banana or a picture of a banana are both likely to have some relationship to the thought we conjure up in response (such as a mental image of someone eating a banana). This is not guaranteed – we may think of someone falling flat on their face – but it is more likely that the signifier and the signified will have something in common (e.g. one will look like the other). These signs are referred to as motivated or iconic signs.

We can also distinguish between levels of meaning, or between denotation and connotation. A denotative meaning is the more literal meaning we give to a sign. In the case of words, this will be a dictionary definition or definitions (a word can have more than one denotative meaning); in the case of more motivated signs like photographs, it will be the mind's attempt to reproduce the image (we connect a picture of a car to a mental image of a car).

A connotative meaning is a more metaphorical or symbolic meaning. So the word 'rose' (or the image of a rose) may connote the idea of romance, love or beauty; a banana may signify a lush, tropical landscape to someone living in a cold climate, or work to an employee on a banana plantation. While denotative meanings tend to be limited, a sign can have an enormous range of connotative meanings (see *Polysemy*).

Semioticians stress that the denotative meaning is no more natural or important than the connotative meaning. It is, however, a level at which there is likely to be more agreement within a culture. It is therefore the realm of connotation that tends to be more contested, and therefore of more interest to those using a semiotic approach in television studies. Does news of a strike connote a recalcitrant workforce or an exploitative employer? Does the word 'welfare' connote images of black people or white people, the deserving or the undeserving poor? What does the use of an extreme close-up of someone's face connote? It is in attempting to answer such questions that semiotics enters the realm of cultural analysis and cultural politics.

Semioticians will explore the way cultural texts, whether the layout of a supermarket, a poem or a situation comedy, create meanings. In media studies the focus will often be on the way a text promotes or prefers one set of meanings over another (see *Encoding and decoding*). Semiology is thus concerned not only with the appearance and cultural meaning of signs, but with their arrangement (see *Narrative*).

One of the most powerful semiotic structures in our culture is what Roland Barthes refers to as 'myth'. Myth, in this context, does not refer to fables or legends, but to the juxtaposition of signs to create a meaning. This meaning is mythical in the sense that it does not operate on the level of logical or causal argument, it simply asserts or implies an association (which may or may not be verifiable). Most *advertisements* use this mythic form. Commercials that present an argument about the merits of a product now look almost quaint and old-fashioned: most contemporary ads simply juxtapose two signs, the product and a sign whose connotations we are intended to associate with the product.

So, for example, a soft drink may be juxtaposed with images of attractive, popular and exuberant young people, or athletics equipment with a well-respected talented athlete. While the commercials do not make any overt claims about the quality of the product, they construct a series of mythic connections: for example, this is the drink that signifies you're young and hip; this is the equipment of superior style and quality that the best athletes use. The great advantage of this semiotic construction is that it gives the advertiser the freedom to make a wide variety of claims (associating cars with sex, breakfast cereals with happy families, cigarettes with active, healthy people, and so on) without apparently claiming anything.

This semiotic device is becoming increasingly significant in contemporary politics. A media event that shows a politician doing ordinary things with ordinary folk creates an association between the two, even if the politician actually favours policies that benefit the rich at the expense of middle- and lower-income wage earners. A series of stories about poor people cheating the welfare or social benefit system creates the myth that such people are typical. Or, in Roland Barthes' famous example, a black soldier saluting the French flag invokes a mythical story about the benefits of French colonialism. One of the aims of semiotics in television and media studies is to identify and disentangle these mythic structures, and to thereby use semiotics to reveal aspects of contemporary ideology and culture.

See also: **Discourse, Polysemy, Sign, Text**

Further reading: Barthes (1988); Eco (1981); Fiske (1987)

SEX/SEXUALITY

All known societies have their own sexual customs and norms, and all operate sanctions on sexual behaviour as well as on sexually explicit images or material (see *Pleasure*). Customs and controls, however, are culturally variable and are liable to change over time. For example, social attitudes to such practices as incest, polygamy or homosexuality have ranged from encouragement to outright demonisation. In most societies, dominant attitudes, articulated through a range of *discourses* such as religion or science, have succeeded in making certain areas of sexuality taboo or subject to high degrees of control. Eventually these ways of thinking can (and have) become institutionalised in law.

It is unsurprising, then, that where sex and television are concerned, public debate has long centred on the extent to which sexually suggestive or explicit material should be allowed on the screens. Interest groups as diverse as fundamentalist religious organisations, anti-censorship lobbies and anti-pornography feminists have pitched in to express strong but contradictory feelings about the subject, and concern has been shown about the moral risks to children and young people in the availability of televised sexual images. In short, sex on television has been subject to committed polemic, strict regulation and censorship.

Within media and television studies, these discussions have been navigated and extended in a variety of ways: for instance, becoming part of a more general debate about media *effects* and influences. Sexuality has also been conceptualised as an aspect of identity, and academic approaches have been dominated by how sexuality is *represented* and signified. Moreover, the subject has been informed by theoretical approaches including *psychoanalysis, feminism* and 'queer theory'. Thus, the public concerns outlined above are only a small part of a broader critical debate.

Before more fully outlining some of the ways in which television studies has picked up this set of issues, it is useful to clarify some terms of reference. 'Sex' has a dual meaning. First, it refers to biological characteristics associated with being male or female. Second, it is used to refer to particular acts (as in 'to have sex'). 'Sexuality' usually refers to sexual orientation, desire, preference or practice, and though linked is distinguishable from both 'sex' (as in the first meaning above) and *'gender'* (meaning the social and cultural roles developed by being male or female). Nonetheless, the potential for overlap of these terms is considerable, not least because sex, gender and sexuality are seen by many as inextricably linked.

It is possible to identify a number of competing perspectives on sex and sexuality which have influenced the direction of recent debate. The essentialist position sees men and women as marked by innate biological (hence 'essential') differences, from which sexuality follows 'naturally'. In this view, heterosexuality is the biological norm, whereas homosexuality is a deviation from the norm. Although this position has been critiqued, both by theorists and by sexual minority activists, it is a view that has been hard to shake, and arguably it has also formed the foundation of the majority of media representations.

The social constructionist approach is a critique of essentialism which holds that sex and gender are in fact separable items, with gender and, by extension, sexual preference being learned in particular cultural contexts. In some forms, the constructionist argument can be somewhat deterministic, though with society rather than biology as the determinant.

Following this rejection of the biological argument, other ways of thinking about sexuality have developed within the less deterministic framework of what might loosely be termed 'identity politics'.

Emerging out of changing social conditions, attitudes and practices from the 1960s onwards, identity politics has also interacted with theoretical debates. From psychoanalysis, for example, debates on sexuality have utilised Freud's emphasis on the role of the unconscious, which, he argued, does not recognise a biological sexual distinction. Rather, Freud suggested that we are born with a 'polymorphous' (unfocused) sexuality, which later solidifies into heterosexuality if we develop 'properly' and learn to associate with one sexual 'side' rather than the other. Although Freud's view of sexuality, with its insistence on male as active and female as passive, has been criticised for being 'phallocentric' (and therefore too focused on male sexuality), it has nonetheless been seen as an important starting point for later debates. For instance, Lacan argued that sexual difference is established at the moment of entry into the symbolic order (see Psychoanalysis), but he in turn has been criticised, particularly by some feminists, for his understanding, borrowed from Saussure, of male and female as binary opposites inscribed in language (Brooker, 1999).

Foucault developed a fully anti-essentialist approach, arguing that sexuality is socially scripted in that we can potentially desire anything or anyone, if the conditions are right. But in conventional modern societies, there is little encouragement to diversify. Instead, sexuality is controlled and regulated so the discourses that support a clear (hetero)sexual identity dominate. While Foucault's account allows for a more fluid conception of sexuality, it can also be seen as a pessimistic view, given its emphasis on the *power* of certain privileged positions (Brooker, 1999).

Garber (1997) and Butler (1990) offer alternative ways of conceptualising sexuality, seeing it as self-determined, as more a matter of choice than of destiny. Garber emphasises bi-sexuality as a 'third kind' of sexual identity, while for Butler sexuality is not so much a fixed position or identity as a process, always subject to contradiction, lack of clarity and the potential for change. In this sense, sexuality is likened to an unfolding performance. These approaches, chiming with *postmodern* accounts of *culture* (including sexual practices and identities) as somewhat free-floating, are nonetheless careful to point to the continuing predominance of heterosexual norms. These norms are generally evident within television and other media *texts*.

The 'compulsory heterosexuality' or 'heterosexual recuperation' embedded in most texts has been the focus of interest for many media and television theorists, but this needs to be understood in the context of more general considerations of ideology and representations of sexuality in media. Sexuality is central to an understanding of how *women* have been represented and signified on television and in other texts such as films and *advertising*. Feminist critics have long commented on the narrow range of roles offered to women, many of which define women according to their sexuality (or more specifically, heterosexual appeal) and as possessions of men. Moreover, the sexual objectification of women is apparent throughout a range of media texts, especially, though by no means exclusively, in relation to stars and celebrities. Some feminist writers have thoroughly implicated sexualised images and especially pornography with a more general degradation of, and violence against, women in patriarchy (Dworkin, 1981). Others argue for greater opportunities for women to gain control over erotic images. From the latter perspective, it is not the availability of sexually explicit material that is the problem, but the type of representations of sexuality involved and the fact that the majority of such material is produced within male-dominated media *institutions* (Lau, 1993).

It is clear that even in television programmes where the main function of a role is not necessarily decorative (such as reading the news), conventional sexual attractiveness, defined by age, size and shape, is usually considered a given for women (Walkowitz, 1997). Additionally, in many television texts female sexuality is often seen as the threat, problem or mystery that sets the narrative in motion. However, female sexuality need not be read negatively. Popular television genres such as *soaps* can empower women by means of roles that link sexuality to economic strength (more usually associated with men) and to self-determination. According to Brown (1987), female soap characters regularly use their sexuality to achieve their ends (such as getting a man to marry them) within a patriarchal world, but rarely are their bodies objectified for male desire in this *genre*. Rather, women's sexuality is associated with female pleasure and control, qualities that female viewers find appealing. Interestingly, this is one of the few television genres where middle-aged and older women are shown to have an active sex life or to show sexual desire.

Men's sexuality, in contrast, has been largely absent from television or cinema screens, and until fairly recently has been discussed only infrequently by academics. Dyer (1985b) argues that, like air, male sexuality has been invisible and taken for granted in media texts, unlike female or supposedly 'deviant' sexuality. Dyer's point is that the sexuality of both men and women tends to be represented indirectly by symbolism. In the past this was for reasons of censorship and public *taste*, but over time the boundaries have changed. Even now, when far more explicit sexual imagery is available for consumption, sexuality and eroticism are still likely to be implied by association with objects or shapes. Dyer argues that where male sexuality is suggested, its symbolism is overwhelmingly centred on the genitals, especially the penis. This suggests that all male sexuality is 'in' the penis and that it is somehow separate from the man, with a will of its own ('the beast below'). Objects used to symbolise male sexuality (in the almost absolute circumstances that ban erections from view) include trains, guns, swords and cigars, so male sexuality comes to be associated 'naturally' with power and domination. In general, then, media representations do not encourage a view of male sexuality as tender or beautiful, especially in the manifold instances where this is equated with economic power.

But in recent years, representations of male sexuality have opened up, along with debates about these representations. Men's bodies are more frequently sexualised, and arguments around the theoretical implications and possibilities of a 'female gaze' have taken their own trajectory (Gamman and Marshment, 1988). Meanwhile, women (and gay men), many of whom are likely to be oblivious to this academic wrangling, have found an increasing number of male bodies to ponder and admire on their television screens. However, increasing narcissism, body-consciousness and eating disorders among men may be unwanted side-effects of some important functional changes in men's lives, many of which have been articulated through media texts (Faludi, 2000).

It can be argued that while male and female sexualities are signified in quite different ways on television, both are chiefly informed by an underlying heterosexual norm. Thus, sexualities which may be regarded as diverse (and possibly liberating) are usually represented as deviant, and have to struggle for space and legitimacy against more conventional notions of heterosexuality and masculine dominance (see *Hegemony*). Larry Gross (1995) has called this the 'symbolic annihilation' of sexual minorities.

Given the prominence of conventional ways of thinking about sexuality, television producers have in the past been cautious about offering points of identification that are not obviously heterosexual. Christianity long ago turned homosexuality into a sin, and this pervasive religious influence has meant that diversity in sexual preference became impossible to discuss within media texts until the 1960s, when censorship rules and attitudes began to relax. Before that, the media industries either steered clear of the subject altogether or dealt with it in such a heavily coded way that only members of sexual minorities themselves would be likely to pick up the references. This clearly had (and has) implications for gay men and lesbians, who have been at the periphery of a number of spheres, including that of representations. As Geraghty and Lusted (1998) have pointed out, the aim of marginalised groups, including 'queers' (renamed from within gay and lesbian communities as a strategic attempt to both acknowledge and wipe out 'difference') has been to open up the possibility of dialogue about the politics of sexual diversity. Gaining more representation is not an end in itself, as can be clearly demonstrated by examining the contradictory ways in which sexual minorities have been represented on television.

From the 1960s, gay men began to gain visibility on television (lesbians were still virtually absent at this time). However, they were almost always shown as figures of fun, usually mincing and effeminate and generally figuring in the context of *comedy* programmes. The emergence of lesbianism was just as problematic. First, there was an almost total denial of the possibility of lesbian experience, followed by predictable butch/femme stereotypes. Shifts in public taste over time, along with important legal changes on both sides of the Atlantic (legalising homosexual acts between consenting adults) have together contributed to a more liberal tendency within mainstream media texts and a greater occurrence of 'sympathetically' treated gay themes. Nevertheless, many programmes offer an anti-homophobic position but at the same time frame this from a heterosexual perspective. In the popular television comedy *Friends*, for example, the 'boys' frequently engage in playful banter that could be read as having homoerotic connotations. But the characters always make it clear that they are neither gay nor homophobic. Their heterosexuality is central.

While there has been recognition that gay sexuality can be titillating to a straight audience, programmers have increasingly come to recognise and value the gay audience. The more visible profile of gay groups, along with recognition of the so-called 'pink pound' and dollar, has led to a desire to reach the gay market without alienating the straight viewer. According to Clark (1995), in a consideration of advertising and other media texts, one move of late is to produce a 'dual marketing strategy': that is, a range of images which are ambiguous or which can be read differently by different groups. These 'gay window ads' avoid overt references to sexual orientation; thus both gay and straight consumers are offered points of identification, allowing them to make sense of cultural forms in ways that are meaningful or pleasurable to them.

So it is possible to chart some move away from gross stereotypes over time. On the other hand, it is still possible to detect in some texts an association between gayness and deviance, perhaps more so since the onset of AIDS and its media-generated link with homosexuality. Thus, a number of *dramas* over the years have featured gays and lesbians as killers, neurotics or misplaced persons (O'Sullivan *et al.*, 1998). Even where popular television has featured apparently 'ordinary' gay characters or actors, broadcasters seem to have lost their nerve, either killing them off (Beth Jordache, a lesbian character in the UK soap *Brookside* committed suicide) or having the programme discontinued altogether, as in Ellen de Generes' fate in *Ellen*.

Nonetheless, it is important to recognise the development of programmes aimed specifically at, and often made by, gay people. In the UK, gay magazine programmes such as *Out on Tuesday* were relatively successful, though short-lived, and the drama series *Queer as Folk* attracted large audiences. Similarly, the *Gay Entertainment Network* in the US has proved highly innovative while testing the limits of free speech in a series of obscenity law suits. Thus, some space is being created for gay viewers, but this is hardly mainstream television as yet.

In general terms, the trend towards deregulation and a proliferation of channels has heralded more opportunity for a range of programmes containing sexually explicit material to be shown, especially in the late-night slots. This has prompted further public debate about the nature and quality of television overall. So, sex and sexuality on television remain controversial subjects while the representation of sexual identities, far from being fixed and solid, may be seen as fluid, variable and contradictory. Sexuality is part of a wider negotiation process between individuals and the media where the meaning of sexual orientation is itself liable to be appropriated and commodified, but this is also an area open to struggle and redefinition.

See also: **Advertising, Effects, Gender, Ideology, Pleasure, Psychoanalysis, Representation, Stereotypes**

Further reading: Dines and Humez (1995); Geraghty and Lusted (1998)

SIGN

The sign, originally identified in the work of the Swiss linguist Saussure, is the basic unit of meaning in *semiotics*. In semiotic terms, it is defined as the joining together of the signifier (something before it has a meaning) and a signified (the meaning someone gives it). Thus, the conceptualisation of a sign in semiotics is generally much broader than the conventional meaning of the word, since it can refer not just to things we conventionally think of as 'signs' – like traffic lights or flags – but to anything that is capable of making meaning.

The distinction between signifier and signified is a theoretical one, since we cannot encounter something – a word, image or object – without giving it some kind of meaning, even if that meaning is somewhat vague. So, for example, if we encounter an unfamiliar word, we will still classify it within a meaningful framework – indeed, the very recognition of a group of letters or sounds as a word is itself a meaningful recognition. The distinction between signifier and signified is nonetheless fundamental to semiotics, which is based on the principle that nothing has a 'natural' or 'essential meaning' because the way we learn to interpret things is based on social or environmental contexts. So, for example, even a natural phenomenon like rainfall is always understood in context, depending on the climate we live in, our relationship to the land, and so forth. It is a distinction that allows us to intervene into the process of meaning formation and examine how signs are formed, and therefore how meaning is fixed by *culture* and *ideology*.

Peirce identifies three categories of sign (Lacey, 1998) identifiable by the nature of the relationship between the signifier and signified. First, iconic signs have a direct representative relationship between the signifier and the signified; for instance, a photograph of a political leader on television news is a *representation* of that person, albeit always a constructed one. Television as a visual medium uses resemblant signs in a way denied to some other cultural media, such as music. Second, indexical signs have a causal relationship between the signifier and signified. That is, the signifier allows the viewer to infer a 'logical' meaning. Early television *drama* often used an aeroplane as a signifier to convey the message that a character was travelling from one country to another (this would often be accompanied by an iconic sign such as Big Ben or the Empire State Building to indicate the character's destination). For the third type, symbolic signs, there is no direct resemblance or link between the signifier and the signified beyond an arbitrary one agreed within a culture, the majority of words within a language being one example.

Signs, like words in a spoken language, are combined in regular or coded ways (see *Code* and *Convention*) to communicate meanings, in what Roland Barthes describes as the process of signification (Barthes, 1972). Many television advertisements, for instance, combine a plethora of signs in a particularly intricate, complex and condensed fashion (see *Advertising*). Barthes claims there can be two levels of relationship between the signifier and signified. At the denotative level, the meaning signified is descriptive or 'obvious': for instance, an advertisement featuring young men and women drinking an alcoholic drink in a bar. But meaning is also signified at a 'deeper' or implied level, which Barthes refers to as connotative. In the case of the advertisement, this might concern gender and sexual relations, the acceptability of alcohol and the nature of leisure. This distinction allows Barthes to suggest that signs contribute to the development of cultural myths (1972). Here he is referring not to the idea of untruths but to the notion that signs have the capacity to constitute the dominant ideas and values – in other words, *ideology* – within a society. He claims that connotative meanings seem to be straightforward and denotative, hence appearing as normal and natural (the representation of women in the 1950s, 1960s and 1970s as passive 'housewifely' consumers would provide an example).

The meaning of *texts* derives from the relations between signs, such as the binary oppositions evident in representations of police and criminals in *crime series*. Signs, though, do not have single and prescribed meanings but are *polysemic*. Any sign can be 'accented' in any number of ways (multi-accentuality) to create different meanings. Much television *comedy* operates by repositioning signs in unusual contexts; see, for instance, signs of Catholicism in *Father Ted* and those of stereotypical children's behaviour in *South Park*.

The concept of sign has taken on a heightened significance in the work of Baudrillard. He has argued that within *postmodernity* members of society live in a mass-media-produced blizzard of signs. People are unable to separate reality from the apparent infinity of signs on television and other media that form a 'hyperreality'. News reports of 'reality' include simulations, while *fans* write to characters in *soap operas* as if they were 'real'. Signs and the real have thus become indistinguishable (Storey, 2001).

See also: **Polysemy, Semiology, Text**

Further reading: Barthes (1972); Fiske (1987); Lacey (1998)

SOAP OPERA

Soap operas began not on television but on commercial radio in the USA in the 1930s. Broadcast during the day, they were aimed at what was assumed to be a largely female audience of 'housewives'. The programmes were generally domestically focused dramas, with a great deal of emphasis on family concerns and personal relationships. They were sponsored by the large detergent companies, who also advertised their products during the shows. This is why they came to be known as 'soap' operas, although it is worth noting that the 'opera' part of the term was an ironic and derogatory reference to the supposed over-dramatisation of everyday life in popular serials of this kind (Western films were also dubbed 'horse operas' for similar reasons). British radio began to broadcast soaps in 1948 with *Mrs Dale's Diary*, and *The Archers*, which began soon afterwards, is still running today. In both Britain and the USA, soaps were first transmitted on television in the 1950s.

Soaps are one of the most popular and common forms of entertainment television world-wide. British television broadcasts soaps both during the day and at peak viewing times in the evenings. Some of these are 'home-grown' soaps like *Coronation Street*, *EastEnders* and *Brookside*, while Britain also imports a number of foreign soaps from America, Australia and, at one time, Brazil. At the peak of their popularity in the late 1970s and early 1980s, American soaps flooded the British market (*Dallas* and *Dynasty* commanding the highest viewing figures). By the late 1980s, however, tired and increasingly 'unreal' storylines (foreign invasions in *Dynasty* and entire plot reversals based on the 'it was all a hideous dream' scenario) appeared to have disenchanted domestic audiences. At this point programme buyers turned to Australia for the cheap and cheerful novelty of the low-budget *Neighbours* and the clean teen fun of *Home and Away*.

The unpredictability of programme *production* and buying is revealed most startlingly in soap operas. The apparent potential of a soap based around 'sun and sangria' on the Spanish Costa encouraged the BBC to build an entire village for the Euro-soap *Eldorado*. Unfortunately the *EastEnders* production team failed to find the right blend of cast, crew and script, and the programme was a giant flop. On the other hand, few would ever have predicted the enormous success of *Neighbours*. In this case scheduling played a vital part. The 5.30 p.m. slot was a dead zone before the nightly six o'clock news, which for several months the BBC filled with *The Flintstones* cartoon. When the slot was taken up by *Neighbours*, the young audience of Fred and Barney fans were captured by the simple plot lines and youthful cast of the Australian soap.

Most recently, the success of teen-orientated soaps has resulted in an influx of more imported examples, such as *Dawson's Creek*, and the production of UK youth soaps such as *Hollyoaks*. Moreover, in the US, the flow has been increasingly two-way with the growing success of Spanish-language soaps, mainly made in Latin America.

From the point of view of the television companies, soaps are relatively cheap to produce and they are also big business in terms of exports, with American, British and Australian soaps being sold and transmitted in many other parts of the world.

In Britain, they regularly attract the largest television audiences, and the lives of many soap characters (as well as the *real* lives of their stars) have become mythologised in our *culture* and incorporated into it via the press and other forms of media such as advertising. Some writers (notably Buckingham, 1987; Morley, 1992; and Ang, 1985) have also pointed to the social function of soaps. In other words, soaps are often a talking point for people. Through them, we are able to communicate with others and to share information, views and feelings about a range of personal or social issues.

When studying soaps, a number of themes are likely to crop up. These include their structure and *conventions* and the role of *women* in soaps. Both of these touch on the relationship between soaps and *audiences* as well as on issues of *pleasure*.

The soap opera features certain recognisable characteristics in terms of narrative structure. Soaps are continuous serials, which means that they have an indefinite run and do not therefore feature a final episode in which the *narrative* is closed or resolved. In contrast, this narrative closure is common in series such as conventional *crime series* or limited-run serials such as some situation *comedies*.

In soaps, it is usual to find overlapping narratives or storylines. In this way, there may be several groups of characters involved in different plots within one episode. These plots do get resolved, but not simultaneously, so that as viewers we are offered a number of different stories to follow. Moreover, soaps frequently use the device of the 'cliff hanger', where a question, decision or piece of information is left unresolved at the close of an episode. In this way, we are invited or 'hooked' into tuning in next time. Part of the pleasure of soaps might well be the anticipation involved in such a structure. Another common device is to end an episode with a revelation connected to one of the current storylines.

It is usual for soaps to feature a regular cast of characters. Sometimes these characters and their attendant storylines can go on for years. If a character is unpopular with the viewing public or the actor leaves the serial – or dies – then the programme-makers have to find ways within the existing narratives to remove the character from the plot. Since soaps work within the conventions of *realism*, an attempt is generally made to find a convincing way for this to happen. Some soaps, however, particularly some of the glossier American-made programmes, have stretched the conventions of both the soap and realism by, for example, bringing characters back to life or having them abducted by space aliens. It can be interesting, therefore, to look at the boundaries of the soap as a *genre* and at the audience's expectations about soaps, and to compare soaps made in different societies.

As well as the familiar characters, soaps typically feature a specific setting such as a street, community, close-knit family or, sometimes, a hospital, school or workplace. It is important that viewers are able to build up familiarity with the settings as well as the characters, and from the point of view of the writers it is necessary to include places where people can realistically meet.

The question of the representation of women in soaps, as well as the soap's appeal to female viewers, has been a rich source of academic enquiry over the years, particularly for *feminist* writers (Ang, 1985; Brunsdon, 1988; Geraghty, 1991, for instance). The soap was conceived as a *drama* that would appeal to women at home (see above) and this early assumption largely shaped the kinds of themes and topics that have become the mainstay of the soap. Today, television companies are quite sophisticated in the ways they target their audiences for different types of programme, and in many cases recognise *gender* differences (among others) in the appeal of specific programmes. However, soaps are watched by large numbers of people of both sexes, and the 'male breadwinner plus housewife' model, which was so central to much audience research on soaps, is no longer the most common form of household, so it may be problematic to persistently regard the soap as a 'feminine' form. Typically, soaps are about everyday life and about the personal, family, work and neighbourhood problems that could arise for many people. The more traditional soaps (*Coronation Street*, for instance, in Britain) are likely to represent life as if not much happens and in a way which places emphasis on personal and intimate conversation and relationships.

On the other hand, critics have sometimes berated soaps for presenting life as if too much happens – in other words, for including too many dramatic events such as marriages, affairs, divorce and death. It may be possible to see these apparently competing views of soaps as equally valid, since the 'dramatic' events are also very often the topics of conversation and gossip for the characters. In any case, both the drama and the everyday detail is said to appeal particularly to women. Moreover, the soap frequently represents women as 'strong', either in their personalities or in terms of their place in the world. Women in soaps are given a range of roles apart from domestic ones, but even in their domestic roles are seen as individuals rather than types. Female viewers are thus offered women characters who may be young, old, glamorous or not, homely or in powerful public positions, alone or with a partner, with or without children and even, latterly, lesbian. It is supposed that some of the pleasure women find in soaps comes from this range of possible identifications. Similarly, in soaps, women, including older women, are often seen as having an active *sexuality* which they enjoy for themselves. Their sexuality is not simply represented as an object of male desire.

But in addition, some writers have suggested that soaps appeal to women not just because of their storylines and characters but also because of their narrative structure (Modleski 1982, 1997; Brunsdon 1984; Fiske 1987), and this takes the academic debate a bit further. It is argued that whereas many traditional forms of popular television present the viewer with a narrative based on a beginning, a middle and an end, the soap instead presents us with what Fiske (1987) describes as 'an infinitely extended middle'. In the former case, the narrative structure is presented in such a way that a state of equilibrium is disturbed and then worked through to a resolution by the end of the plot. In the case of soaps, having an infinitely extended middle means that the plot never gets fully resolved (overlapping storylines) so there is never a climax that ends the narrative and ties up loose ends. The soap is all loose ends, and that is its attraction.

Some commentators have made a link between women's and men's real social positions and the ways they respond to television texts. Put simply, in patriarchal societies women continue to have less power than men and are less likely to 'succeed' in the same way as men. The soap is said to reflect this imbalance partly by the way success, in the final resolution of the plot, is endlessly deferred, but it also offers female viewers the pleasure of watching how people struggle with the difficulties they come across in their lives. This too is said to have particular resonances for many women and their own struggles.

See also: **Code, Convention, Feminism, Gender, Narrative, Realism**

Further reading: Allen (1995); Ang (1985); Brunsdon *et al.* (1997); Buckingham (1987); Geraghty (1991); Sijl (1988)

SPORT

Historically, the development of formal sport has been intimately interwoven with the emergence of a number of media forms. Both mass circulation newspapers and radio owed some of their significance to their coverage of modern formal sport, which similarly was partially shaped by that same relationship. But it is in television's coverage of sport that the relationship has reached its zenith. Most of the largest global television *audiences* have been for sporting events and particularly football's World Cup finals, while in individual societies television has organised sport as a 'national event' – for example, the Superbowl in the US. Notably, many strategies for developing and selling new television *technology* have had sport at their core: for instance, satellite, cable, digital and most recently, pay-per-view.

Some commentators writing from a functionalist position (see, for instance, Birrell and Loy, 1979) have argued that the mass media play a positive role with regard to sport by informing viewers about sport, integrating them within social groups, providing them with excitement and offering them an escape from everyday existence.

Conversely, much research with a *Marxist* genealogy has focused on the role of television as an agent of *commercialisation* within sport. It is argued that in the pursuit of capital, and hence audiences, television has influenced sport in various ways. Attention has been drawn to the *power* of television in its relationship with sport, sport-related industries (agents, sponsors, services, gambling, etc.) and audiences. Media transnationals thus have the capacity to determine audiences' experience of sport. Contemporary Marxists have talked about a sports–media axis in terms of what Cashmore has referred to as a match made in heaven (Cashmore, 1996).

Thus, it is argued that television corporations are able to influence which sports flourish commercially. While football globally, cricket in Britain and American football in the US have all benefited from lucrative television deals, other sports have failed to acquire backing and have been more likely to remain grass-roots concerns. For example, squash, because it is not 'good television', and netball, because it is perceived as a female sport which will attract neither audiences nor sponsors, have not flourished commercially.

Similarly, television has also done much to shape the structure and *culture* of sport as an institution. In pursuit of higher audiences, sports have been persuaded to change *conventions* and rules. This is epitomised in the way that American sports such as basketball and American football have become peppered with time-outs. Other examples might be the introduction of 'non-standard' distances for track events in athletics (thereby heightening the possibility of world records being broken and audiences being attracted), the requirement that major football matches kick off at particularly hot times of the day to increase global audiences, and the shift towards one-day cricket on the grounds that it is 'more exciting'.

Within the field of *cultural studies* there has been a continuing debate around what the focus of analysis should be, with some arguing for the primacy of the economic and others stressing the importance of the *text*. The latter school has used *semiology* to reject the more simplistic view that the media has somehow contaminated 'pure' sport and to investigate the sense in which sport is mediated by television. Whannel (1992a), combining an economic and a textual approach, has looked at ways in which sport is visually constructed for television. For instance, television is able to transform time by compressing events into edited highlights or using slow motion to prolong, say, a 100-metre race. Similarly, cameras can take the viewer over considerable distance (as with golf coverage) or can zoom in to focus on individuals' faces. Equally, modes of presentation and commentary act to mediate 'the event'. Whannel considers how presenters can offer viewers frames of reference in the context of competition. Contests may be set up as cup giants versus minnows, elder statesman (*sic*) against brash newcomer, or, nationally as 'us' versus 'them'.

Textually specific analysis has developed this sort of work. In particular, it has considered how sports teams and individuals are characterised and personalised by television. Wren-Lewis and Clarke (1983) concentrate on how commentators constructed football teams at the 1982 World Cup via *discourses* of national 'characteristics', political systems and footballing history. Other work focuses on the constitution of sporting events in terms of the clash of constructed personalities – for example, Carl Lewis versus Ben Johnson at the 1988 Olympics, or Diego Maradona of Argentina against Gary Lineker of England during the 1986 football World Cup.

Television, then, is able to use these invented personalities and characteristics in combination with the specific sporting context to produce sporting *narratives* that can emphasise drama, spectacle and significance. Whannel draws attention to the *ideological* work under-taken by the narrativisation of sport, especially in the context of nationalist ideology which may organise and emphasise the discursive unities of being British, American or any other nationality. Jenny Hargreaves (1994), in discussing the wider question of the relative absence of female sport in the media, notes how television tends to represent sportswomen in ways that stress their sexuality ('normal' and 'deviant') and domestic identity.

Contradictorily, while television has been accused of peddling national stereotypes, it has also acted to undermine local national identities. Concern has been expressed that participation and interest in 'traditional' sports is being threatened with the onslaught of satellite television. Thus, young men in the Caribbean are turning from cricket, a 'traditional' sport (though, of course, originally transplanted by English colonialists) to NBA basketball transmitted from the US. Television is variously seen as an agent of *cultural imperialism* or *globalisation*. What is clear, though, is that audiences are showing an abiding demand for sport in its various guises.

See also: **Cultural imperialism, Globalisation**

Further reading: Goldlust (1987); Wenner (1989); Whannel (1992a)

STEREOTYPES

Most people recognise and utilise stereotypes. They are often regarded as a harmless form of social shorthand: a fast track to recognising the characteristics of a person, group or situation. The term itself is derived from the Greek (*stereos*, meaning 'solid', and *typos*, meaning 'mark') but the concept was developed in the twentieth century by the American journalist Walter Lippmann in his book *Public Opinion* (1922) to mean fixed and narrow 'pictures in our head'. Lippmann recognised two crucial aspects of stereotyping which have formed a basis for a contemporary understanding of the way media stereotypes carry meaning. First, stereotypes tend to be resistant to change; second, they generally carry a pejorative and narrow range of meanings (O'Sullivan *et al.*, 1994). Today, it is widely recognised that stereotypes are inaccurate, simplistic generalisations about a group of individuals that may lead to particular perceptions of the group by others. Moreover, holding stereotyped views, particularly about marginalised or disenfranchised people, can have serious implications for actual treatment. In other words, categorising members of a group in narrow ways may lead to the group being treated prejudicially and according to narrow expectations.

Conceptualised in this way, stereotyping can be linked to issues of *power*, in that it may be easier to stereotype less powerful groups in society than it is to stereotype those with greater power. But this understanding of how stereotyping works requires caution. It may be too simplistic given the variety of social groups that can be subject to humorous ridicule (the 'upper-class twit' or the 'computer nerd' are not necessarily economically or culturally powerless). What it may be possible to assert is that the media process of reducing humans to stereotypes at the very least acts as a means of establishing boundaries between 'insiders' and 'outsiders'. The audience is encouraged to identify with 'positive' rather than 'negative' characters. Put simply, viewers are asked to see themselves as 'us' and not 'them'. Richard Dyer (1985a) has made the point that one of the most significant aspects of media stereotypes is that they carry a suggestion that the characteristics represented are somehow 'natural' and are shared by the whole group. Thus characterising one male ballet dancer as effeminate or one city dweller as selfish and money-grabbing suggests that this is the natural, normal and inevitable condition of all male ballet dancers or city dwellers. This 'naturalising' process can be seen as ideological in its function. On the other hand, Tessa Perkins (1979) suggests that stereotypes can often express something about real social relations – not that all blonde women are really 'dumb', for instance, but that this stereotype reflects women's inferior position in society as well as the importance of their appearance (and youth and passivity) for gaining any kind of status. So stereotypes have a complex relationship to 'reality'. While stereotypes may be partial, they are not necessarily false: they generally contain a grain of truth.

Many cultural commentators have argued that television helps construct and perpetuate stereotypes, and there is a good deal of evidence to support this view. Stereotypes of *gender, race, class, sexuality*, political stance, disability and so on are common in popular television genres such as sitcoms and *soaps*, and may also be detected in more 'serious' programmes such as *news* bulletins. In *comedy* programmes, in particular, the stereotype is used as an economical way of establishing character types (the mincing gay man, the petulant teenager or domineering mother-in-law) who can be instantly recognised by the *audience* without the need for background information. *Advertising* similarly needs to direct the audience's understanding for immediate impact and advertisers are therefore not generally concerned with developing depth of character or notions of individuality.

Although stereotyping as a mechanism is persistent, the form stereotypes take must change with shifting cultural norms and expectations. For instance, many racial stereotypes common in the 1950s and 1960s would be regarded as offensive, unacceptable and probably unlawful today. However, a difficult question is whether the widespread circulation of stereotypes creates cultural norms in the first instance, or whether cultural norms are established independently of stereotyping and stereotyping follows as a consequence. In this view, it takes a shift in cultural norms to make certain stereotypical representations seem out of place and thus unacceptable.

Much research has been undertaken on variants of this question. The '*effects*' of audience exposure to stereotypes are difficult to measure although the 'cultural effects' theorists suggest that rather than instant or immediate effects, repetition of a narrow range of representations of any group may over time give rise to a distorted and 'negative' view of that group. This is particularly the case, according to Hartmann and Husband (1973), if members of an audience gain their primary ideas about the stereotyped group from media sources, rather than from personal experience. Hartmann and Husband's research focused on racial stereotyping and the long-term influence of the media. However, families, communities and peer groups can also exert an important socialising mechanism on ideas and attitudes, so the relative influence of television is difficult to isolate and pin down. Thus, while it is evident that effects are difficult to prove, so too it is possible that stereotypes are not always or necessarily caused by television (or other media) texts. Rather, an interrelationship between audience, text and media industry operates in a circular manner, each influencing and responding to the other.

The development of debate around the uses and meanings of media stereotypes has led to a number of responses by television writers, programmers and commissioning editors. An early defensive position, commonly taken, hinged on the idea of the narrative necessity for stereotypes as cultural shorthand. This is a view that also defends stereotyping as 'light-hearted good fun' and tends to regard those who object to stereotyping as 'humourless'. An alternative stance has been to overturn 'negative' images and replace them with more 'positive' ones (see *Representation*). One of the perceived dangers of this approach is that of tokenism: that is, the tendency to insert, for example one black person, one lesbian or one political activist into a programme as a 'positive' character regardless of their relevance to the narrative. Another weakness of the 'positive images' approach is that it tends to de-politicise and trivialise the experiences of the stereotyped group. This 'we are all alike' approach can run the risk of ignoring specific cultural conditions in the effort to provide pleasant, acceptable images for an assumed 'mainstream' audience and raises a number of questions. For instance, can one sympathetic, non-camp homosexual character wipe out decades of representing homosexuals as figures of fun? And what levels of responsibility should programmers take to ensure that gay (or other stereotyped) people are 'positively' represented? Is this possible or even desirable?

Moving away from a 'positive images' approach, a more recent response has been to focus on the important underlying issue of who actually produces stereotypes. The continuing dominance of the television industries by white middle-class men has led to the recognition of the link between stereotyping and the relative lack of minority groups working in television. Interestingly, there is some evidence to suggest that when under-represented groups gain *access* to the creation and production of television programmes, the preferred strategy is not necessarily to provide 'positive' images, but may involve the production of a range and variety of characterisations. In Britain, the comedy show *Goodness Gracious Me* has broken new ground, not only by introducing audiences to a variety of Asian characters but by utilising stereotypes of British Asian life and turning them on their head. *Goodness Gracious Me* has not abandoned stereotyping as a mechanism for recognition: instead it understands and interrogates traditional stereotypes, and introduces a range of new ones developed by Asian writers and performers from within British Asian culture. The difference in point of origin is significant and allows for certain representations – such as the Asian mother, excessively proud of her sons – to be humorously undertaken. Taboos can be broken from 'the inside' that would otherwise be regarded as racist.

Some of the issues around stereotyping are now largely outmoded. This is not to say that there are no more stereotypes, but that academic arguments have moved on. The existence and persistence of stereotypes is well established; the need to provide 'positive' alternatives has been considered, and the focus now is more on how viewers use/understand/make meaning from cultural stereotypes. Issues of identity are paramount – what is a television *text* offering the viewer in terms of identification? Can viewers resist these offerings? Do viewers 'see through' stereotypes? Have stereotypes lost their power, given that they have been so widely and publicly debated?

Certainly, an increasing awareness by both the viewing public and media professionals of the potentially damaging influence of stereotypes may have led to a reduction in their more blatant use and a slight increase in opportunities for people from groups commonly stereotyped to make alternative representations. In general, those making television programmes are choosing to become more sensitive to the sensibilities of sections of the viewing public rather than risk complaint and possibly falling viewing figures. On the other hand, programmers and advertisers, despite the existence of regulatory bodies, continue to utilise certain stereotypes – particularly sexualised images of women – as a form of 'shorthand' fairly persistently, albeit sometimes in more subtle forms.

The question remains: what is the relationship between television and the existence of cultural stereotypes? Television's roles in *agenda-*

setting, gatekeeping and cultural leadership clearly continue to be crucial, but television can offer a site for progressive as well as regressive texts, for the possibility of going beyond and breaking with stereotypes as well as contributing to their persistence. And viewers are capable of reading stereotypes in a range of ways and according to the context in which they appear.

See also: **Comedy, Gender, Ideology, Representation, Soap opera**

Further reading: Dyer (1985a); Lacey (1998); Perkins (1979)

STRUCTURALISM AND POST-STRUCTURALISM

Structuralism is principally derived from the linguistic work of Ferdinand de Saussure (1857–1913) and is concerned with ways of making visible the invisible framework and structures which constitute *culture* and social reality. Society and culture are seen as being determined by deep social and psychological structures that are independent of human thought and action. Structuralism became very popular in the 1960s, and its presence was felt throughout a range of approaches including Marxist theory, psychoanalysis, literary theory and anthropology. By the end of the 1970s, structuralism had become so diverse that it could no longer be considered a unified approach or method. But some of its concepts are still widely employed, particularly within the field of *textual* analysis, and the structuralist legacy lives on within the post–structuralist tradition (see below).

For structuralists, social and cultural life can be scientifically studied analogously to language. This fundamental proposition can be detected in the work of Saussure, who maintained that language is a system of mutually dependent *signs*. He divided language into two parts: langue (the total system of language) and parole (individual speech acts). For Saussure, analysis should be focused on the structure of language as a system of relationships and should be synchronic. That is, language should be studied without reference to the past (as opposed to diachronic analysis, which focuses on language with reference to history and social change). He argued that language works through signs (such as words or images) which are composed conceptually of signifiers, objects or phenomena, and signifieds, or the meanings which attach to the signifier. The relationship between signifiers and signifieds is usually arbitrary, so that the meaning of any sign is often produced through convention, that is to say cultural agreement. Further, meaning is 'put together' from the relationships between signs which produce difference, and from processes of selection, combination and opposition. These are the codes and conventions of languages. Thus, language as a system does not reflect reality but rather, because we conceptualise social life through language, constructs our sense of reality. For writers such as Roland Barthes this is vital, because it points to the way in which meanings are constituted in society so that language is not a neutral and 'innocent' reflection of reality but the source of what he calls 'myths' or *ideology*.

There are, then, several basic principles underlying the structuralist approach. First, structures are privileged over and above individual purposeful action. The unobservable but detectable underlying structural relations underpinning the surface appearance of social reality are seen as determining social relations and social life. For structuralists, what at first appears to be 'natural' is in fact socially constructed. The implications of this give rise to the second basic premise of structuralist approaches, which is that social actors are not the authors of their intentions but are the products of structures, *discourses* and social relationships. From this comes the difficult idea that we do not speak language, language speaks us. Third, a striking feature of structuralist approaches has been the contention that structures are universal and remain more or less constant.

For structuralists, their model of language analysis can be extended to all cultural practices and texts, which are seen as aspects of wider structural systems. It is argued that at any one time what we eat, what we wear, which television programmes we watch and our kinship networks are not isolated individual choices but aspects of the operation of rules, laws and structures which function to produce meaning in any given cultural sphere. Similarly, media texts are not seen primarily as the product of an author's intentions but as examples of the workings of textual rules and *conventions*. Analysis of this kind allows identification of certain structures common to a wide range of myths, *narratives*, stories, legends, folktales and so on, Propp's work on Russian folk tales providing a lasting example. Structuralism, then, is primarily concerned with 'how' texts mean rather than with 'what' they mean.

Structuralism has proved to be a useful method for understanding television because it provides a framework for understanding the internal rules for the production of televisual meaning (Seiter, 1992). For example Jones (1996) applies a structuralist analysis to *The X-Files*, locating deep structures which are also identifiable in Indo–European mythology and which, in turn, can be situated within a broader framework of mythic narratives. Her reading of *The X-Files* allows her to suggest that the programme embodies a mythological structure constructed around the basic opposition of culture and nature as represented in the characters of Scully and Mulder.

Structuralists have been criticised for closing down the diversity of readings a text may produce (see post-structuralism, below). Also, the structuralist emphasis on unobservable but underlying structures which determine social relations and social life has led to accusations that it adopts a profoundly 'anti-humanist' approach: that is, the individual has no agency to organise and interpret the world. Finally, structuralism has been condemned for being ahistorical – the structuralist notion that all social phenomena are linked and can be explained in terms of underlying, universal structures results in a mechanistic approach to understanding culture and society which cannot cope with the sheer complexity of contemporary cultural life. On another level, structuralism seems unable to answer the common-sense question of how structures originate.

Post-structuralism both shares and rejects some of the basic propositions of structuralism. Following Derrida (1967) post-structuralists see meaning as always being in a constant state of flux, rather than being final or fixed. For Derrida, texts are contradictory and the meanings they produce are both plural and fluid. The 'true' meaning of a text can never be really known and all texts bear traces of other texts, being defined as chains of signifiers. The concept of 'difference' is crucial to Derrida's work. He suggests that there is a disparity (or a slippage) between signifiers and signifieds as the meaning of any one sign is partly determined by what it represses or omits. Thus, the meaning of a text can be understood by looking at what it puts outside of itself as well as by what it contains. Post-structuralists use a form of criticism known as deconstruction, which posits that texts can support multiple readings (some of which may be contradictory). This demonstrates that a preference for any particular reading is, in part, constructed out of and based upon certain beliefs and values (which are culturally determined) and is not guaranteed by the text itself. Ultimately, then, what is provided is a provisional account of the intertextual nature of all texts.

Using *The X-Files* again as an example, it is possible to identify the ways in which a post-structuralist reading of a text differs from a structuralist reading. A deconstructionist analysis of *The X-Files* would produce a fluid and dynamic reading and would pay attention to the complex strategies of *intertextuality* at work. Hersey (1998) proposes that far from guaranteeing that 'the truth is out there' (the slogan associated with the programme) *The X-Files* articulates multiple truths structured around cultural, *racial* and *gendered* perceptions. It is also common for the programme to leave many of its narratives unresolved as well as to use either coded language or the indigenous language of native American cultures (without explaining or providing a translation for audiences). The way in which *The X-Files* knits together and articulates a variety of discourses without privileging any particular one also suggests that attempts to impose a final or preferred reading would be inappropriate. Thus, post–structuralists pay attention to the role of the viewer in the process of producing meaning and the regimes of intertextual knowledge that are brought to the viewing experience. Meaning in *The X-Files*, then, is refracted not only through the multiple discourses of the text but also through those which the viewer brings to the text. Meaning is produced at the point where text and reader 'meet' and is not simply a property of the text itself.

Structuralism claimed to provide a scientific method which located unity and order in the underlying structures of texts but assumed that analysts' meanings coincided with those of the reader. Post–structuralism is characterised by a shift away from the determining structures of texts, a concern with signifiers as against signifieds, and a foregrounding of the role of the reader in the process of producing meaning which is the product of our interactions with texts. Here there is a focus on the *polysemic* nature of cultural texts and the range of possible readings available to readers. Post-structuralism also pays attention to the categories of *class*, gender and race as well as to *pleasure* and the role of history in the processes of meaning production. In doing this, post-structuralism offers a critique of structuralism's all-encompassing approach, of the notion of the self as a unified subject and of the 'stability' of signs. This opens up questions concerning identity and truth which are pursued in the work of *postmodernists*.

See also: **Discourse, Ideology, Intertextuality, Polysemy, Postmodernism, Semiology**

Further reading: Fiske (1987); Sarup (1993); Seiter (1992); Storey (1993)

SYNERGY

A 'synergy' occurs when different parts of an organisation come together in a mutually beneficial way to work as a whole. This means that a greater value is added to products than would have been the case had those parts remained separate. Burnett (1996) has looked at this process in respect to the music industry. Often, he suggests, hits in the pop charts are actually a part of a wider 'package' that is produced by an entertainment company as it 'ties-in', 'cross-promotes' or 'cross-pollinates' a range of different commodities. Burnett cites Whitney Houston's song and video, 'I Will Always Love You', which was released as a part of the soundtrack for the film *The Bodyguard*, as an example of this practice.

The exploitation of synergies is now a prime motivation for people working in the media and entertainment industries, including television. The ability of an organisation to achieve this, however, depends very much on its economic *power*. To capture a synergy from within one company, a process of 'multimedia integration' or 'diversification' needs to have occurred, which involves a large 'parent company' or corporation owning interests in more than one type of media. For example, the large global conglomerate Time Warner currently owns Warner Music Group, the magazines *People* and *Sports Illustrated*, the book publisher Time Life Books, the film producers Warner Bros Film and New Line Cinema, and the Warner Brothers Television Network. More recently, Time Warner has also merged with the Internet Service Provider (ISP) America On-Line (AOL). Potential synergies offered by this new alliance centre on the provision of existing content from Time Warner on the internet, including being able to view CNN news on screen, and the ability to download films from a video-library archive. The economic power of conglomerates allows for synergies to occur, and these in turn consolidate their position as leaders in the highly concentrated global marketplace (see *Globalisation*).

On a smaller scale, national television networks, such as the BBC, have also attempted to exploit synergies. Recently, the cookery show format has proved extremely popular, with spin-off recipe books topping the bestseller lists. The tie-in between a popular show and a book, with one effectively marketing and helping to sell the other, is a lucrative prospect. A good example of this is the BBC's ownership of BBC Books, an imprint of a larger company, BBC Worldwide Publishing. This has allowed for the publication of books such as *Ainsley Harriot's Barbecue Bible* to 'accompany' a television series. For a smaller organisation like the BBC, however, the costs of diversifying may be prohibitive, which may partly explain why many of its books are still produced in alliance with other companies, such as Penguin Books.

It is not essential, however, for a synergy to occur exclusively via cross-media ownership, although this is how the concept is usually discussed. Often, synergies happen because of the mutually beneficial undertakings of quite separate companies. For example, the makers of television guides, such as *TV Quick*, provide previews of upcoming shows and publish *schedules*. These guides offer a good deal of publicity to television networks and can clearly help particular shows to capture audiences, especially if they enjoy good reviews. In return, the magazine may interview a television personality from a featured programme or may have a high-profile star on its front cover, which will help to boost its sales. Daily and weekly newspapers, both national and regional, provide a similar function through previews and interviews. For example, the British Sunday paper *The Observer* publishes a short television guide in which there is a sport preview, a documentaries preview and a list of 'films of the week', along with all of the usual schedules for television and radio. The publication of this guide suggests that covering television is advantageous to the newspaper in securing readers. These processes are obviously working together, but are not often accounted for in discussions of synergies, which tend to look only at *ownership* and integration.

See also: **Globalisation, Ownership**

Further reading: Burnett (1996); Turow (1992)

TASTE

If we are told that someone has 'impeccable taste' we are likely to think of a person who is well versed in the arts rather than being a *fan* of popular culture, preferring Mozart to Madonna or Shakespeare to Sidney Sheldon. They may, if British, also holiday in Italy or France rather than in Florida, are likely to enjoy cricket rather than football, drink wine rather than beer, or eat hummus rather than hamburgers. Even if we do not enjoy or participate in those activities associated with taste, which are often minority pursuits, we may still share similar ideas about what 'good taste' is supposed to be. More problematically, we may even feel slightly guilty about our own cultural preferences if they do not fit into this accepted standard of what is tasteful. It is clear, then, that our *culture* has developed so that certain practices and activities have accrued a higher status than others, with those people who are culturally and aesthetically discerning seen as having taste. This locates the concept of taste within debates about *mass culture* and the impact, in particular, of commercial forms of popular culture upon values and attitudes. It is usually pursuits that fall within the sphere of popular culture, exemplified by *commercial television*, that are found wanting when it comes to being tasteful.

In terms of the media, the cultural status of texts is usually determined by whether they measure up to exacting intellectual or aesthetic standards. At an intellectual level, 'serious' television *genres*, particularly *news* and *documentary* programming, are often critically revered while others, such as *soap opera* and *sports* programming, are denigrated. At an aesthetic level, shows that challenge or break strict genre conventions, such as *Twin Peaks* in America or *The Singing Detective* in Britain, are celebrated as works of art. This differing status is also reflected in the *production* practices that surround different television genres. For example, Abercrombie (1996) claims that British documentary producers tend to be men and are recruited from elite universities such as Oxford or Cambridge. They also enjoy large budgets despite low viewing figures compared to other popular genres. Documentary producers are themselves committed to a *public service* ethos in which their role is to educate and inform viewers, rather than provide them with 'trivial' material. In turn, the *pleasures* that viewers take from different texts are also located within this hierarchy of taste and status. For example, our emotional engagement with a soap is often perceived as being less 'worthy' than our intellectual appreciation of an informative documentary. Measuring taste, therefore, is a tool of cultural segregation that is used to discriminate both *between* the 'high arts' and popular culture and *within* popular culture itself. In the case of television, this is usually to differentiate between different genres.

Efforts to validate the high status of specific texts or genres are usually made by those 'with taste' in a bid to construct themselves in opposition to those 'without'. Until the post-war era, this tended to include intellectuals and academics, who venerated the high arts over and above forms of popular culture. This was because intellectuals enjoyed a degree of 'cultural capital' accrued through their education and class backgrounds. The French sociologist Pierre Bourdieu (1986) has argued that culture is organised in an equivalent way to the economy, in that resources within the 'cultural economy' are shared unequally between different people. Individuals from separate class backgrounds thus tend to enjoy varying degrees of cultural capital as well, manifested in the distinctive cultural habits, lifestyles and preferences that they engage in. Bourdieu collectively refers to these predilections as the 'habitus'. Our taste in cultural pursuits, including our choice of viewing on the television, is part and parcel of the habitus that we fit into. We do not, however, have a free choice over which habitus we occupy, as depending on our class backgrounds our lifestyle is likely to be, in part at least, pre-determined and inherited. We can thus predict that working-class people are more likely to read tabloid newspapers rather than broadsheets, or watch sitcoms rather than avant-garde art films shown late at night. While social mobility can, to some extent, shift us between one lifestyle and another, it cannot erase traces of the habitus that we have inherited. For example, wealthy working-class people who have gained economic capital (the 'nouveau riche') are often frowned upon by people with 'old money' (the landed or aristocratic classes) for trying to imitate good taste. For those doing the frowning, successful cultural simulation is impossible to achieve as taste is innate and ingrained and cannot be bought.

The problem for Bourdieu, however, is that these different lifestyle patterns, or 'habituses', are not given equal value in our culture. The dominant cultural system, expressed through education and cultural institutions such as art galleries and opera houses, legitimates certain forms of culture and taste which, over time, have combined to make up the 'high arts'. These cultural practices have come to stand at the summit of cultural status. It is of little surprise that those people who 'appreciate' them also enjoy the highest levels of economic capital. In this respect the notion of taste is used to justify inequalities and acts as an *ideological* benchmark that sets out the boundaries between different cultural and economic classes. Where some think that taste is natural and innate, Bourdieu's argument is that it is not. Rather, it has developed as a tool that is used to legitimate and reproduce social hierarchies (Bourdieu 1986).

Fiske (1992) has drawn on Bourdieu's work to explain how *fans* distinguish between good and bad television texts at an aesthetic level. Fiske's work demonstrates that audiences of subordinate (i.e. popular) culture also absorb dominant cultural categories of taste and apply them to popular texts, including television. He refers to those texts legitimated by the dominant system (i.e. the high arts) as 'official culture'. Although television texts may never become official culture, Fiske suggests that there is an equivalent 'popular cultural capital' that also acts to establish a hierarchy of taste. Effectively this creates a 'pseudo-official' yet subordinate culture that also venerates some texts over and above others. Television fans, by gaining an intimate knowledge of a particular text, can set up a canon of good taste in the same way that a literary critic or a film critic is able to. Consequently, they can possess high levels of popular cultural capital. Brower (1992) has explored how some television fans in America have acted as 'tastemakers', forming themselves into an influential lobby group called Viewers for Quality Television. This well-organised and articulate group is made up of older, middle-class intellectuals and engages in aesthetic criticism through discriminating between good and bad television texts. It also lobbies commercial television networks to maintain a commitment to 'quality television'. As a result, the group emulates and rehearses the language and practices of official culture. Their use of a *discourse* of 'quality', for example, coupled with referring to themselves as 'viewers' rather than fans, provides them with a sense of intellectual gravity and import. In most cases, the texts that they have campaigned to preserve have faced being axed, usually for being economically unfeasible due to low ratings. These have included *Cagney and Lacey* and *St Elsewhere*, both regarded as offering the viewer challenging, thought-provoking material rather than the mediocre fare of popular *genre*-based programming.

The conflation of popular commercial programming with poor taste and inferior quality has, in Britain, manifested itself in the way that the television industry has been regulated. As a result, taste has been an important political as well as theoretical and aesthetic issue. The regulation of the television industry has effectively positioned the BBC, from its inception, as a cultural authority that has attempted to organise the taste of the nation through its commitment to public service broadcasting. Here, the BBC has acted as a bulwark against the gradual encroachment of a commercial television system in which the imperatives of profit maximisation have been presented as a threat to the 'quality' of programming. The BBC's traditional role has not been to give people what they want according to the demands of public taste, but to elevate that taste to a higher level.

Williams proposes that this view reflects fears about the *Americanisation* of television (particularly in pandering to the whims of *advertisers*) that were prevalent in Britain when commercial television was first established via the 1954 Television Act (K. Williams, 1997). The ITV regional television network that emerged out of this legislation was quick to develop popular programming, including cheap imports from America (e.g. *I Love Lucy*, *Gunsmoke* and *Dragnet*). At the time this was seen by self-appointed cultural guardians, including the National Television Council, as an affront to taste, and was regarded as evidence of a general cultural decline. Curran and Seaton (1997) describe how opponents of commercial television were particularly enraged by American television channel NBC's treatment of the Queen's coronation. The station interspersed pictures of this prominent event, which symbolised the best of establishment culture and tradition, with images of a cartoon chimp, J. Fred Muggs, selling tea. A greater affront to taste and decency, at the time anyway, was difficult to imagine.

Those who campaigned against commercial television argued for the maintenance of a monopoly for the BBC. Despite being viewed by some as reactionary elitists, their concerns were powerfully articulated and had some influence. Even after the monopoly was broken by ITV, the free market was not allowed to determine the full diet of programming and the BBC's privileged position, maintained by the collection of the licence fee, was preserved. The continuing commitment to public service, so the argument went, would allow for a greater variety of more challenging material to be produced. The Pilkington Committee (1961), set up to explore the future of broadcasting in the wake of commercial television, addressed concerns that ITV's *scheduling* had led to a decline in cultural standards. The report, published in 1962, was in effect an official eulogy to the BBC and a 'thumbs-down' to ITV. This was reflected in the Committee's decision to reward the BBC with a new channel, BBC2. The report singled out popular genres, including quiz shows, for particular condemnation. As a result, the powers of ITV's official regulator, the Independent Television Authority (ITA), were expanded to include a role in overseeing schedules in order to maintain standards of quality and, by implication, taste.

The emergence of cable and satellite programming, however, has made it much harder for traditional cultural authorities such as the BBC to make convincing pronouncements upon good taste. It has also made it much more impractical to regulate the television industry with anything other than a 'light touch'. The increasing access to a range of programming, at least for those who can afford it, has also coincided with the emergence of a *postmodern* cultural aesthetic in which distinctions about the value or quality of different texts have become blurred. In these eclectic and ironic times it is not unusual to have opera singers such as Luciano Pavarotti providing theme tunes for a football tournament, or for classical violin players such as Nigel Kennedy to be reworking the songs of Jimi Hendrix. By the same token, television has also helped to obscure the conventional boundaries between high art and popular culture, and the tasteful and tasteless. In particular, MTV, with its varied flow of programming, has allowed 'art-rock' and 'pop' texts to sit comfortably alongside one another, while many music videos have 'played' with avant-garde film-making techniques, such as the abandonment of conventional *narrative* form (Goodwin, 1993). All of this has made it much harder to confidently categorise texts in terms of value or quality. In turn, it is perhaps not so easy to discriminate between different social groups in terms of their taste or lack of it. Given the social inequalities that have traditionally been legitimated by distinctions of taste, we might see this as a thoroughly welcome change.

See also: **Americanisation, Commercial television, Documentary, Fans, Mass culture, News, Public service broadcasting**

Further reading: Abercrombie (1996); Bourdieu (1986); Brower (1992); Curran and Seaton (1997); Fiske (1992); Williams (1997)

TECHNOLOGY

The role and place of technology (in its various forms) in *culture* and social change has been a prime concern within the social sciences and of specific interest in the field of media and communications research. This concern with and interest in technology has created a growing body of research literature of various kinds. A good deal of recent research within media and *cultural studies* has been ethnographic in kind and has aimed to secure a greater understanding of the role of technology in 'everyday life'. This approach is symptomatic of a broader shift within media and cultural studies in general and is sometimes referred to as the 'domestic technology paradigm' (Eldridge et al., 1997).

Early approaches to technology were generally of the technological determinist variety – constructed around the premise that technology is in some way autonomous and has determinate *effects* upon society. Technology was assumed to play a key role in shaping the social structures of advanced industrial societies, with technological progress also seen as inevitable. Technological determinism has since been discredited in that it downplayed the wider social and cultural processes that impact on which technologies are developed and how they are used. The determinist approach also overlooked the diverse range of social arrangements and relationships formed with different technologies. Any approach which conceptualises technology as being somehow separate or outside of society will inevitably be limiting and itself deterministic. McQuail (1994) points out that technologies themselves are cultural artefacts, and as such they are imbued with cultural meanings. The notion that technologies are developed in some sort of hermetically sealed environment and then 'introduced' into society with instantaneous and directly observable social and cultural effects fails to take into account that technology itself is social and therefore is socially shaped. Technologies develop within societies – not autonomously.

This shift in theorising in no way detracts from the significance and impact of technology on social life but, rather, emphasises the importance of conceptualising technology within societies and the ways in which social, political, economic and cultural factors have shaped (and will continue to shape) technology. Silverstone (1994) suggests that technologies themselves are effects – of social, cultural, political and economic circumstances as well as of structures, actions and decisions. By analysing technology within a wider social and cultural context it is possible to begin to better understand the extent to which these contextual factors influence the ways in which we interact with and attach meaning to different technologies.

In very broad terms, since the mid 1980s research into television as technology and as a medium of communication has shifted away from exploring how the characteristics of the medium influence message form and content. Instead, work has focused on television as a technology that occupies a prominent cultural space in the homes and everyday lives of the majority of people living in advanced industrial societies. Similarly, the focus of audience reception theories, and audience research in general, has shifted to the significance (and problematics) of the consumption of a wide range of cultural products via different communication technologies (television, *video*, satellite, cable, digital, CD systems and computers) situated within the domestic environment of the home and set within the routine interactions of everyday life. What is highlighted in this type of research is that our relationships with different technologies are quite complex, subject to wider contextual factors, and notoriously difficult (conceptually and theoretically) to explain in simple terms of cause and effect.

On the one hand, these studies indicate that communication technologies enter into already existing social relationships and patterns of power distribution in the home (Morley, 1986; Gray, 1992; Moores, 1995). But these studies also highlight the potential *pleasures*, conflicts, struggles and opportunities for resistance that technology engenders. Research studies into the uses (and abuses) of television, the remote control buttons and VCRs are abundant. What this research foregrounds is that very often when the television is on people do not always pay attention to it, or that they channel surf – taking fragmented bits of information from whatever happens to catch their attention. Who gets to watch what, access to television and video, and control of the remote control give rise to power struggles in the home.

This type of research has not been without its critics, who see the general trend in micro-level studies as being uncritical and almost celebratory of consumption and technology. Eldridge *et al.* (1997) suggest that the importance and significance of media *institutions, power* structures and *ideological* analysis of media texts should not be discarded in favour of studies which foreground active consumption, pleasure and resistance based around minor intergenerational and gender conflicts in the home. For Eldridge *et al.,* the main problem with the domestic technology approach lies in its emphasis on the medium rather than the message. By focusing mainly on television as technology and processes of consumption, these studies fail to engage critically with the content of programmes.

In spite of such criticisms, these approaches are valuable in that they point to the ways in which, as Silverstone (1994) puts it, technologies are embedded in the cultural, social, political and economic matrices of society. If we are going to consider the 'effects' of technology, these effects have to be conceptualised within the context of what already exists – the structures, institutions, values, beliefs, customs and ideas which serve to structure and give meaning to people's lives. In the case of television, the institutions it embodies and in which it is embedded are constantly changing and will continue to do so. As the trend towards convergence (institutional and technological) and *globalisation* illustrates, television cannot be explained purely in terms of reference to its status as technology or simply in terms of technological developments. Any form of explanation must also take into account the social, political, economic and cultural dimensions of the medium as well as the nature of its relationship to other technologies.

See also: **Audiences, Culture, Family viewing, Video**

Further reading: Gauntlett and Hill (1999); Gray (1992); Moores (1995); Silverstone and Hirsch (1994)

T

the term 'text' is used in common parlance to refer to a first instance, a television programme. Texts can take including written, aural and visual, within media and

research on texts has, unsurprisingly, been a central concern of television tex on. Contradictorily, though, early work on from literary studies and was eager to point and danger of what was seen as a popular, and even vulgar, cultural medium (Hartley, 1998). Since then, textual analysis has been at the core of television studies, particularly those of a *semiological* bent.

Roland Barthes makes a distinction between the initial production of a cultural phenomenon and the resulting text as it is experienced by a reader or viewer in the form of, for instance, a television programme (Barthes, 1972). The text is composed of *signs* which are used together according to a set of *codes* and *conventions*, including those of *narrative*, technique (for instance, lighting, editing and camera use) and characterisation. Together they can generate a set of meanings or a message. The point of semiology is to deconstruct texts to understand how they and their constituent parts work to create this meaning.

Barthes is clear that the meaning of texts is not fixed. They are *polysemic* in that they may be interpreted by *audiences* in diverse ways. However, texts may be more or less closed or open to interpretation. Closed texts, such as television *news* programmes, are structured to confine potential meanings and therefore tend to be more predictable for audiences. Conversely, open texts – examples might be *The X-Files* or many British television *advertisements* – provide greater space for audiences to make meaning and are therefore less 'reassuring'. Even here, though, audiences evolve their understanding, gradually learning more about the structures and processes of texts. For example, viewers become familiar with the enigma codes by which narratives steadily reveal information required to solve textual problems such as 'who did the crime?' This comprises part of the *pleasure* of a text.

Baudrillard claims that *postmodernity* is characterised by a 'blizzard' of signs and texts that relate to each other in an increasingly tangled web of *intertextuality* (Watson, 1998). Viewers, however, are skilled enough to understand or at least experience single texts in the context of other texts from across the mass media. A typical episode of *The Simpsons*, for example, relies for some of its humour on sophisticated references to television programmes, films and other media text.

Television study that restricts itself to textual analysis have criticised, first for neglecting an account of who or what produced, text and in what social, historical and political circumstance. For second, for ignoring the question of how audiences react of a example, a focus on the text as a solitary unit will not take over an network's concern to capture and shape an audience's viate the evening or longer (see *Scheduling*). Neither will it channel audience's experience of viewing, which might television surfing and 'doing other things' while watch*it*–led work (Geraghty and Lusted, 1998). Accordingly, the b in television studies shows, at the least, an awareness of production contexts and active audiences.

See also: **Intertextuality, Semiology, Sign**

Further reading: Fiske (1987); Geraghty and Lusted (1998); Lacey (1998)

USES AND GRATIFICATIONS

'Uses and gratifications' is the term given to an audience research model which became particularly influential from the late 1950s to the 1970s in both Britain – by researchers such as Jay Blumler – and the United States – notably by Elihu Katz. The uses and gratifications approach developed partly in response to the failure of early 'effects' research to produce consistent or persuasive findings (see *Effects*). One of the main problems with early 'effects' research, critics argued, was that the role of *audiences* in the creation of meaning was not sufficiently well developed. Audiences would be seen as passive recipients of media messages rather than active consumers of those messages.

The uses and gratifications approach reversed the question asked by early media researchers. Rather than asking what the media do to people, they asked what people did with the media. In this formulation, audiences are seen as individuals with values, interests and needs – people who play a variety of social roles that inform how, when and why they consume media. Media use does not just happen, it performs a specific set of functions. It might be used to inform, to entertain or to provide something to do while eating an evening meal. Television can then be seen in terms of how, and how far, it gratifies those using it. So, for example, those people who watch the *news* seeking to be entertained may interpret what they see differently from those who watch seeking to be informed. Or those people who are highly motivated viewers of news may form a different impression from those who are watching it merely because it's on. A uses and gratifications approach thereby allows researchers to differentiate between audience members not merely in terms of demographic characteristics, but in terms of their pattern of media use.

The development of this approach is regarded by many as a significant step forward in the study of media influence. Rather than seeing audiences as merely accepting or refusing media messages, uses and gratifications conceptualises a more complex, interactive relationship between media and audiences. Audiences, in short, are seen as an active part of the process. This model is a notable departure from the pessimism of some of the early *mass culture* or mass persuasion theories of media influence, which saw media as a potential source of manipulation and propaganda. It is, in this sense, more in tune with a consumerist model of market research, in which people are seen as having certain needs (the need to do housework efficiently, the need to be popular, the need to be attractive, etc.) which may be gratified by selling them certain products.

Critics of the uses and gratifications approach argue that the consumerist aspect of uses and gratifications can ignore the role the media play in creating needs. Many adolescent girls, for example, may feel an intense need to conform to certain notions of attractiveness – a need that the media have helped create and reinforce with relentless portrayals of ideal women with a particular look and body type (see *Gender*). In contemporary consumer culture, relatively few needs could be regarded as fairly universal (such as the need to eat or the need to sleep). Most are socially constructed by *ideological* agencies like television or the cultural industries. Critics have also argued that if early mass culture theories gave the media too much power, uses and gratifications has merely shifted the problem by granting audiences too much power. The role of media, accordingly, is reduced to a function of audience needs or motivation – thus the news is judged partly by whether it does or does not perform an 'information function' or an 'entertainment function'. The fact that people use media to fulfil certain functions or that they approach it with certain motivations, critics argue, does not mean that the media might not also be exerting an influence.

Not all uses and gratifications research, however, can be dismissed for a failure to consider the question of media effects. The model has also been used as a way of refining a media effects approach – particularly by developing the notion of motivation. Media influence is, in this instance, seen as something that is mediated by the way people use media or by their motivations. Studies have focused, for example, on the way political messages have influenced different people in different ways. Groups of highly motivated viewers with an interest in politics tended to be influenced by one type of message, while less interested viewers with less motivation to watch were more persuaded by another type of message. Where a traditional effects study might have produced data that was confused and difficult to interpret, this type of study establishes clear and intelligible patterns of media influence.

As audience research has evolved, many researchers have dropped the functional focus of the uses and gratifications model but retained and developed the idea that the influence of a medium like television is mediated by patterns of media use. Media are therefore studied within specific social contexts. The work of researchers such as David Morley in Britain and James Lull in the United States have used ethnographic approaches to establish patterns of TV viewing – patterns with, for example, systematic variations between men and women – and to investigate the social role media technology plays in people's everyday lives.

The *cultural studies* approach to media audiences (see *Encoding and decoding*) has also retained the notion of active audiences, but has focused less on the idea of motivation and more on the notion of ideology. Audiences are seen as having a set of ideological assumptions, and these assumptions will play a part in the way in which they engage with media, what media messages or *texts* mean to them and how they may be influenced by media. While uses and gratifications has tended to see these kinds of assumption as pre-given, cultural studies stresses that the media can also play an ideological role in creating or reinforcing certain assumptions.

See also: **Audiences, Effects, Encoding and decoding**

Further reading: Berger (1991); Blumler and Katz (1974); J. Lewis (1991)

VIDEO

The term 'video' is derived from the Latin *videre*, which means 'to see'. Developments in video *technology* have had an impact in all spheres of moving image production but the most significant of these developments have been in relation to television. However, while video and television have developed in close association with each other since the 1950s and seem to have a symbiotic relationship, it is misleading to think of video as simply being a by-product or 'subset' (Cubitt, 1993) of television. Since the 1980s and the availability of relatively low-priced video hardware and software (VCRs, camcorders, videotapes, editing decks) on domestic markets, relations between television producers, texts and audiences have been considerably reconfigured. Audiences are able to timeshift programmes, rent (or buy) pre-recorded videotapes or, alternatively, produce their own viewing material. Thus, as Wyver (1989) suggests, historically the relationship between television and video has been an uneasy one.

Due to the flexibility of video in the recording and reproduction of visual images (with the added facility of instant playback), broadcasters expressed an interest in video technology from the outset. The main developments in video technology took place in the USA in the 1950s and were principally developed through the work of Charles Ginsburg and the Ampex Corporation. By 1958, Ampex-produced video equipment was being used by broadcasters in America (particularly in the areas of *sport* and *news*) as well as being imported into Britain and parts of Europe. Initially, the problems incurred through the very basic design of early video technology meant that the disadvantages of using video often outweighed the advantages. The magnetic recording of images on to videotape offered a cheap alternative to film stock (because videotape is reusable) but it was, to begin with, notoriously difficult and time-consuming to edit. Furthermore, the cumbersome cameras and recording technology meant that quite often working with video was more of a hindrance than a benefit. It was not until the 1960s, with the invention of lightweight and smaller camera kits (portapaks) and more sophisticated electronic editing equipment, that video technology became more widespread throughout the television industry.

During the mid to late 1960s some artists began to experiment with video as a means of exploring new creative possibilities in the field of moving image *production*. Quite often, practitioners were concerned with constructing avant-garde/experimental non-narrative pieces that challenged (aesthetically and ideologically) the *codes* and *conventions* of mainstream film and television. Alongside these developments a distinctive social/*documentary* strand of video production also emerged – the influences of which can be identified in current variations of *access* and *community television* programming. Film-makers were able to get out of the studios and 'document' aspects of people's lives in a way which was previously unthought of, since with the new lightweight video equipment location shooting became much easier. There was a general sense, for those working in the margins of the media industries as well for some media professionals, that video was an important medium that would fundamentally transform production. It was widely perceived as being the technology that could lead to the democratisation of television (Hood, 1987). The video 'revolution', however, was short-lived, and the utopian dimensions of the new technology quickly diminished as it became apparent that, in spite of its portability and relative ease of use, video technology needed the support systems of more sophisticated (and more expensive) technologies which were largely unavailable to ordinary people.

The 1970s saw the emergence of VCRs (video-cassette recorders) on the domestic market and the subsequent struggle for an industry standard between competing manufacturers which continued into the 1980s. Consumer demand for VCRs increased dramatically and continued to do so into the 1990s.

The significance of video technology being available on domestic markets should not be underestimated. Video has significantly altered the time/space characteristics of television. Timeshifting gives audiences more control over their viewing, while choice for audiences increases as one channel can be watched while another is being recorded. Audiences are no longer 'locked into' broadcasters' *schedules*. Indeed, viewers can choose to opt out of schedules altogether by choosing to hire (or purchase) a pre-recorded tape such as a Hollywood movie or a special interest videotape (which may encompass a variety of choices from exercise and fitness to pornography). The availability of camcorders (lightweight video camera-recorders) in the late 1980s also means that audiences can now produce their own videotapes (the 'home video' being the most popular domestic use of camcorder technology). Moreover, video game systems give audiences a strategy wherein the television set simply becomes a 'channel' for the playing of video games.

While there is no specific body of theory relating to video in the sense that there is for film and television, there is a growing body of diverse and interdisciplinary literature concerning various aspects of video production. The reason for this, according to Cubitt (1993), is that there is no essential form of video – it is difficult to pin down to a precise set of meanings or a fixed identity. The diverse applications of video technology and the number of uses to which it can be put all point to video as a means of transcending boundaries (Brocker and Brooker, 1997). The eclecticism and sheer diversity of video mean that it has been deployed in a variety of areas from the blatantly commercial to the avant-garde/experimental. Its ability to fuse and therefore blur the cultural boundaries between these two categories, as in *music video*, makes it a somewhat elusive technology to categorise. It is precisely these qualities that have inspired some theorists to cite video as a *postmodern* phenomenon.

In spite of the eclectic nature and the politically and aesthetically transgressive potential of video, it has, more or less, been successfully incorporated into mainstream media production. Like all new technologies, video has been subject to various laws and restrictions concerning copyright, licensing, classification, distribution and circulation. Anxieties concerning 'video nasties' and their '*effects*' on audiences (particularly *children*) led to the implementation of the Video Recording Act (1984) in the UK and the creation of related censorship laws. This legislation also worked to limit and marginalise independent and alternative video production.

The two most popular uses for video in a domestic context, then, are first the recording of mainstream television programmes, and second the viewing of mainstream Hollywood movies. Even the 'home video' has been successfully packaged for audiences in popular programmes such as *America's Funniest Home Videos* and (in Britain) *You've Been Framed*. Recent developments in satellite and digital delivery systems, along with the introduction of DVD (Digital Video Discs) and VOD (Video On Demand) systems, will no doubt further change the ways in which producers, distributors and consumers utilise, and interact with, video technology.

See also: **Access, Music video, Postmodernism, Technology**

Further reading: Armes (1988); Cubitt (1993); Gray (1992); Wyver (1989)

VIOLENCE

Concern about the relationship between mediated violence and its *effects* on *audiences* has been levelled at various 'new' media – including the cinema and comics – for over a century. Debates surrounding television violence and its consequences have often been close to the top of political and academic agendas in a range of societies. Opinions on the subject vary from those who express disquiet about the incursions into personal freedom that censorship entails to those who attribute the breakdown of social and cultural relations or indeed the abandonment of entire value systems to the violent media images audiences consume. The causal relationship between televised violence and juvenile crime in particular is a constant source of media and political debate.

As a media commodity, violence is popular with many film and television producers because of its suitability for a global audience. In short, unlike many forms of *comedy* or *drama*, violence requires little translation and therefore travels well. At a political level, a vociferous lobby against televised violence has been very influential across the channels and the airwaves in Britain and the US. The argument often involves emotive language concerned with notions of innocence, corruption and protection – especially with regard to *children*. In Britain, a familiar source of anti-violence rhetoric has been Mary Whitehouse and the National Viewers and Listeners Association (NVLA) which has held the torch for 'standards' on the televising of violence (as well as language and *sexuality*) and its *scheduling*. Similarly, the American critic Michael Medved has argued that the Hollywood entertainment industry feeds audiences a diet of extreme violence and sexual immorality which then has an unambiguously negative effect on behaviour (Medved, 1992). The popular press has made much of 'copycat violence'. For example, in America John Hinckley was alleged to have thought he was Travis Bickle, the avenging protagonist in Scorsese's film *Taxi Driver*, while the judge in the Bulger child-murder case in Britain laid some of the blame at the door of *Child's Play III*. Similarly, *Beavis and Butthead* has excited a great deal of moral indignation following dubious allegations that it was directly responsible for instances of arson. Indeed, the notion that screen violence can lead to copycat behaviour is now so familiar that it has been the subject of various television fictions, from episodes of *The Simpsons* (in which Maggie mimics violent moments from the *Itchy and Scratchy* cartoon) to *Law and Order* (in which the defendant in a murder trial blames his behaviour on media images).

While criticisms of media violence have traditionally come from the political right (often becoming blurred with discussions of sex), many more progressive voices have seen media violence as gratuitous, unimaginative and potentially a cause of anti-social or anti-democratic ways of thinking – one that, for example, makes aggressive foreign policy more palatable as a popular form of conflict resolution.

Academically, various studies have concluded that television violence causes or heightens the likelihood of actual violence. The Newsom Report, published in the aftermath of the Bulger case, asserted that what is experienced vicariously will have *some* effect on *some* people, and pointed at the millions of pounds spent on advertising as proof. The report expressed concern that the viewer is made to identify with the perpetrator of the act and not with the victim, and, further, that watching acts of violence which they otherwise could not have imagined results in mimicry of behaviour by children and adolescents (Newsom, 1994). In rigorous research based on a variety of techniques, Belsen (1978) found a positive correlation between watching television violence and seriously violent acts by adolescent boys. In a rather more diluted form, some effects research has suggested that prolonged exposure to television, whether television *news*, *crime series*, pornography or whatever, will have a gradual 'desensitising' influence on audiences.

While, as we shall see, there are powerful criticisms of this stance, it is worth noting that research using a similarly positivist methodology has argued that some kinds of television may also have a positive effect on audiences. For example, children might learn more co-operative behaviour after watching relevant programmes in which such values are stressed.

Opponents of this position have begun by criticising the largely behavioural orientation of much of the research. The limitations are numerous and include the artificiality of laboratory settings, the showing of clips out of context (since most people watch television amid various other social activities), and, in some cases, the under-representation of working-class people and females among participants.

Critics have also gone on to question the unclear articulation of terms, asking what exactly is being talked about as violence. Underpinning both these criticisms is the idea that violence should be considered as an essentially cultural concept with a meaning and significance dependent on a complexity of social, cultural and historical circumstances. Violence is many-faceted and encompasses varied forms of behaviour (political, sexual, physical, emotional, and so on) in numerous contexts. The full meaning or, more importantly, our understanding of a violent act depends – as does any act – upon its context. The perpetrator, the victim, the severity of the act, the justification behind the act and the wider cultural concepts of morality and justice (such as the acceptability of certain legitimate, legalised forms of violence by the state), all contribute to the full weight of the meaning behind the act itself.

This argument can be extended to the relationship between a violent *text* and its alleged effect. Consequences may be influenced by the individual character of the viewer and his or her social identity, with *gender* being especially significant. Similarly, media violence occurs in a context that is separable from the text itself. So, for television to affect our behaviour we need to be in a particular frame of mind, of a certain orientation, at a certain moment, in a specific grouping, and so forth (Messenger Davies, 1989). Life experiences, then, can be argued to be more important than mediated experiences.

Textual analysis has also pointed to the contextualised definition of violence, which in any programme has a specific and variable meaning. Buckingham (1993b) argues that meaning has been fundamentally neglected in much of the research, it being seen as inherent in the 'message' and transmittable directly into the mind and thence, somehow, to the behaviour of the viewer. But in fact violence within the narrative might be represented as immoral, for instance where it is carried out by anonymous criminals, or moral, where it is perpetrated by police. It might be graphic but 'wrong', as in hospital dramas, veiled, as on some television news, or indeed comic, as in cartoons. Quantitative *content analysis* might miss these distinctions by comparing the incomparable. It might class together scenes that are essentially different in nature. The violence in *Tom and Jerry*, in one sense, far outstretches even the worst video nasties, but in its system of signification it is recognisably different from the realistic portrayal of a brutal rape.

Cultivation analysis has taken a rather different stance in the analysis of television violence, focusing not on the relationship between violence and behaviour but on the portrayal of violence and people's perceptions of the world. In the US, researchers have discovered what they call the 'Mean World Syndrome' in that heavy viewing of television appears to encourage a fear of violence that may be out of proportion with the actual risk people face. This, they argue, has political consequences, in that it may incline people towards politicians who promote a hard-line approach to law and order. Research suggests that this pattern is not necessarily replicated elsewhere, which may be a reflection of the greater volume of violence in US television.

The debate, then, has tended to polarity, with the more extreme opposition to violent television setting mutually influential academic, political and moral agendas. What is apparent is that any discussion of violent television needs to begin with a developed understanding of the relationship between texts and audiences and a lengthy discussion of methodology.

See also: **Audiences, Children and television, Content analysis, Effects**

Further reading: Braham (1987); Buckingham (1993b); Petley (1997); Signorielli and Morgan (1990)

WOMEN IN TELEVISION

There is no getting away from the fact that traditionally, and world-wide, the television industries have been dominated by men (Unesco, 1987). While men were predominant in most occupations earlier in the twentieth century, it is probably of some additional significance that the early period of television coincided with a time when (at least in the developed western world) prevailing ideologies of womanhood kept women largely confined to the home. Thus it is no real surprise that there were few women in positions of authority or *power* in the early days of television. Certain significant changes have taken place in the last thirty years, and these have raised awareness about gender inequalities within the industry, but the question remains whether the gender map of the industry has been irrevocably changed. Television now provides a range of career opportunities for women, but it may be premature to talk of equality within this domain.

Focusing on this area raises a number of related issues: what, if anything, is the relationship between employment patterns within television organisations and televisual *representations*? Has the presence of more women in television made any difference to actual programmes? Or are numbers less important than whether women are able to occupy positions of influence and power? What are the opportunities and limitations presented by having more women in television?

Research into these questions on both sides of the Atlantic tells much the same story. In Britain, the 1975 enquiry into equal opportunities carried out by the Association of Cinematograph, Television and Allied Technicians within the industry showed that the position of women had not improved but had deteriorated since the 1950s, when women represented 18 per cent of the workforce in TV. By 1975, the figure had decreased to 15 per cent, with women concentrated in areas such as costume, make-up and production secretary, with very few in technical production roles. In 1986, figures by ITCA (Independent Television Companies Association) found that out of 306 cameramen (*sic*) only 12 were women; of 269 sound technicians, 8 were women; and of 1,395 engineers, 19 were women (Muir, 1988).

Monica Simms' survey of the BBC in 1985 reached similar conclusions. Looking at the BBC top grades, she found that 159 were men while only 6 were women. Simms came up with nineteen recommendations, one of which was the establishment of a women's employment officer, so issues such as job-sharing and flexible hours were put on the agenda. The BBC today has vastly improved its equal opportunities policy, but even so relatively few women make it to the top. Long hours, unsociable shifts, having to jump up and move at a moment's notice, all still apply; and so, while women continue to be major child-carers, it is not surprising that few women ascend to the most powerful jobs in television (Muir, 1988). In *commercial television* too, developments have been significant though mixed. The 1990 Broadcasting Act ruled that Channels 3, 4 and 5 must, as a licence condition, provide an annual statement of action taken to put equal opportunities into effect and the 1996 Broadcasting Act up-dated these conditions.

Channel 4's remit to provide a forum for innovative programmes has worked in favour of some women, especially through encouragement to set up their own *production* companies. But in the proliferation of satellite, cable and digital channels, early indications show little evidence of the promotion of work by women (as opposed to more conventional women-focused lifestyle and shopping programmes). Unless there is a stated determination to provide equal opportunities, then, the new companies have so far tended to adopt old ways, in both employment patterns and in gender representations. With the increasing fragmentation of the TV industries and the tendency for 'project-based' or short-term contracts, many women are going into or setting up their own independent production companies. But even in this sector women are in the minority, with only about 15 per cent of top management places being occupied by women.

In the USA, a similar pattern has emerged. Following the struggles for various forms of civil rights during the 1960s and 1970s, the US Federal Communications Commission made discrimination on the grounds of gender illegal in 1969, and this began to come into force in 1971. Other legal measures introduced in this period were assessed by later research, showing that by 1980, women held 21.5 per cent of top jobs (defined in four categories) in commercial television stations, and by 1985 this had increased to 26.7 per cent (Castro, 1988). While on the face of it this appeared to represent a considerable improvement, further investigations found that the figures were somewhat deceptive because the four categories used for analysis included more than 80 per cent of all television jobs. Moreover, many jobs had been given new labels in order for them to appear in these categories.

Affirmative action programmes in the USA have had varying degrees of success at different periods of time with, for instance, gains being made (particularly for women from minority groups) in the 1970s, followed by a period of stagnation during the Reagan administration (Stone, 1988). Additionally, an abundance of research shows that women have tended to earn significantly less on average than men in all sectors of the television industries, a pattern that has been largely consistent on both sides of the Atlantic and in other countries. Moreover, in areas where women have entered the television industries in larger numbers, this has been accompanied by an overall decline in salary levels and status (van Zoonen, 1994).

It might be assumed that this 'feminisation' of television has resulted in profound cultural, organisational and representational change. But even with increasing numbers of women employed in the industry, the culture of television is still considered by many to be highly masculine. In her controversial McTaggart Lecture at the Edinburgh Television Festival in the mid 1990s, Janet Street-Porter asserted that the industry is dominated by the 'Three Ms' – male, middle class and mediocre. Similarly, Anne Ross Muir (1988) has argued that if women are clustered in the lower-paid and lower-status positions within the industry, then they are less likely to be able to influence the kinds of representations we see on television. Television companies, therefore, far from challenging sexism, tend to reproduce it. She argues that most television programmes exhibit a masculine point of view because men control the industry.

This is evident in a number of ways, from the kinds of programmes that are commissioned to the decisions about who makes them. Chaudhuri (1999) has argued that the last bastion of male supremacy on television may be the *game show*. Taking popular shows such as *Who Wants to Be a Millionaire?* she argues that women are far less likely to apply to be contestants, are less likely to be chosen and are less likely to win larger prizes. Moreover, this is unsurprising because most programmes still have men as their producers, presenters and question compilers. Women contestants may be treated differently from men, and most of the questions have a male orientation. So it is possible to argue that even though many more women now work in the television industries, the culture is still overwhelmingly masculine and organisational patterns and cultures within television companies inevitably influence programming content and values.

Research by van Zoonen on feminism and journalism (1989) showed a conflict between professional norms and individual intentions. Women journalists who espoused *feminist* ethics found that although such ideas were included in their training, they became difficult to apply in a professional setting. The work culture was conservative and masculine; feminism was not seen as relevant to producing the news. Although these women reported a high degree of autonomy in their work, they also found that there were insurmountable obstacles to producing any work that focused on improving the position of women, and after a while the women began to see this as 'normal' and taken for granted. Thus, the influence of organisational socialisation might go some way towards explaining the limitations on women in altering the content or style of programmes.

It would be naïve to assume that increasing the numbers of women (or any other less powerful group) will automatically change the nature of programming. Too many other factors are involved, including the influence of generic *codes* and *conventions* as well as the collective nature of much work in television. Some would argue that identifying a common 'feminine approach' would also be needed, and this may prove difficult. But equally, it is over-pessimistic to argue that women who work in television simply adopt a dominant set of values. Squire's (1997) study of *The Oprah Winfrey Show* has demonstrated that as a powerful figure in television production, Winfrey uses her show to question common assumptions about *class*, *gender* and *race*, and overtly attempts to empower women. In this popular and influential US daytime television talk show, with a predominantly female audience and a majority of female guests, Winfrey utilises traditionally feminine traits such as touching, laughing and crying to connect with her audience. But, Squire argues, Winfrey also links personal issues with a clear interest in women's advancement, giving the show a feminist agenda. Winfrey occupies a privileged space in the television hierarchy, a space that is not typically held by women, but her example raises possibilities for others. Despite some reservations, then, it can be concluded that in certain conditions, work produced by women may well focus on particular kinds of subject matter or foreground particular concerns that have been taken up less frequently by men (Real, 1989; Erens, 1990).

In summary, changes in the legal framework around employment opportunities have been crucial, but these do not guarantee that women will achieve equality with men in the masculine culture of television. Women are not necessarily racing to the top, and most women in television are still working in the lower echelons of their organisations. Nonetheless, in organisations with a higher proportion of women in the primary positions, there is greater likelihood of more women in the next layer down: that is, in senior production jobs. Whether the presence of more women working in television directly influences television output is at present difficult to establish, with factors working for and against change. It is evident, though, that some changes have taken place, with a greater proportion of programmes featuring women in central roles and in a wider range of roles (see Gender).

The most persistent patterns of employment discrimination tend to be those that are also most difficult to identify and prove. These are culturally based factors such as the operation of informal (male) networks and the attitudes of some men to their female colleagues. Van Zoonen (1994) has added that, in many countries, perceived clashes between the norms and expectations of femininity and motherhood and those of professionalism work against equal opportunities for women in broadcasting.

The overall picture at the beginning of the twenty-first century is that women are offered greater legal protection and have made huge strides in some areas of broadcasting. Information on patterns of employment has frequently come from the television industries themselves, who have initiated research into employment patterns, often as a means of generating and monitoring equal opportunities policy. There is no doubt that there are more women in television today, and many authoritative and respected figures in television are now women. But institutional and cultural obstacles, not least the informal operation of a masculine *hegemony*, persist, and the power base remains overwhelmingly male.

See also: **Gender, Power**

Further reading: Brunsdon *et al.* (1997); van Zoonen (1994)

BIBLIOGRAPHY

Abercrombie, N. (1996) *Television and Society*, Cambridge: Polity.

Allen, D. and Kaur, R. (1993) 'Race and racism', in K. McLeish (ed.) *Bloomsbury Guide to Human Thought: Ideas that Shaped the World*, London: Bloomsbury.

Allen, R. (1985) *Speaking of Soap Operas*, Chapel Hill: University of North Carolina Press.

——(1987) *Channels of Discourse*, London: Methuen.

——(ed.) (1992) *Channels of Discourse Reassembled*, London: Routledge.

——(ed.) (1995) *To Be Continued: Soap Operas Around the World*, London and New York: Routledge.

Althusser, L. (1971) 'Ideology and ideological state apparatuses', in L. Althusser, *Lenin and Philosophy*, London: New Left Books.

Ang, I. (1985) *Watching Dallas: Soap Opera and the Melodramatic Imagination*, London: Methuen.

Appadurai, A. (1990) 'Disjuncture and difference in the global cultural economy', in M. Featherstone (ed.) *Global Culture: Nationalism, Globalization and Modernity*, London: Sage.

Arbuthnot, L. and Seneca, G. (1990) 'Pretext and text in *Gentlemen Prefer Blondes*', in P. Erens (ed.) *Issues in Feminist Film Criticism*, Bloomington: Indiana University Press.

Ariés, R. (1973) *Centuries of Childhood*, Harmondsworth: Penguin.

Armes, R. (1988) *On Video*, London: Routledge.

Arnold, M. (1960 [1869]) *Culture and Anarchy*, London: Cambridge University Press.

Baehr, H. and Dyer, G. (eds) (1987) *Boxed In: Women and Television*, New York and London: Pandora.

Barker, C. (1997) *Global Television: An Introduction*, Oxford: Blackwell.

Barthes, R. (1972) *Mythologies*, New York: Noonday Press.

——(1974) *S/Z*, New York: Hill and Wang.

——(1988) 'The old rhetoric: an aide-memoire', in R. Barthes, *The Semiotic Challenge*, tr. Richard Howard, New York: Hill and Wang.

Baudrillard, J. (1983) *Simulations*, New York: Semiotext.

——(1988) *Selected Writings*, ed. M. Poster, Stanford: Stanford University Press.

Bell, A. (1991) *The Language of News Media*, Oxford: Blackwell.

Belsen, W. (1978) *Television Violence and the Adolescent Boy*, Farnborough: Saxon House.

Benjamin, W. (1973) *Illuminations*, London: Fontana.

Bennett, T. (1981) 'Popular culture: defining our terms', in T. Bennett, *Popular Culture: Themes and Issues*, Unit 1/2, Milton Keynes: Open University Press.

Bennett, T., Boyd-Bowman, S., Mercer, C. and Woollacott, J. (eds) (1981) *Popular Television and Film*, London: BFI/Open University Press.

Bennett, T., Martin, G., Mercer, C. and Woollacott, J. (eds) (1981) *Culture, Ideology and Social Process*, Milton Keynes: Open University Press.

Berger, A. (1991) *Media Analysis Techniques*, California, London, Delhi: Sage.

——(1995) *Cultural Criticism: A Primer of Key Concepts, Foundations of Popular Culture, Vol. 4*, Thousand Oaks, London, Delhi: Sage.

Bettelheim, B. (1969) *The Children of the Dream*, London: Thames and Hudson.

Bhaba, H. (1994) *The Location of Culture*, London: Routledge.

Birrell, S. and Loy, J. (1979) 'Media sport: hot and cool', *International Review of Sport Sociology*, 14(1): 5–19.

Blumler, J. (1991) 'The new television marketplace: imperatives, implications, issues', in J. Curran and M. Gurevitch (eds) *Mass Media and Society*, London: Methuen.

Blumler, J. and Katz, E. (eds) (1974) *The Uses of Mass Communications*, London: Sage.

Bogle, D. (1973) *Toms, Coons, Mulattoes, Mammies and Bucks: An Interpretative History of Blacks in American Films*, New York: Viking.

Bourdieu, P. (1986) *Distinction: A Social Critique of the Judgement of Taste*, trans. R. Nice, Cambridge, Mass.: Harvard University Press.

Bowes, M. (1990) 'Only when I laugh', in A. Goodwin and G. Whannel (eds) *Understanding Television*, London: Routledge.

Boyd-Barrett, O. and Newbold, C. (eds) (1995) *Approaches to Media: A Reader*, London and New York: Arnold.

Braham, P. (1987) *Media Effects*, Buckingham: Open University Press.

Brandt, G. (ed.) (1993) *British Television Drama in the 1980s*, Cambridge: Cambridge University Press.

Branston, G. (1998) 'Histories of British television', in C. Geraghty and D. Lusted (eds) *The Television Studies Book*, London and New York: Arnold.

Branston, G. and Stafford, R. (1996) *The Media Student's Book*, London and New York: Routledge.

Broadcasting Act (1990) *Public General Acts – Elizabeth II*, chapter 42, London: The Stationery Office.

Brooker, M. and Brooker, W. (eds) (1997) *Postmodern Afterimages*, London: Arnold.

Brooker, P. (1999) *A Concise Glossary of Cultural Theory*, London: Arnold.

Brooker, W. (1998) *Teach Yourself Cultural Studies*, London: Hodder Headline.

Brower, S. (1992) 'Fans as tastemakers: viewers for quality television', in L. Lewis (ed.) *The Adoring Audience: Fan Culture and Popular Media*, London: Routledge.

Brown, M.E. (1987) 'The politics of soaps: pleasure and feminine empowerment', *Australian Journal of Cultural Studies*, 4(2): 1–25.

Brunsdon, C. (1981) 'Crossroads: notes on soap opera', *Screen*, 22(4): 32–7.

——(1984) 'Writing about soap opera', in L. Masterman (ed.) *Television Mythologies: Stars, Shows, and Signs*, London: Comedia/MK Media Press.

——(1988) 'Feminism and soap opera', in K. Davies, J. Dickey and T. Stratford (eds) *Out of Focus: Writing on Women and the Media*, London: The Women's Press.

——(1998) 'What is the "television" of television studies?', in C. Geraghty and D. Lusted (eds) *The Television Studies Book*, London and New York: Arnold.

Brunsdon, C., D'Acci, J. and Spigel, L. (eds) (1997) *Feminist Television Criticism: A Reader*, Oxford: Oxford University Press.

Buckingham, D. (1987) *Public Secrets: EastEnders and its Audience*, London: BFI.

——(1993a) *Children Talking Television: The Making of Television Literacy*, London: Falmer Press.

——(1993b) *Reading Audiences; Young People and the Media*, Manchester and New York: Manchester University Press.

Burnett, R. (1996) *The Global Jukebox: The International Music Industry*, London: Routledge.

Burns, T. (1977) *The BBC: Public Institution and Private World*, London: Macmillan.

Butler, J. (1990) *Gender Trouble: Feminism and the Subversion of Identity*, London and New York: Routledge.

Butsch, R. (1995) 'Ralph, Fred, Archie and Homer: why television keeps recreating the white male working-class buffoon', in G. Dines and J. Humez (eds) *Gender, Race and Class in Media* Thousand Oaks, London, New Delhi: Sage.

Byars, J. (1991) *All that Hollywood Allows: Re-reading Gender in 1950s Melodrama*, Chapell Hill, NC: University of North Carolina Press.

Cantor, M. and Pingree, S. (1983) *The Soap Opera*, Beverly Hills, California: Sage.

Cashmore, E. (1996) *Making Sense of Sports*, London: Routledge.

Castro, J. (1988) 'Women in television: an uphill battle', *Channels*, January: 43–52.

Caughie, J. (1980) 'Progressive television and documentary drama', *Screen* 21(3): 9–35.

Certeau, M. de (1984) *The Practice of Everyday Life*, Berkeley: University of California Press.

Chapman, D. (1998) 'Downloading the documentary', in M. Wayne (ed.) *Dissident Voices: The Politics of Television and Political Change*, London: Pluto Press.

Chaudhuri, A. (1999) 'Who wants to be a quiz show contestant?', *Guardian*, 29 November.

Clark, D. (1995) 'Commodity lesbianism', in G. Dines and J.M. Humez (eds) (1995) *Gender, Race and Class in Media*, Thousand Oaks and London: Sage.

Clarke, A. (1986) ' "This is not the boy scouts": television police series and definitions of law and order', in T. Bennett (ed.) *Popular Culture and Social Relations*, Milton Keynes and Philadelphia: Open University Press.

Clarke, J. (1996) 'Crime and social order: interrogating the detective story', in J. Muncie and E. McLaughlin (eds) *The Problem of Crime*, London: Sage.

Cohen, S. and Hark, I. (1993) *Screening the Male: Exploring Masculinities in Hollywood Cinema*, London and New York: Routledge.

Commission of the European Communities (1987) *Equal Opportunities in European Broadcasting*, Brussels: Commission of the European Communities.

Communications Research Group, University of Aston (1990) *Television Advertising and Sex Role Stereotyping*, London: Broadcasting Standards Council.

Comstock, G. (1991) *Television in America*, Newbury Park and London: Sage.

Corner, J. (ed.) (1986) *Documentary and the Mass Media*, London: Arnold.

——(1991) 'Documentary voices', in J. Corner (ed.) *Popular Television in Britain*, London: BFI.

——(1996) 'Mediating the ordinary: the access idea and television form', in J. Corner and S. Harvey (eds) *Television Times: A Reader*, London: Arnold.

——(1999) *Critical Ideas in Television Studies*, Oxford: Oxford University Press.

Corner, J. and Harvey, S. (eds) (1996) *Television Times: A Reader*, London: Arnold.

Cottle, S. (1993) *TV News: Urban Conflict and the Inner City*, Leicester: Leicester University Press.

Crisell, A. (1997) *An Introductory History of British Broadcasting*, London: Routledge.

Cubitt, S. (1993) *Videography: Video Media as Art and Culture*, London: Macmillan.

Curran, J. and Gurevitch, M. (1996) *Mass Media and Society*, London: Arnold.

Curran, J. and Seaton, J. (1997) *Power Without Responsibility: The Press and Broadcasting in Britain*, London: Routledge.

Curtis, L. (1984) *Ireland: The Propaganda War. The British Media and the Battle for Hearts and Minds*, London: Pluto Press.

Dahlgren, P. (1995) *Television and the Public Sphere*, London: Sage.

Daniels, T. (1998) 'Television studies and race', in C. Geraghty and D. Lusted (eds) *The Television Studies Book*, London and New York: Arnold.

Derrida, J. (1978 [1967]) *Writing and Difference*, trans. Alan Bass, Chicago: University of Chicago Press.

Dickinson, R., Harindranath, R. and Linne, O. (eds) (1998) *Approaches to Audiences*, London: Arnold.

Dines, G. and Humez, J. (1995) *Gender, Race and Class in Media*, Thousand Oaks and London: Sage.

Doane, M. (1990) 'Film and the masquerade: theorizing the female spectator', in P. Erens (ed.) *Issues in Feminist Film Criticism*, Bloomington: Indiana University Press.

Docherty, T. (ed.) (1993) *Postmodernism: A Reader*, London: Harvester Wheatsheaf.

Dorfman, A. and Mattelart, A. (1975) *How to Read Donald Duck. Imperialist Ideology in the Disney Comic*, New York: International General Editions.

Dovey, J. (2000) *Freakshow: First Person Media and Factual Television*, London: Pluto Press.

Dowmunt, T. (ed.) (1994) *Channels of Resistance*, London: BFI.

During, S. (ed.) (1993) *The Cultural Studies Reader*, London: Routledge.

Dworkin, A. (1981) *Pornography: Men Possessing Women*, New York: Perigee.

Dyer, R. (1985a) 'Taking popular television seriously', in D. Lusted and P. Drummond (eds) *TV and Schooling*, London: BFI.

——(1985b) 'Male sexuality in the media', in A. Metcalf and M. Humphries (eds) *The Sexuality of Men*, London: Pluto Press.

——(1989) 'Don't look now', in A. McRobbie (ed.) *Zoot Suits and Second Hand Dresses: An Anthology of Fashion and Music*, London: Macmillan.

Dyer, R., Geraghty, C., Jordan, M., Lovell, T., Paterson, R. and Stewart, J. (1980) *Coronation Street*, London: BFI.

Easthope, A. (1986) *What a Man's Gotta Do: The Masculinity Myth in Popular Culture*, London: Paladin.

Eaton, M. (1981) 'Television situation comedy', in T. Bennett, S. Boyd-Bowman, C. Mercer and J. Woollacott (eds) *Popular Television and Film*, London: BFI.

Eco, U. (1972) 'Towards a semiotic inquiry into the television message', *Working Papers in Cultural Studies*, 3: 103–21.

——(1979) 'Can television teach?', *Screen Education*, 31: 15–25.

——(1981) *The Role of the Reader*, London: Hutchinson.

Ehrenreich, B. (1995) 'The silenced majority: why the average working person has disappeared from American media and culture', in G. Dines and J. Humez (eds) *Gender, Race and Class in Media*, Thousand Oaks and London: Sage.

Eldridge, J. (ed.) (1995) *News Content, Language and Visuals, Glasgow University Media Reader, vol. 1*, London: Routledge.

Eldridge, J., Kitzinger, J. and Williams, K. (1997) *The Mass Media and Power in Modern Britain*, Oxford: Oxford University Press.

Ellis, J. (1982) *Visible Fictions*, London: Routledge.

——(2000) 'Scheduling: the last creative act in television', *Media, Culture and Society*, 22(1).

Emerson, A. (1993) *Teaching Media in the Primary School*, Cassell: London.

Erens, P. (ed.) (1990) *Issues in Feminist Film Criticism*, Bloomington: Indiana University Press.

Ewen, S. (1976) *Captains of Consciousness*, New York: McGraw Hill.

Fairclough, N. (1992) *Discourse and Social Change*, Cambridge: Polity.

——(1995) *Media Discourse*, London: Arnold.

Faludi, S. (1991) *Backlash: The Undeclared War Against Women*, New York: Crown.

——(2000) *Stiffed: The Betrayal of Modern Man*, London: Random House, Vintage.

Ferguson, B. (1984) 'Black Blue Peter', in L. Masterman (ed.) *Television Mythologies*, London: Comedia.

——(1998) *Representing 'Race': Ideology, Identity and the Media*, London and New York: Arnold.

Fiske, J. (1987) *Television Culture*, London and New York: Routledge.

——(1989) *Reading the Popular*, London, Sydney, Wellington: Unwin Hyman.

——(1991) 'Moments of television: neither the text nor the audience', in E. Seiter, H. Borchers, G. Kreutzner and E. Warth (eds) *Remote Control: Television, Audiences and Cultural Power*, London and New York: Routledge.

——(1992) 'The cultural economy of fandom', in L. Lewis (ed.) *The Adoring Audience: Fan Culture and Popular Media*, London: Routledge.

Fiske, J. and Hartley, J. (1978) *Reading Television*, London: Routledge.

Flitterman-Lewis, S. (1987) 'Psychoanalysis, film and television', in R. Allen (ed.) *Channels of Discourse*, London: Methuen.

Freud, S. (1922) *Beyond the Pleasure Principle*, London: International Psycho-analytical Press.

Frith, S., Goodwin, A. and Grossberg, L. (eds) (1993) *Sound and Vision: The Music Video Reader*, London: Routledge.

Galtung, J. and Ruge, M. (1981) 'Structuring and selecting news', in S. Cohen and J. Young (eds) *The Manufacture of News; Social Problems, Deviance and the Mass Media*, London: Constable.

Gamman, L. (1988) 'Watching the detectives: the enigma of the female gaze', in L. Gamman and M. Marchment (eds) *The Female Gaze: Women as Viewers of Popular Culture*, London: The Women's Press.

Gamman, L. and Marshment, M. (eds) (1988) *The Female Gaze: Women as Viewers of Popular Culture*, London: The Women's Press.

Gans, H. (1979) *Deciding What's News*, New York: Vintage Books.

Garber, M. (1997) *Vice Versa: Bisexuality and the Eroticism of Everyday Life*, London: Hamish Hamilton.

Garnham, N. (1987) 'Concepts of culture: public policy and the cultural industries', *Cultural Studies* 1(1): 23–7.

——(1992) *Capitalism and Communication. Global Culture and the Economics of Information*, London: Sage.

Gauntlett, D. (1995) *Moving Experiences: Understanding Television's Influences and Effects*, London: John Libbey.

Gauntlett, D. and Hill, A. (1999) *TV Living: Television, Culture and Everyday Life*, London: Routledge.

Geraghty, C. (1991) *Women and Soap Opera: A Study of Prime-Time Soaps*, Cambridge: Polity.

Geraghty, C. and Lusted, D. (eds) (1998) *The Television Studies Book*, London and New York: Arnold.

Gerbner, G. and Signorielli, N. (1979) *Ageing with Television: Images of Television Drama and Conceptions of Social Reality*, Philadelphia: University of Pennsylvania, Annenberg School of Communication.

Giddens, A. (1990) *The Consequences of Modernity*, Cambridge: Polity.

Gillespie, M. (1995) *Television, Ethnicity and Cultural Change*, London: Routledge.

Gitlin, T. (1985) *Inside Primetime*, New York: Pantheon Books.

Glasgow University Media Group (1976) *Bad News*, London: Routledge and Kegan Paul.

——(1985) *War and Peace News*, Buckingham: Open University Press.

Goddard, P. (1991) 'Hancock's Half Hour: a watershed in British television comedy', in J. Corner (ed.) *Popular Television in Britain*, London: BFI.

Goffman, E. (1979) *Gender Advertisements*, New York: Harper and Row.

Goldlust, J. (1987) *Playing for Keeps: Sport, the Media and Society*, Melbourne: Longman Cheshire.

Goodwin, A. (1990) 'TV news: striking the right balance', in A. Goodwin and G. Whannel (eds) *Understanding Television*, London: Routledge.

——(1993) *Dancing in the Distraction Factory*, London: Routledge.

Goodwin, A. and Whannel, G. (eds) (1990) *Understanding Television*, London: Routledge.

Gramsci, A. (1971) *Selections from the Prison Notebooks*, ed. and trans. by Q. Hoare and G. Nowell-Smith, London: Lawrence and Wishart.

Gray, A. (1987) 'Behind closed doors: video recorders in the home', in H. Baehr and G. Dyer (eds) *Boxed In: Women and Television*, London: Pandora.

——(1992) *Video Playtime: The Gendering of a Leisure Technology*, London: Routledge.

Greer, G. (1971) *The Female Eunuch*, London: Paladin Press.

Gripsrud, J. (1998) 'Television, broadcasting, flow: key metaphors in TV theory', in C. Geraghty and D. Lusted (eds) *The Television Studies Book*, London: Arnold.

Groombridge, B. (1972) *Television and the People: A Programme for Democratic Participation*, Middlesex: Penguin.

Gross, L. (1995) 'Out of the mainstream: sexual minorities and the mass media', in G. Dines and J.M. Humez (eds) *Gender, Race and Class in Media*, Thousand Oaks and London: Sage.

Gunter, B. and McAleer, J. (1997) *Children and Television*, London: Routledge.

Gurevitch, M. (1991) 'The globalisation of electronic journalism', in J. Curran and M. Gurevitch, *Mass Media and Society*, London: Arnold.

Hall, S. (1980) 'Encoding/decoding', in S. Hall, D. Hobson, A. Lowe and P. Willis (eds) *Culture, Media, Language*, London: Routledge.

——(1981) 'The whites of their eyes: racist ideologies and the media', in G. Bridges and R. Brunt (eds) *Silver Linings*, London: Lawrence and Wishart.

——(1988) *The Hard Road to Renewal*. London: Verso.

——(1992) 'The question of cultural identity', in S. Hall, D. Held and T. McGrew (eds) *Modernity and its Futures*, Cambridge: Polity.

——(1997a) *Representation and the Media*, Northampton, Massachusetts: Media Education Foundation (video lecture).

——(ed.) (1997b) *Representation: Cultural Representations and Signifying Practices*, London, Thousand Oaks, New Delhi: Sage/Open University Press.

Hall, S. and Whannel, P. (1964) *The Popular Arts*, London: Hutchinson.

Hall, S. and Jefferson, T. (eds) (1976) *Resistance through Rituals*, London: Hutchinson.

Hall, S., Critcher, C., Jefferson, T., Clarke, J. and Roberts, B. (1978) *Policing the Crisis: Mugging, the State and Law and Order*, London: Macmillan.

Hall, S., Hobson, D., Lowe, A. and Willis, P. (eds) (1980) *Culture, Media, Language*, London: Hutchinson.

Hansen, A., Cottle, S., Negrine, R. and Newbold, C. (1998) *Mass Communication Research Methods*, London and Hampshire: Macmillan.

Hargreaves, J. (1994) *Sporting Females: Critical Issues in the History and Sociology of Women's Sports*, London: Routledge.

Harrison, M. (1985) *TV News, Whose Bias?*, London: Policy Journals.

Hartley, J. (1982) *Understanding News*, London: Methuen.

——(1998) 'Housing television: textual traditions in TV and cultural studies', in C. Geraghty and D. Lusted (eds) *The Television Studies Book*, London and New York: Arnold.

——(1999) *Uses of Television*, London: Routledge.

Hartmann, P. and Husband, C. (1973) 'The mass media and racial conflict', in S. Cohen and J. Young (eds) *The Manufacture of News*, London: Constable.

Haskell, M. (1987) *From Reverence to Rape: The Treatment of Women in the Movies*, Chicago: University of Chicago Press.

Hayward, S. (1996) *Key Concepts in Cinema Studies*, London: Routledge.

Hebdige, D. (1979) *Subculture: The Meaning of Style*, London and New York: Methuen, New Accents.

——(1988) *Hiding in the Light*, London: Comedia.

——(1998) 'Postmodernism and "the other side" ', in J. Storey (ed.) *Cultural Theory and Popular Culture: A Reader*, Hemel Hempstead: Prentice Hall.

Herman, E. and Chomsky, N. (1988) *Manufacturing Consent: The Political Economy of the Mass Media*, New York: Pantheon Books.

Hersey, E. (1998) 'Word-healers and code-talkers: Native Americans in *The X-Files*', *Journal of Popular Film and Television*, 26(3): 109–19.

Hiebert, R., Ungurait, D. and Bohn, T. (1991) *Mass Media VI: An Introduction to Modern Communication*, New York and London: Longman.

Hobson, D. (1982) *Crossroads: The Drama of a Soap Opera*, London: Methuen.

Hodge, R. and Tripp, D. (1986) *Children and Television: A Semiotic Approach*, Stanford: Stanford University Press.

Hoggart, R. (1957) *The Uses of Literacy*, London: Chatto & Windus.

Hollander, E. (1992) 'The emergence of small scale media', in N. Jankowski, O. Prehn and J. Stappers (eds) *The People's Voice: Local Radio and Television in Europe*, London: John Libbey.

Hollows, J. (2000) *Feminism, Femininity and Popular Culture*, Manchester and New York: Manchester University Press.

Hood, S. (1987) *On Television*, London: Pluto Press.

hooks, b. (1989) *Feminist Theory: From Margin to Center*, Boston: South End Press.

——(1990) *Yearning: Race, Gender and Cultural Politics*, Boston: South End Press.

——(1992) *Black Looks: Race and Representation*, Boston: South End Press.

Hurd, G. (1981) 'The television presentation of the police', in T. Bennett, S. Boyd-Bowman, C. Mercer and J. Woollacott (eds) *Popular Television and Film*, London: BFI/Open University Press.

Huston, A., Donnerstein, E., Fairchild, H., Feschbach, N., Katz, P., Murray, J., Rubenstein, E., Wilcox, B. and Zuckerman, D. (1992) *Big World, Small Screen: The Role of Television in American Society*, Lincoln: University of Nebraska Press.

Iyengar, S. and Kinder, D. (1987) *News That Matters*, Chicago: University of Chicago Press.

Jameson, F. (1984) 'Postmodernism, or the cultural logic of late capitalism', *New Left Review*, 146: 53–92.

Jankowski, N., Prehn, O. and Stappers, J. (eds) (1992) *The People's Voice: Local Radio and Television in Europe*, London: John Libbey.

Jenkins, H. (1992) *Textual Poachers*, London: Routledge.

Jensen, K. and Jankowski, N. (1993) *Qualitative Methodologies for Mass Communication Research*, London: Routledge.

Jenson, J. (1992) 'Fandom as pathology: the consequences of characterisation', in L. Lewis (ed.) *The Adoring Audience: Fan Culture and Popular Media*, London: Routledge.

Jhally, S. and Lewis, J. (1992) *Enlightened Racism:* The Cosby Show *, Audiences, and the Myth of the American Dream*, Boulder and Oxford: Westview.

Jones, L. (1996) 'Last week we had an omen: the mythological X-Files', in D. Laverty, H. Hague and M. Cartwright (eds) *Deny All Knowledge: Reading the X-Files*, London: Faber and Faber.

Kaplan, E.A. (1987) *Rocking around the Clock: Music Television, Postmodernism and Consumer Culture*, New York: Methuen.

Keighron, P. (1998) 'The politics of ridicule: satire and television', in M. Wayne (ed.) *Dissident Voices: The Politics of Television and Cultural Change*, London: Pluto Press.

Kellner, D. (1990) *Television and the Crisis of Democracy*, Colorado: Westview.

Kilborn, R. and Izod, J. (1997) *An Introduction to Television Documentary: Confronting Reality*, New York: St Martins Press.

Kinder, M. (1991) *Playing With Power in Movies, Television and Video Games*, Los Angeles: University of California Press.

Kirkham, P. and Skeggs, B. (1998) '*Absolutely Fabulous*: absolutely feminist?', in C. Geraghty and D. Lusted (eds) *The Television Studies Book*, London: Arnold.

Kubek, E. (1996) 'You only expose your father: the imaginary, voyeurism and the symbolic order in *The X-Files*', in D. Laverty, H. Hague and M. Cartwright (eds) *Deny All Knowledge: Reading the X-Files*, London: Faber and Faber.

Kuhn, A. with Radstone, S. (eds) (1990) *The Women's Companion to International Film*, London: Virago.

Lacey, N. (1998) *Image and Representation: Key Concepts in Media Studies*, Basingstoke: Macmillan.

Langer, J. (1998) *Tabloid Television*, London: Routledge.

Lau, G. (1993) 'Confessions of a complete scopophiliac', in P. Gibson and R. Gibson (eds) *Dirty Looks: Women Pornography, Power*, London: BFI.

Lavery, D., Hague, A. and Cartwright, M. (1996) *Deny All Knowledge: Reading the X-Files*, London: Faber and Faber.

Lazarsfeld, P. and Katz, E. (1955) *Personal Influence*, Glencoe Free Press.

Lazarsfeld, P., Berelson, B. and Gaudet, H. (1944) *The People's Choice*, New York: Columbia University Press.

Leavis, F.R. (1930) *Mass Civilisation and Minority Culture*, Cambridge: Minority Press.

Leiss, W., Kline, S. and Jhally, S. (1990) *Social Communication in Advertising*, New York: Methuen.

Leman, J. (1991) 'Wise scientists and female androids: class and gender in science fiction', in J. Corner (ed.) *Popular Television in Britain*, London: BFI.

Lewis, J. (1991) *The Ideological Octopus: Explorations into the Television Audience*, New York: Routledge.

Lewis, L. (ed.) (1992) *The Adoring Audience: Fan Culture and Popular Media*, London: Routledge.

——(1993) 'Emergence of female address on MTV', in S. Frith, A. Goodwin and L. Grossberg (eds) *Sound and Vision: The Music Video Reader*, London: Routledge.

Lewis, P. (1986) *Media and Power*, London: Camden Press.

Liebes, T. and Katz, E. (1993) *The Export of Meaning*, Oxford: Oxford University Press.

Lippmann, W. (1922, republished 1965) *Public Opinion*, New York: Free Press.

Livingstone, S. (1999) 'Mediated knowledge', in J. Gripsrud (ed.) *Television and Common Knowledge*, London: Routledge.

Lull, J. (1990) *Inside Family Viewing*, London: Routledge.

Lundby, K. (1992) 'Community television as a tool of local culture', in N. Jankowski, O. Prehn and J. Stappers (eds) *The People's Voice: Local Radio and Television in Europe*, London: John Libbey.

Lyotard, J. (1984) *The Postmodern Condition*, Manchester: Manchester University Press.

McArthur, C. (1978) *Television and History*, London: BFI.

McChesney, R. (2000) *Rich Media, Poor Democracy*, Chicago: University of Illinois Press.

McCombs, M. (1981) 'The agenda-setting approach', in D. Nimmo and K. Saunders (eds) *Handbook of Political Communication*, California: Sage.

Macionis, J. and Plummer, K. (1998) *Sociology: A Global Introduction*, New York: Prentice Hall Europe.

McLeish, K. (ed.) (1993) *Bloomsbury Guide to Human Thought: Ideas that Shaped the World*, London: Bloomsbury.

McQuail, D. (1994) *Mass Communication Theory*, London: Sage.

McQuail, D. and Windahl, S. (1993) *Communication Models for the Study of Mass Communication*, London: Longman.

McQueen, D. (1998) *Television: A Media Student's Guide*, London: Arnold.

Maltby, R. and Craven, I. (1995) *Hollywood Cinema*, Oxford and Cambridge, Mass.: Blackwell.

Marc, D. (1989) *Comic Visions: Television Comedy and American Culture*, London: Unwin Hyman.

Marcuse, H. (1964) *One Dimensional Man*, London: Routledge and Kegan Paul.

Marris, P. and Thornham, S. (1996) *Media Studies: A Reader*, Edinburgh: Edinburgh University Press.

Marshall, G. (ed.) (1994) *The Concise Oxford Dictionary of Sociology*, Oxford and New York: Oxford University Press.

Masterman, L. (1985) *Teaching the Media*, London: Comedia.

——(1992) 'The case for television studies', in M. Alvarado and O. Boyd-Barrett (eds) *Media Education*, London: BFI and Open University.

Mattelart, A., Delcourt, X. and Mattelart, M. (1984) *International Image Markets*, London: Comedia.

Medhurst, A. and Tuck, L. (1996) 'Situation comedy and stereotyping', in J. Corner and S. Harvey (eds) *Television Times: A Reader*, London: Arnold.

Medved, M. (1992) *Hollywood versus America: Popular Culture and the War on Traditional Values*, Zondervan: HarperCollins.

Mercer, K. (1994) *Welcome to the Jungle*, London and New York: Routledge.

Messenger Davies, M. (1989) *Television is Good for Kids*, London: Hilary Shipman.

Miles, R. (1989) *Racism*, London: Routledge.

Millett, K. (1970) *Sexual Politics*, London: Abacus.

Milner, A. (1994) *Contemporary Cultural Theory: An Introduction*, London: UCL Press.

Modleski, T. (1982) *Loving with a Vengeance: Mass Produced Fantasies for Women*, London: Methuen.

——(1991) *Feminism without Women*, London: Routledge.

——(1997) 'The search for tomorrow in today's soap operas', in C. Brunsdon, J. D'Acci and L. Spigel (1997) *Feminist Television Criticism: A Reader*, Oxford: Oxford University Press.

Moores, S. (1995) *Satellite Television and Everyday Life: Articulating Technology*, London: John Libbey.

Morgan, M. and Shanahan, J. (1995) *Democracy Tango: Television, Adolescents, and Authoritarian Tensions in Argentina*, Cresskill, NJ: Hampton Press.

Morley, D. (1980) *The Nationwide Audience*, London: BFI.

——(1986) *Family Television*, London: Comedia.

——(1992) *Television, Audiences and Cultural Studies*, London: Routledge.

Morley, D. and Robbins, K. (1995) *Spaces of Identity: Global Media, Electronic Landscapes and Cultural Boundaries*, London and New York: Routledge.

Mosco, V. (1996) *The Political Economy of Communication: Rethinking and Renewal*, California: Sage.

Muir, A.R. (1988) 'The status of women working in film and television', in L. Gamman and M. Marshment (eds) *The Female Gaze: Women as Viewers of Popular Culture*, London: The Women's Press.

Mullan, B. (1997) *Consuming Television*, Oxford and Cambridge, Mass.: Blackwell.

Mulvey, L. (1975) 'Visual pleasure and narrative cinema', *Screen*. 16(3): 6–19.

——(1979) 'Afterthoughts on "Visual Pleasure and Narrative Cinema" inspired by *Duel in the Sun*', *Framework*, 10: 3–10.

Murdock, G. and Golding, P. (1995) 'For a political economy of mass communications', in O. Boyd-Barrett and C. Newbold (eds) *Approaches to Media: A Reader*, London: Arnold.

Neale, S. (1980) *Genre*, London: BFI.

——(1993) 'Masculinity as spectacle: reflections on men and mainstream cinema', in S. Cohen and I.R. Hark (eds) *Screening the Male: Exploring Masculinities in Hollywood Cinema*, London and New York: Routledge.

Nelson, R. (1997) *TV Drama in Transition: Forms, Values and Cultural Change*, Basingstoke: Macmillan.

Newcomb, H. and Alley, R. (1983) *The Producer's Medium: Conversation with America's Leading Producers*, New York: Oxford University Press.

Newsom, E. (1994) *Video Violence and the Protection of Children*, Nottingham: University of Nottingham Press.

Nichols, B. (1991) *Representing Reality: Issues and Concepts in Documentary*, Bloomington: Indiana University Press.

——(1994) *Blurred Boundaries: Questions of Meaning in Contemporary Culture*, Bloomington: Indiana University Press.

Nixon, S. (1996) *Hard Looks: Masculinities, Spectatorship and Contemporary Consumption*, London: UCL Press.

O'Malley, T. and Treharne, J. (1993) *Selling the Beeb*, London: Campaign for Press and Broadcasting Freedom (CPBF).

O'Shaughnessy, M. (1990) 'Box pop: popular television and hegemony', in A. Goodwin and G. Whannel (eds) *Understanding Television*, London and New York: Routledge.

O'Sullivan, T., Hartley, J., Saunders, D., Montgomery, M. and Fiske, J. (1994) *Key Concepts in Communication and Cultural Studies*, London: Routledge.

O'Sullivan, T., Dutton, B. and Rayner, P. (1998) *Studying the Media: An Introduction*, London: Arnold.

Paget, D. (1998) *No Other Way to Tell It: Dramadoc/Docudrama on Television*, Manchester: Manchester University Press.

Paglia, C. (1990) *Sexual Personae*, New Haven, New Jersey: Yale University Press.

Paterson, R. (1990) 'A suitable schedule for the family', in A. Goodwin and G. Whannel (eds) *Understanding Television*, London: Routledge.

Perkins, T. (1979) 'Rethinking stereotypes', in M. Barrett, P. Corrigan, A. Kuhn and V. Wolff (eds) *Ideology and Cultural Production*, London: Croom Helm.

Petley, J. (1997) *Ill-Effects: The Media Violence Debate*, London: Routledge.

Postman, N. (1985) *Amusing Ourselves to Death: Public Discourse in the Age of Show Business*, London: Methuen.

Potter, D. (1984) *Waiting for the Boat: On Television*, London: Faber and Faber.

Press, A. (1991) *Women Watching Television*, Philadelphia: University of Pennsylvania Press.

Pribram, E. (ed.) (1988) *Female Spectators: Looking at Film and Television*, London: Verso.

Priest, S.H. (1996) *Doing Media Research – an Introduction*, Thousand Oaks and London: Sage.

Propp, V. (1979) *Morphology of the Folktale*, Austin: University of Texas.

Radway, J. (1984) *Reading the Romance: Women, Patriarchy and Popular Literature*, Chapel Hill: University of North Carolina Press.

Ransome, P. (1992) *Antonio Gramsci: A New Introduction*, Hemel Hempstead: Harvester Wheatsheaf.

Real, M. (1989) *Supermedia: A Cultural Studies Approach*, Newbury Park, London, New Delhi: Sage.

Renov, M. (1993) *Theorizing Documentary*, New York: American Film Institute/Routledge.

Ritzer, G. (1993) *The McDonaldization of Society*, London: Sage.

Rogers, E. and Dearing, J. (1987) 'Agenda-setting: where it has been, where is it going?' *Communication Yearbook 11*, London: Sage.

Rushton, D. (ed.) (1993) *Citizen Television: A Local Dimension to Public Service Broadcasting*, London: John Libbey.

Sarup, M. (1993) *An Introductory Guide to Post-Structuralism and Post-Modernism*, Hemel Hempstead: Harvester Wheatsheaf.

——(1996) *Identity, Culture and the Postmodern World*, Edinburgh: Edinburgh University Press.

Scannell, P. (1990) 'Public service broadcasting: the history of a concept', in A. Goodwin and G. Whannel (eds) *Understanding Television*, London: Routledge.

Scannell, P., Schlesinger, P. and Sparks, C. (1992) *Culture and Power*, London: Sage.

Schiller, H. (1995) 'The international commercialization of broadcasting', in O. Boyd-Barrett and C. Newbold (eds) *Approaches to Media: A Reader*, London: Arnold.

Schlesinger, P. (1978) *Putting 'Reality' Together – BBC News*, London: Constable.

Seiter, E. (1992) 'Semiotics, structuralism and television', in R. Allen (ed.) *Channels of Discourse Reassembled*, London: Routledge.

Seiter, E., Borchers, H., Kreutzner, G. and Warth, E. (1991) *Remote Control: Television, Audiences and Cultural Power*, London and New York: Routledge.

Shanahan, J., Morgan, M. and Shanahan, J. (1999) *Television and its Viewers: Cultivation Theory and Research*, London: Cambridge University Press.

Shohat, E. and Stam, R. (1994) *Unthinking Eurocentrism: Multiculturalism and the Media*, London and New York: Routledge.

Shuker, R. (1994) *Understanding Popular Music*, London: Routledge.

Signorielli, N. and Morgan, M. (eds) (1990) *Cultivation Analysis: New Directions in Media Effects Research*, Newbury Park: Sage.

Sijl, A. (1988) *East of Dallas: The European Challenge to American Television*, London: BFI.

Silverstone, R. (1994) *Television and Everyday Life*, London: Routledge.

Silverstone, R. and Hirsch, E. (eds) (1994) *Consuming Technologies: Media and Information in Domestic Spaces*, London: Routledge.

Simatos, A. and Spencer, K. (1992) *Children and Media: Learning From Television*, Liverpool: Mantius Press.

Sklair, L. (1991) *Sociology and the Global Process*, Hemel Hempstead: Harvester Wheatsheaf.

Smythe, D. (1981) *Dependency Road: Communications, Capitalism, Consciousness and Canada*, Norwood NJ: Ablex.

Sparks, R. (1992) *Television and the Drama of Crime*, Buckingham: Open University Press.

Squire, C. (1997) 'Empowering women? *The Oprah Winfrey Show*', in C. Brunsdon, J. D'Acci and L. Spigel (eds) *Feminist Television Criticism: A Reader*, Oxford: Oxford University Press.

Sreberny-Mohammadi, A. (1991) 'The global and the local in international communications', in J. Curran and M. Gurevitch (eds) *Mass Media and Society*, London: Arnold.

Sreberny-Mohammadi, A., Winseck, D., McKenna, J. and Boyd-Barrett, O. (eds) (1997) *Media in Global Context: A Reader*, London and New York: Arnold.

Stacey, J. (1990) 'Desperately seeking difference', in P. Erens (ed.) *Issues in Feminist Film Criticism*, Bloomington: Indiana University Press.

Stempel, G. (1989) 'Content analysis', in G. Stempel and B. Westley (eds) *Research Methods in Mass Communication*, Englewood Cliffs, NJ: Prentice Hall.

Stevenson, N. (1995) *Understanding Media Cultures: Social Theory and Mass Communications*, London: Sage.

Stokes, J. (1999) *On Screen Rivals: Television and Cinema in the United States and Britain*, Basingstoke: Macmillan.

Stokes, J. and Reading, A. (1999) *The Media in Britain: Current Debates and Developments*, Basingstoke: Macmillan.

Stone, V. (1988) 'Trends in the status of minorities and women in broadcast news', *Journalism Quarterly*, 65: 288–93.

Storey, J. (1993) *An Introductory Guide to Cultural Theory and Popular Culture*, Hemel Hempstead: Harvester Wheatsheaf.

——(1996) *Cultural Studies and the Study of Popular Culture: Theories and Methods*, Edinburgh: Edinburgh University Press.

——(2001) *Cultural Theory and Popular Culture: An Introduction*, Harlow: Prentice Hall.

Streeter, T. (1996) *Selling the Air*, Chicago: University of Chicago Press.

Strinati, D. (1995) *An Introduction to Theories of Popular Culture*, London: Routledge.

——(2000) *An Introduction to Studying Popular Culture*, London: Routledge.

Strinati, D. and Wagg, S. (eds) (1992) *Come On Down? Popular Media Culture in Post-War Britain*, London: Routledge.

Swanson, G. (1991) 'Representations', in D. Lusted (ed.) *The Media Studies Book*, London: Routledge.

Tasker, Y. (1993) *Spectacular Bodies: Gender, Genre and Action Cinema*, London and New York: Comedia/Routledge.

Taylor, L. and Willis, A. (1999) *Media Studies: Texts, Institutions and Audiences*, Oxford: Blackwell.

Thompson, E.P. (1980 [1968]) *The Making of the English Working Class*, Harmondsworth: Penguin.

Thwaites, T., Davis, L. and Mules, W. (1994) *Tools For Cultural Studies: An Introduction*, Melbourne: Macmillan.

Tomlinson, J. (1991) *Cultural Imperialism*, London: Pinter.

Tuchman, G. (1978) *Making News*, New York: Free Press.

Tulloch, J. (1990) *Television Drama: Agency, Audience and Myth*, London and New York: Routledge.

Tulloch, J. and Alvarado, M. (1983) *Dr Who, the Unfolding Text*, London: Macmillan.

Tumber, H. (ed.) (2000) *Media Power, Professionals and Policies*, London: Routledge.

Tunstall, J. (1977) *The Media are American*, London: Constable.

——(1993) *Television Producers*, London: Routledge.

——(1996) 'Producers in British television', in P. Marris and S. Thornham (eds) *Media Studies: A Reader*, Edinburgh: Edinburgh University Press.

Tunstall, J. and Palmer M. (1991) *Media Moguls*, London: Routledge.

Turner, G. (1990) *British Cultural Studies: An Introduction*, London: Routledge.

Turow, J. (1992) 'The organisational underpinnings of contemporary media conglomerates', *Communication Research*, 19: 682–704.

Unesco (1987) *Women and Decision Making: The Invisible Barriers*, Paris: Unesco.

van Dijk, T.A. (1993) *Elite Discourse and Racism*, London: Sage.

van Zoonen, L. (1989) 'Professional socialization of feminist journalists in the Netherlands', *Women's Studies in Communication*, 12(3): 1–23.

——(1994) *Feminist Media Studies*, London and Thousand Oaks: Sage.

Wagg, S. (1992) 'You've never had it so silly: the politics of British satirical comedy from *Beyond the Fringe* to *Spitting Image*', in D. Strinati and S. Wagg (eds) *Come On Down? Popular Media Culture in Post-War Britain*, London: Routledge.

Walkowitz, R. (1997) 'Reproducing reality: Murphy Brown and illegitimate politics', in C. Brunsdon, J. D'Acci and L. Spigel (eds) *Feminist Television Criticism: A Reader*, Oxford: Oxford University Press.

Watson, J. (1998) *Media Communication*, Basingstoke: Macmillan.

Wayne, M. (ed.) (1998) *Dissident Voices: The Politics of Television and Political Change*, London: Pluto Press.

Wenner, L. (1989) *Media, Sports and Society*, London: Sage.

Whannel, G. (1990) 'Winner takes all: competition', in A. Goodwin and G. Whannel (eds) *Understanding Television*, London: Routledge.

——(1992a) *Fields in Vision: Television Sport and Cultural Transformation*, London: Routledge.

——(1992b) 'The price is right but the moments are sticky: television quiz shows and popular culture', in D. Strinati and S. Wagg (eds) *Come On Down? Popular Media Culture in Post-War Britain*, London: Routledge.

White, M. (1987) 'Ideological analysis and television', in R. Allen (ed.) *Channels of Discourse*, London: Methuen.

Williams, G. (1994) *Britain's Media: How They Are Related*, London: Campaign for Press and Broadcasting Freedom (CPBF).

Williams, K. (1997) *Get Me a Murder a Day! A History of Mass Communication in Britain*, London: Arnold.

Williams, R. (1958) *Culture and Society*, London: Chatto and Windus.

——(1963) *Culture and Society*, London: Penguin.

——(1974) *Television, Technology and Cultural Form*, Glasgow: Fontana.

——(1976) *Keywords*, London: Fontana.

——(1980) 'Advertising: the magic system', in *Problems in Materialism and Culture*, London: New Left Books.

Williamson, J. (1990) 'Ads nauseam', *Cosmopolitan*, January.

Wilson, R. (1994) *Local Television: Finding a Voice*, Church Stretton: Dragonflair Publishing.

Winston, B. (1998) 'Not a lot of laughs: documentary and public service', in M. Wayne (ed.) *Dissident Voices: The Politics of Television and Political Change*, London: Pluto Press.

Wodak, R. (1996) *Disorders of Discourse*, New York: Longman.

Wollen, P. (1997) 'Ways of thinking about music video (and postmodernism)', in M. Brooker and W. Brooker (eds) (1997) *Postmodern Afterimages*, London: Arnold.

Woollacott, J. (1986) 'Fictions and ideologies: the case of situation comedy', in T. Bennett, C. Mercer and J. Woollacott (eds) *Popular Culture and Social Relations*, Milton Keynes: Open University Press.

Wren-Lewis, J. and Clarke, A. (1983) 'The World Cup – a political football', *Theory, Culture and Society*, 1(3): 123–32.

Wyver, J. (1989) *The Moving Image: An International History of Film, Television and Video*, London: Blackwell and BFI.

INDEX

Page numbers in italic indicate specific topics covered in the book.

everyday life 59, 84–9, 196–7, 225, 243, 244
Ewen, S. 6
Experience 98
experimental methods 79
exploitation 122
expressionism 190
Eye Witness News 147

Fairclough, N. 64, 65, 67
false consciousness 23–4, 56, 117, 121
false needs 130
Faludi, S. 98, 107, 218
Families at War 103
family and domestic viewing 72, *84–9*, 97, 154, 184–5, 205, 206, 207, 244–5
fans 20, *89–95*, 127–8, 138, 172, 208, 209, 222, 238–9, 240–1, 243
fantasy 182, 193–4, 207
fascism 133–4
Father Ted 222
Federal Communications Commission 1, 160, 257
Federal Radio Commission 160
female gaze 97, 107, 184, 218
female texts 97
femininity 89, 105–7, 109, 230, 248
feminisation 257
feminism 46–7, 56–7, 65, 83, 89, *95–9*, 104–8, 109, 118, 122–3, 126, 137, 149–150, 154, 174, 183–4, 185, 190, 206, 208, 214–16, 225, 226, 258–9
Ferguson, B. 77, 189, 193
Feuer, J. 109–10
film theory 180–3
Fininvest 151
first-person narration texts 2
Fiske, J. 15, 27–8, 29, 43, 47, 63, 64, 65, 66, 67, 84, 94, 95, 99, 100–1, 103, 127, 128, 136, 142, 153, 154–5, 168, 173, 174, 175, 185, 214, 222, 226, 236, 240, 243, 247
flagship programmes 142
flexiad drama 73–4
Flintstones, The 223
Flitterman-Lewis, S. 182, 184–5
folk culture 12, 18, 55, 62
folk devils 45
football 115

formality 28
Foucault, M. 64, 216
Fox 52, 125, 164
fragmentation 59, 63, 91, 137, 159, 170, 172, 174, 206, 244, 257
Frankenstein 207
Frankfurt School 13, 18, 20, 24, 56, 62, 91, 129–130, 133–4
Frazier 30
Freescreen 1
Fresh Prince of Bel Air, The 191
Freud, S, 153–4, 180–2, 216
Friends 10, 30, 32, 53, 74, 86, 110, 172, 219
Frith, S. 138
Frye, N. 108
functional analysis 19,
functionalism 227
funding 159

Gallup, G. 133
Galtung, J. 144–5
game shows 24, 28, 87, 99–103, 119, 124, 131, 140–1, 142, 163, 197, 242, 258
Gamman, L. 47, 97, 107, 184, 185, 218
gangster films 109
Gans, H. 147, 149
Garber, M. 216
Garnett, T. 26
Garnham, N. 3, 177
gatekeeping 2, 7, 143, 233
Gates, H. 190
Gauntlett, D. 23, 245
Gay Entertainment Network 220
gay representation 230, 231
gay sexuality 219–20
gay stereotypes 32–3
gender 20, 24, 27, 46–8, 49, 50, 65, 67, 80, 82, 88–9, 95–9, 102, *103–8*, 118, 122, 126, 146–7, 151, 174, 175, 179, 183–4, 185, 190, 200, 205–6, 208, 215, 216–18, 220, 225–6, 228, 230, 233, 236, 248, 249, 254, 255–60
gendered genres 46–8, 109
General Electric Company 73
genre 7, 10, 20, 28, 30, 34, 43, 44–8, 67, 70, 71, 74, 76, 99, 103, *108–111*,